Homegrown Lessons

Edward Pauly
Hilary Kopp
Joshua Haimson

Homegrown Lessons

Innovative Programs Linking School and Work

A Manpower Demonstration Research Corporation Study

Jossey-Bass Publishers • San Francisco

Substantial discounts on bulk quantities of Jossey-Bass books are available to corporations, professional associations, and other organizations. For details and discount information, contact the special sales department at Jossey-Bass Inc., Publishers. (415) 433–1740; Fax (800) 605–2665.

For sales outside the United States, please contact your local Paramount Publishing International Office.

TCF   Manufactured in the United States of America on Lyons Falls Pathfinder Tradebook. This paper is acid-free and 100 percent totally chlorine-free.

Library of Congress Cataloging-in-Publication Data

Pauly, Edward.
    [Home-grown lessons]
    Homegrown lessons : innovative programs linking school and work / Edward Pauly, Hilary Kopp, Joshua Haimson.— 1st ed.
        p.   cm.— (The Jossey-Bass education series)
    Previously published as: Home-grown lessons.
    Includes bibliographical references and index.
    ISBN 0-7879-0074-5 (acid-free paper)
    1. Career education—United States—Case studies.   2. School-to-work transition—United States—Case studies.   3. Practicums—United States—Case studies.   I. Kopp, Hilary.   II. Haimson, Joshua.   III. Title.   IV. Series.
LC1037.5.P375   1995
370.11'3'0973--dc20   94-47966
                                                                                    CIP

FIRST EDITION
HB Printing   10 9 8 7 6 5 4 3 2 1   Code 9534

The Jossey-Bass Education Series

Contents

List of Tables

List of Abbreviations

ABA   American Bankers Association
ABC   Association of Building Contractors
AFDC   Aid to Families with Dependent Children
CCSSO   Council of Chief State School Officers
CD   Career development course
CIM   Certificate of initial mastery
HVAC   Heating, ventilation, and air conditioning
JFF   Jobs for the Future
JTPA   Job Training Partnership Act (1982)
MDRC   Manpower Demonstration Research Corporation
NAM   National Association of Manufacturers
NCRVE   National Center for Research in Vocational Education
NTMA   National Tooling and Machining Association
PaCE   Professional and Career Experience (Fort Collins, Colorado)
PACE   Partnership for Academic and Career Education (Tri-County Technical College, South Carolina)
PIA   Printing Industries of America
SCANS   Department of Labor Secretary's Commission on Achieving Necessary Skills
SHSHP   Socorro High School for the Health Professions

Preface

In the new global marketplace, economic rewards are reserved for those with the best skills and the most valuable knowledge. To prepare young people for productive and satisfying adult lives in this competitive environment, many local high schools and employers, working as partners, are taking the lead in developing and implementing effective school-to-work programs. These programs will play an important role in the expanding school reform movement because they change the nature of high school by incorporating the knowledge and skills found in modern workplaces—combining classroom courses and work-based learning into an integrated curriculum. This new approach is called school-to-work.

Yet this emerging school-to-work movement is handicapped by a lack of information on the experiences of the U.S. communities that have already created innovative combinations of improved high school education and work-based learning. These pioneers can teach the rest of us important lessons about the challenges that will soon confront employers, educators, and community leaders across the nation as they start building their own school-to-work programs. These lessons are also directly relevant to the policy decisions and program development efforts that are already underway.

Two years ago—working with partners at Jobs for the Future, BW Associates, and Workforce Policy Associates—the Manpower Demonstration Research Corporation (MDRC) began the School-to-Work Transition Project, an investigation of sixteen of the nation's most promising school-to-work programs. These programs were chosen because they represent a wide variety of approaches, and have enough operational experience to provide startup and implementation lessons for others.

The findings from the School-to-Work Transition Project address many critical concerns of policy makers, educators, and employers. These sixteen pioneers can teach us:

- Why and how these innovative school-to-work programs created unexpected combinations of activities and approaches.

- How these programs were able to build the local support they needed to get started.

- How a broad range of students, including a substantial number of disadvantaged and low-achieving students, are able to participate in school-to-work programs; and how marketing and student selection methods can attract a diverse enrollment.

- How programs that start early in high school can reach at-risk students before they become disengaged or drop out.

- How students' educational experiences can be improved through changing the nature and content of instruction in high school; providing extra, personalized support for students; fostering the sense that they belong to a program with a special identity; and creating contextual learning experiences in workplaces.

- How local employers can contribute to the programs, providing both the essential work-based learning activities and the no-less-valuable knowledge, coordination, and resources that programs need to survive.

- How new school-to-work programs overcome key implementation challenges.

In writing this book we have listened carefully to the voices of educators, employers, students, and parents in communities across the nation. As a result this book is able to shed new light on the impressive accomplishments of the promising educational reforms that these constituencies have come together to build.

The lessons in this book are directly relevant to the concerns of everyone working to build the next generation of school-to-work programs, as states and localities implement the School-to-Work Opportunities Act (which became law in May 1994): educators, including academic and vocational teachers and administrators; employers, particularly those who currently employ and train young people and those who are considering doing so; leaders of trade associations and other industry groups; and all those concerned about the role of the schools and employers in helping young people start their careers.

An Overview of the Contents

The intense interest in establishing a U.S. school-to-work transition system and the rising tide of legislative proposals, state initiatives, and local programs indicate that major policy action on this front is already underway. Each chapter highlights a major area of concern that policy makers and practitioners are likely to confront and presents lessons learned from innovators in the field.

Chapter One describes the growing interest in school-to-work programs in response to current education problems and worldwide economic conditions. It also describes and categorizes the sixteen school-to-work initiatives included in this book and discusses the way programs were chosen for the study and how the study was carried out. In particular, it explores the phenomenon of hybrid programs that the research team discovered to be characteristic of school-to-work initiatives—contradicting the conventional assumption that these programs fit into the carefully defined models and categories that are discussed and debated by policy makers.

Chapter Two describes the lessons learned by program operators about how to develop and start up a program. For those who will soon initiate their own programs, this chapter explains how policies and contextual factors shape the initial experience of school-to-work programs. For those in existing programs, this chapter may reveal causes of persistent problems.

Chapter Three examines the lessons on student participation, including which students participate and why they are attracted to these programs, and addresses issues related to recruiting, selecting, and serving a broad range of students.

Chapter Four looks at the way the school-to-work initiatives change students' daily experiences. It focuses on the characteristics of students' instructional experiences, their social supports in school, and their workplace experiences. Students' and parents' views about their program experiences are also described, and the limited data on the programs' outcomes is summarized.

Chapter Five analyzes the role of employers in school-to-work programs, looking closely at the reasons that employers participate and the factors that affect their participation. It describes how employers have contributed to developing and implementing the programs and the nature of the work-based experiences they provide for participating students. In addition, the role of business intermediary organizations in facilitating employer involvement is explored, and early evidence on the potential scale of employer participation in a national school-to-work system is considered.

The challenges that schools and employers have experienced in implementing school-to-work programs are identified and analyzed in Chapter Six, including the ways teachers are refining the curriculum and instructional techniques, adapting the program to existing school requirements and regulations, dealing with the problems of program expansion, and the effort of employers to adjust to working with high school students.

Chapter Seven summarizes our recommendations for policy makers and practitioners.

An appendix contains more detailed information about each of the sixteen school-to-work programs on which this book is based.

Manpower Demonstration Research Corporation

The Manpower Demonstration Research Corporation (MDRC) is a nonprofit social policy research organization founded in 1974 and located in New York City and San Francisco. Its mission is to design and rigorously field test promising education and employment-related programs aimed at improving the well-being of disadvantaged adults and youth, and to provide policy makers and practitioners with reliable evidence on the effectiveness of social programs. Through this work, and its technical assistance to program administrators, MDRC seeks to enhance the quality of public policies and programs.

MDRC actively disseminates the results of its research through its publications and through interchange with policy makers, administrators, practitioners, and the public. Over the past two decades, working in partnership with more than forty states, the federal government, scores of communities, and numerous private philanthropies, MDRC has developed and studied more than three dozen promising social policy initiatives.

In addition to this book, MDRC's School-to-Work Transition Project has produced two other major research products during its two years of field research and analysis. Thomas Bailey and Donna Merritt of Teachers College and Conservation of Human Resources, Columbia University, reviewed the existing analyses of the agricultural education, cooperative education, tech prep, and career academy programs in their monograph, *The School-to-Work Transition and Youth Apprenticeship: Lessons from the U.S. Experience* (MDRC, 1993). Jobs for the Future (a nonprofit organization headquartered in Boston that supports school-to-work reform) produced *Learning Through Work: Designing and Implementing Quality Worksite Learning for High School Students* (MDRC, 1994), a companion volume to the present book offering much-needed technical assistance for local developers of work-based learning experiences.

MDRC hopes that these three documents prove to be useful

resources for educators and employers in local communities, state agencies, and the federal government as they work to improve the prospects and opportunities for today's youth. As MDRC's staff continue their work on the school-to-work transition through a major longitudinal evaluation of the high school career academies, they look forward to bringing additional policy-relevant information to bear on the challenges confronting the school-to-work movement. For the present, *Homegrown Lessons* offers the invaluable experiences of pioneering school-to-work programs for all those who will be planning and implementing the future generations of these programs, and want the advantage of building on the practical and important lessons already learned.

MDRC's work on this project received major support and funding from The Commonwealth Fund, the DeWitt Wallace–Reader's Digest Fund, and The Pew Charitable Trusts. Additional support for publication and dissemination of the project's reports was provided by the Aetna Foundation, Inc., the Metropolitan Life Foundation, the Bristol-Myers Squibb Foundation, Inc., the Prudential Foundation, the S. H. Cowell Foundation, and The Travelers Foundation. It was the funders' understanding of the importance of the school-to-work transition that made this project possible.

Acknowledgments

We could not have written this book without the generous assistance of the several hundred teachers, students, parents, employer staff, school and district officials, state agency officials, and trade and industry association leaders who were interviewed by the research team. They allowed us to observe their classrooms, visit their workplaces, and talk with them about their pioneering school-to-work program experiences.

We are particularly indebted to the program leaders who arranged for us to visit and learn about their programs: Kathy Floyd (the Academy of Finance at Lake Clifton–Eastern High School in Baltimore, Maryland); Larry Rosenstock and Maria Ferri (the restructured Rindge School of Technical Arts in Cambridge, Massachusetts); Christine Reising (the cluster program at Crater High School in Central Point, Oregon); John Polto (the cluster program at Dauphin County Technical School near Harrisburg, Pennsylvania); Linda Williams (Poudre R-1 School District's Professional and Career Experience [PaCE] program in Fort Collins, Colorado); Lynn Peters and William Decker (the Fox Cities Youth Apprenticeship program in Appleton, Wisconsin); Doris Jones and Martha Allen (the youth apprenticeship program at Metropolitan Vocational Center in Little Rock, Arkansas); Shirley Starke (King-Drew Medical Magnet High School in Los Angeles, California); Patricia Clark (the Health and Bioscience Academy at Oakland Technical High School in Oakland, California); Mendel Stewart, Frances Stokes, and Diana Walter (the tech prep and youth apprenticeship programs in Pickens County, South Carolina); Jim Wernsing (Roosevelt Renaissance 2000 at Roosevelt High School in Portland, Oregon); Carl Cooper, Nancy Sochet, Jan Kehoe, and Paula Mitchell (the Socorro High School for the Health Professions at Socorro High School near El Paso, Texas); Wayne Rowley (Craftsmanship 2000 in Tulsa, Oklahoma); Rick Adcock (the tech prep program at Wayne Township's Ben Davis High School near Indianapolis, Indiana); and Mary Skalecki and Marilyn Orlopp (the West Bend Youth Apprenticeship program in West Bend, Wisconsin).

We also thank Ricky Takai of the U.S. Department of Education and Leslie Loble of the U.S. Department of Labor for sharing information on the federal government's developing school-to-work policy agenda.

The Manpower Demonstration Research Corporation's (MDRC's) partners in the School-to-Work Transition Project—Jobs for the Future, Workforce Policy Associates, and BW Associates—contributed throughout the study. BW Associates shared in the field research on three local programs. Workforce Policy Associates helped relate the project's findings to the policy debates on school-to-work programs, and gathered the information on the role of national trade associations in school-to-work programs. Jobs for the Future shared in the field research, provided access to programs participating in their National Youth Apprenticeship Initiative, and led the focus groups with students and parents. We were fortunate to be able to work with Jeanne Adair, Erin Flynn, Susan Goldberger, Richard Kazis, John Niles, Mary O'Flanagan, Hilary Pennington, Barbara Roche, and Estevan Rodriguez of Jobs for the Future; Patricia McNeil and Christine Kulick of Workforce Policy Associates; and Paul Berman and Beryl Nelson of BW Associates. Alan Weisberg assisted us in conducting the focus groups, and Elspeth MacHattie provided a skilled editorial eye.

We benefited from very helpful and thoughtful reviews of an earlier version of this book by David Stern, Thomas Bailey, Richard Kazis, and Richard Murnane. We are also very grateful for the advice and guidance of the foundation leaders whose commitment to improving the life chances of high school students made possible the research that led to this book: Thomas Moloney, Mo Katz, Andrew Fisher, Robert Schwartz, and Susannah Cohan.

At MDRC, we received the support and assistance of many people. Rob Ivry ably planned, led, and managed the School-to-Work Transition Project from start to finish, and focused particularly on linking the field research with policy issues. The field research team included the authors, Rachel Pedraza, and Deborah Thompson (who also reviewed the literature for us). Our senior reviewers were Judith Gueron, Robert Granger, James Kemple, and John Wallace. Lynn Miyazaki prepared our survey data. We received research assistance from Melissa Barnes, Michel Broudo, and Karen Trister. Suzanne Wagner and Michael Wilde carefully edited the book, which was prepared for publication by Stephanie Cowell and Patt Pontevolpe.

The Authors

Edward Pauly is senior education researcher for the Manpower Demonstration Research Corporation, where he was the principal investigator for its three-year School-to-Work Transition Project. His current research focuses on school-to-work initiatives and other reforms aimed at improving the achievement of at-risk students. Previously he was on the faculty of Yale University. He is the author of *The Classroom Crucible: What Really Works, What Doesn't, and Why* (Basic Books, 1991) and the coauthor, with Judith M. Gueron, of *From Welfare to Work* (Russell Sage Foundation, 1991).

Hilary Kopp and **Joshua Haimson** were staff members of the School-to-Work Transition Project.

The nonprofit Manpower Demonstration Research Corporation designs and evaluates promising social policy initiatives. Its projects include major studies of education, youth employment, welfare-to-work, and adolescent parent programs.

Homegrown Lessons

Chapter One

Introduction:
Preparing Students for the Future

It is now undeniably clear that many students in the United States need help making the transition from high school to postsecondary learning opportunities and to meaningful, productive, skilled work. State and federal policy makers recognize this, educators recognize it, and so does the general public. In the words of the National Center for Education and the Economy's Commission on the Skills of the American Workforce (1990, pp. 23, 42), "The cry from America's board rooms, education think tanks and government officials is two-fold: America's workers are ill-equipped to meet employers' current needs and ill-prepared for the rapidly approaching high technology, service-oriented future. . . . We are not now providing the education and skills to a majority of our students and workers which will be required to support a move to new high performance work organizations."

In the United States, approximately three-fourths of our young people do not receive a four-year college degree, yet often they leave high schools inadequately prepared either for postsecondary education or training programs, or for direct entry into the workforce. These students are rarely taught the skills that are valued in the labor market, they have few opportunities to explore potentially rewarding careers, and they are frequently unaware of the postsecondary training programs that are available.

In the spring of 1994, Congress passed and the president signed into law the School-to-Work Opportunities Act, which seeks to create a national system of school-to-work transition programs. The movement that led to this legislation was fed by reports about the well-established employment preparation systems in most European nations and Australia and by compelling descriptions of the absence of such systems, and the education problems that this absence fosters, in this country. *A Nation at Risk* (National Commission on Excellence in Education, 1983), *The Forgotten Half* (Grant Foundation Commission, 1988), and *America's Choice: High Skills or Low Wages!* (Commission on the Skills of the American Workforce, 1990) drew attention to the need for schools that effectively prepare *all* students for rewarding work lives. Studies by labor economists point to the likelihood that employers will "dumb down" new jobs unless they know that future workers will have better skills than current entry-level workers (Murnane and Levy, 1992). Because other nations have based their economic strength and growth on systematically improving the skills of each cohort of workers, the United States may not be able to compete in the global market of the future unless its education policies change.

These carefully researched reports underscore the nation's increasingly obvious social and economic circumstances: One-quarter of young people drop out of high school; unemployment rates hover around 7 percent nationally and 10 percent in many cities, with higher rates for younger workers; and overall economic growth—the engine of future employment opportunities—remains sluggish in many industries. In most communities, the economic prospects of young people who lack highly marketable knowledge and skills are grim. One does not need to read the experts' reports to realize that many young people need more and better preparation for their lives in the labor force.

This book was written in the midst of a groundswell of school-to-work initiatives. States and local communities are planning and implementing new school-to-work programs in response to the School-to-Work Opportunities Act. Innovative legislation and broad-ranging projects have been undertaken by states (led by Arkansas, California, Florida, Illinois, Indiana, Kentucky, Maine, Massachusetts, Michigan, New Jersey, New York, Oregon, Pennsylvania, and Wisconsin), by the Council of Chief State School Officers (CCSSO), and by private-sector organizations including foundations and Jobs for the Future (JFF, a nonprofit organization that supports school-to-work reforms).

At the same time, scholars have deepened society's understanding of how education can prepare students for productive adult lives. Berryman and Bailey (1992, pp. 91, 93) summarize the emerging conclusions of a large body of research that points to the need to build new educational methods into all schooling, including school-to-work transition programs: "Teaching methods should be designed to give students the chance to observe, engage in, invent, or discover expert strategies in context. . . . The learning environment should reproduce the technological, social, chronological, and motivational characteristics of the real-world situations in which what is being learned will be used."

Thus, schools, employers, states, and the federal government are developing new programs just at the time that experts are demonstrating the need for contextual, experiential learning opportunities that enable students to apply their lessons in practical situations.

The rising interest in new educational methods reflects a broad recognition that the secondary education system in the United States has serious problems. There is reason to believe that many students are not learning the critical-thinking, problem-solving, technical, and teamwork skills required of productive adults in a globally competitive work environment. The Department of Labor Secretary's Commission on Achieving Necessary Skills (SCANS, 1991) argued strongly that less than half of the nation's youths leave school equipped to find and hold a good job. SCANS identified educational needs in five areas that schools typically treat lightly, if at all: managing and using information, allocating resources, understanding systems (that is, using several specialized tasks to solve complex, interconnected problems at work and in everyday life), using technologies, and working effectively with others.

These important high-tech skills are most often learned by students who go to college, and meaningful training opportunities are provided most often to people who are already at the top of the earnings hierarchy (Marshall and Tucker, 1992). In contrast, education and training for low-achieving students typically emphasize drills, memorization, and basic skills rather than problem-solving, critical-thinking, and higher-order skills. These differential practices have contributed to a growing gap between the earnings of workers who have a college diploma and those without one; for high school dropouts the gap is even larger (Levy and Murnane, 1992). Unless *all* young people are given substantially upgraded preparation for adult life and work, the gulf between the haves and the have-nots will inevitably widen.

This book draws on the efforts of pioneering U.S. school districts and employers who have built their own programs to help students make the transition from school to work. Previous research has documented both the accomplishments of the European school-to-work systems (see Hamilton, 1990; Council of Chief State School Officers, 1991; Nothdurft, 1990) and the difficulties facing American youths who do not attend college (see Grant Foundation Commission on Work, Family and Citizenship, 1988; Osterman, 1991; Levy and Murnane, 1992). In our study, we extended the foundation laid by these researchers by documenting the experiences of sixteen school-to-work programs in twelve states, programs that combine high school instruction with workplace learning to facilitate the school-to-work transition. Our goal is to present the "homegrown" lessons from these sixteen programs on the key issues facing policy makers, schools, and employers. Efforts to establish a national school-to-work system will require a high degree of cooperation among these three groups, and we have sought to identify lessons useful to all of them, to help them understand each other's roles and concerns and work together fruitfully. Consequently, this book contains both policy lessons and more detailed discussions for practitioners creating and working in school-to-work programs. The experiences of these programs show clearly that school-to-work programs *can* work with a diverse student body; they *can* provide students with qualitatively different kinds of learning experiences; they *can* get teachers excited about applications-based education; they *can* recruit employers to supply exciting work-based learning experiences geared to adolescents.

Three topics are discussed in the balance of this introductory chapter. First, we describe the basic school-to-work models used in our sixteen programs. Then we discuss how we selected and then explored these programs. Finally, we give an overview of a central issue, and an unnoticed benefit, of school-to-work programs—their sheer diversity, which gives evidence of the flexibility and adaptability that they can bring to the wide range of circumstances characterizing the United States.

Five School-to-Work Program Models

The universe of school-to-work programs includes many new and updated approaches ranging from employment-agency–style job referrals to distinctive instructional methods and multiyear education and training activities.

Even a cursory exposure to the experiences of students, teachers, and employers who are melding academic and workplace learning makes it clear that the term *school-to-work* is an oversimplification. For most youths there is no single transition from school to work; young people use a wide variety of combinations of schooling, postsecondary education and training, and employment to enter the adult world. The term is used here because it is widely accepted in the education and employment communities and because it underscores the importance of providing students with the knowledge, skills, and understanding to navigate this difficult passage successfully.

For our study, we sought programs that differed substantially from traditional approaches and that included learning in both high school and the workplace. Some prominent efforts to restructure vocational education have emphasized school-based activities rather than work-based learning activities; these approaches were not included in our study. The sixteen case studies were chosen from five major types of innovative school-to-work programs: high school career academies, occupational-academic cluster programs, restructured vocational education and cooperative education programs, tech prep programs, and youth apprenticeships. (All sixteen case study programs are described in detail in the Appendix.)

Career Academies

Each academy is a school-within-a-school that takes approximately fifty entering students a year and provides them with a three- or four-year program that integrates their academic learning with the study of an industry and the careers of the people who work in it (such as health care or financial services). The students in an academy are grouped together for many of their high school courses and stay with a small group of academy teachers for several years. Academic courses use a curriculum that draws from the academy's occupational field. Instructional techniques include hands-on and team projects. On-the-job learning occurs when local employers provide mentors and summer internships to introduce students to the academy's field. Some academies seek college-bound high school students, while others target a wide range of students, including some who are at risk of school failure.

Four career academies are discussed in this book:

1. Academy of Finance, Lake Clifton–Eastern High School, Baltimore, Maryland: broad preparation for varied financial occupations.
2. King-Drew Medical Magnet High School, Los Angeles, California: broad preparation for varied health occupations.

3. Health and Bioscience Academy, Oakland Technical High School, Oakland, California: broad preparation for varied health and science occupations.

4. Socorro High School for the Health Professions, Socorro High School, El Paso, Texas: broad preparation for varied health occupations.

Occupational-Academic Cluster Programs

Cluster programs typically are large-scale efforts to offer all of the students in a high school a choice among several career pathways. Each pathway uses a sequence of related courses tied to a cluster of occupations (such as environment-related industries, service industries, or manufacturing and engineering occupations). Students are usually exposed to a wide variety of careers before choosing an occupational cluster, and they may switch clusters in the course of the program. Each cluster offers occupation-related courses; students receive training in broad, work-related skills after taking introductory career exploration courses. Academic and occupational instruction are integrated and applied learning techniques are sometimes used. Work-based experiences enable students to explore potential careers. Students may take several classes in their cluster each year, so the clusters resemble schools within a school (although if the student clusters are large, this effect may be diminished).

Education reformers affiliated with the National Center for Education and the Economy have argued that this approach can be used to provide school-to-work learning experiences for a large proportion of U.S. high school students, and some states, including Oregon, have officially endorsed the approach. Vocational educators view the cluster approach as a way to integrate academic and vocational instruction.

The three occupational-academic cluster programs that we studied are:

1. Crater High School, Central Point, Oregon: business, social services, and ecology clusters.
2. Dauphin County Technical School, Harrisburg, Pennsylvania: technical, service, construction, and communications/transportation clusters.
3. Roosevelt Renaissance 2000, Roosevelt High School, Portland, Oregon: six technical and service career clusters.

Restructured Vocational Education Programs

In restructured vocational programs, the job skills training and school-supervised work experiences found in traditional vocational education programs are reshaped. Students are given earlier and broader opportunities to learn about varied careers, more opportunities for career exploration through job shadowing and visits to workplaces, structured reflection on workplace experiences, and closer linkages between occupational and academic courses. The goals of this new approach are to include a larger and more diverse group of students in vocational programs, to make career exploration a central part of their education, and to prepare them for a wide range of career opportunities.

These programs may employ cooperative education (often known simply as "co-op"), a widely used form of school-supervised work experience linked to classroom learning. Typically, participating students receive job-related instruction in school, followed by on-the-job training in a part-time job while they continue to attend school. Specialized teachers work with employers to identify co-op jobs that provide good training opportunities for students, and they prepare a formal training agreement that specifies the work that students will perform and the training that students will receive. The co-op teacher visits the workplace to facilitate the student's and the supervisor's work together and to make sure that the training agreement is being followed. In most co-op programs, students are paid by employers and (if they comply with the training agreement) receive credit toward high school graduation.

We examined two restructured vocational education programs:

1. Rindge School of Technical Arts, Cambridge, Massachusetts: career exploration; technical training in communication, design, construction, transportation, and food.
2. Professional and Career Experience, Poudre R-1 School District, Fort Collins, Colorado: career exploration and internships in varied fields.

Tech Prep Programs

Tech prep programs upgrade both the general track and vocational high school curricula to emphasize technology-related instruction in science, math, and other courses; coursework includes hands-on, applications-based instruction, using workplace problems. These programs aim to prepare students for postsecondary technical training programs by aligning their high school courses with community college requirements; students can receive credit toward an associate's degree based on their tech prep work. Because they connect the last two years of high school with two-year community college programs, tech prep programs are often called 2 + 2 programs.

Two tech prep programs are included in this study:

1. Pickens County School District, Easley, South Carolina: broad preparation for high-technology careers.
2. Ben Davis High School, Wayne Township (Indianapolis), Indiana: broad preparation for high-technology careers; optional job skills training.

Youth Apprenticeship Programs

Youth apprenticeship programs use the workplace as a learning environment to provide students with competencies in technical skills and related math, science, communication, and problem-solving skills. Students learn by doing in paid employment and training with an expert adult mentor and supervisor who works closely with them on job-related and general employment-related skills. Classroom vocational instruction and related courses that integrate academic and vocational learning are part of youth apprenticeships, and most programs link secondary and postsecondary institutions to provide this instruction. Qualified students receive a recognized occupational credential when they complete the program.

The five youth apprenticeship programs discussed here are:

1. Fox Cities Printing Youth Apprenticeship, Appleton, Wisconsin: technical and job skills training in printing.
2. Metropolitan Vocational Center, Little Rock, Arkansas: technical and job skills training in health occupations and heating/ventilation.
3. Pickens County School District, Easley, South Carolina: technical and job skills training in electronics.
4. Craftsmanship 2000, Tulsa, Oklahoma: technical and job skills training in metalworking.
5. West Bend Printing Youth Apprenticeship, West Bend, Wisconsin: technical and job skills training in printing.

Table 1.1 compares the key elements of the five program approaches as put forth by their developers and advocates. Later in the chapter, these "ideal" program models are compared to the actual programs included in this study.

As Table 1.1 shows, the five generic models have seven possible components: a new curriculum or an emphasis on applications-based instruction; preemployment preparation classes; career

Table 1.1. School-to-Work Transition Programs: Key Elements of Five Models.

Program	New Curriculum, Applications-Based Instruction	Preemployment Preparation	Career Exploration	Work-Based Learning	School-Within-a-School	Mentors	Link to Post-Secondary Programs[a]
Career academies	Present		Present	Present	Dominant element	Present	
Occupational clusters	Present		Present	Present	Dominant element		
Restructured vocational education	Present	Present	Dominant element	Present			
Tech prep	Dominant element						Present
Youth apprenticeship	Present	Present		Dominant element		Present	Present

Source: MDRC field research.

Notes: [a]Available as an option in most programs.

exploration classes and activities such as workplace visits and job shadowing; work-based learning experiences; a school-within-a-school organization; student activities with adult mentors who work for cooperating employers and help students learn about the world of work; and linkages to postsecondary programs, including community and technical colleges. Most of these components are self-explanatory, but a few require some definition.

Applications-based instruction uses knowledge from the academic disciplines to solve concrete problems that workers might encounter. These lessons are demanding but relatively brief, typically requiring one to five class hours to complete. Applications might include having the students write clear instructions for operating a piece of equipment (in English and communication courses), solve measurement problems using mathematical formulas and graphs (in mathematics), and remove impurities from a chemical sample (in chemistry). In *job shadowing*, a student visits a workplace to accompany and observe a skilled adult worker. The adult demonstrates and explains the tasks that make up his or her particular job; the student sees the specific skills and tasks that are required for the job and how such workers spend their time during the workday.

In a *school-within-a-school*, students take several courses with the same classmates each day; teachers base their instruction on a shared theme, work to build strong relationships with their students, and use shared planning time to make many decisions usually reserved for departments or school administrators. In many schools-within-a-school, these clusters of students and teachers continue to work together for several years. Students are more likely to form friendships with classmates who are in several of their courses, friendships that are likely to focus on shared school experiences. This organizational approach aims to provide students with educational and social support by reinforcing pro-school values and students' engagement in school tasks.

Table 1.1 underscores the fact that each school-to-work

approach is a combination of elements, many of which are used in several approaches but to different degrees. For example, all of the models use a new curriculum, but this is the dominant feature only in the tech prep model. Career academies and occupational-academic clusters incorporate essentially the same program elements, but academies are typically relatively self-contained programs within a comprehensive high school, while cluster programs attempt to include all or most of the students in a school. The table shows that the models often overlap with one another, despite their different emphases and their particular combinations of curricular reforms, instructional methods, and organizational features. Although the models are somewhat abstract and idealized, they are the starting point for the creation of most school-to-work initiatives. Local school officials, teachers, and employers typically begin developing their own school-to-work program with one of these models in mind.

The school-to-work movement has often sought to differentiate itself from vocational education, for two reasons. First, vocational education has a problematic public image. It is often thought of as a program that provides training in low-status and dead-end jobs to unmotivated and low-achieving students. This perception both stigmatizes the students and severely limits the growth potential of vocational education. Second, advocates of school-to-work initiatives see themselves as having a different goal. They seek to replace much existing high school education with a system of innovative, career-oriented educational approaches, rather than simply upgrading and expanding vocational courses that supplement, but do not alter, the basic high school program.

Both of these reasons ignore the fact that vocational educators have done a great deal to lay the foundation for ambitious school-to-work programs, shifting their training toward fast-growing high-tech careers, working to integrate academic and vocational instruction, and reaching beyond the lowest-achieving track to recruit students (see National Assessment of Vocational Education,

1989 and 1994). In other words, vocational education is undergoing rapid change, and its leaders seek the same goals as the school-to-work movement.

If the school-to-work movement is to succeed, it will need the vigorous participation of vocational educators and their cooperating employers to build a *new* approach to educating high school students. That approach will mix academic and occupation-related instruction, school-based and work-based learning, broad career preparation oriented to large industrial sectors rather than narrowly specified jobs, and an expectation that most careers will require postsecondary learning—all of which are the (still largely unrealized) goals of many vocational educators.

Vocational educators played leading roles in creating and implementing many of the school-to-work programs described in this book, and they deserve much of the credit for these programs' accomplishments. It would be both false and destructive to sever school-to-work initiatives from the ongoing renewal of vocational education; they are proceeding together, as many of the examples in this book clearly show. In an important sense, the school-to-work movement *is* the new vocational education.

Choosing the Case Study Programs

We set out to identify a diverse group of programs that represent the range of innovative school-to-work approaches found in the United States today, and to draw on their rich body of experience to learn about the challenges they have confronted. This goal did not require that a statistically representative sample of programs be selected. In fact, at this early stage in the development of school-to-work programs around the nation, such a sample would probably be composed mostly of developing programs that could contribute few lessons based on their experience to date. Many of the programs recommended to us for consideration were still in the planning phase, and even more had started only the school-based part of their program or the work-based part but not both.

To identify potential case study programs, we reviewed published accounts of school-to-work programs and sought referrals from national organizations, including the American Association of Community and Junior Colleges, Jobs for the Future, the National Academy Foundation, the National Association of State Directors of Vocational-Technical Education, and the National Center for Work and Learning. We also received referrals from state education departments and leading researchers, including Sue Berryman, Thomas Bailey, Charles Dayton, David Stern, Stephen Hamilton, Robert Glover, Robert Lerman, and others. To avoid redundancy, several programs that were participating in other studies were excluded. Programs serving very rural areas were also excluded because their issues are unique. That decision led to the exclusion of programs using a school-based enterprise approach (see Stern, 1991); many (but not all) school-based enterprises are in rural schools. This model has received relatively little attention but is significant because it relies on work experience opportunities created within the school setting, a valuable tool when limitations in the local labor market make it impossible to provide students with actual work-based learning opportunities.

More than one hundred referrals were received, and we collected information on more than sixty programs by telephoning program staff. Specifically, we looked for programs with the following characteristics:

- Enrolls students starting at least two years before their scheduled high school graduation.
- Provides both high school instruction and work-based experience, and uses the combined efforts of schools and employers.
- Differs substantially from most U.S. high school education in content and instructional methods.
- Serves a broad range of students, including both disadvantaged or low-achieving and nondisadvantaged students.
- Has enough operational experience to provide startup and

implementation lessons for others (programs were excluded if they did not have students enrolled by fall 1992).

For the programs that met these criteria, we collected descriptive information on their main activities, students, linkages to employers, and scale of operations. We focused on those programs that appeared to differ from conventional high school activities and to represent the broad range of school-to-work approaches, and asked the program directors for permission to conduct a day-long visit. Twenty-seven programs were visited and, from these, sixteen were asked to participate. All of them agreed to be part of the study. Taken together, they represented the diversity of innovative school-to-work approaches being developed in this country.

The selection criteria were intended to focus the study on some of the major unresolved questions that concern school officials, employers, and policy makers now developing school-to-work programs. These questions, all of which we address later, include:

- What is the feasibility of introducing innovative, occupation-related instruction into traditional U.S. secondary school programs?
- What is the nature of the adaptations that schools and employers must make to carry out school-to-work programs?
- What design features and selection processes are necessary to include disadvantaged, low-achieving students among those served by school-to-work programs?
- How can employers be recruited to participate in school-to-work programs?
- How do the new work-based learning experiences function?
- What factors increase the prospects for successful program operations and expansion to serve a large proportion of U.S. youths?

In addition, we sought to identify and highlight the innovative structural and curricular features of these home-grown programs so that others can benefit from their experience and vision. The relevant major characteristics of the sixteen programs are displayed in Table 1.2.

Because our analysis was qualitative, we present descriptions of programs rather than measurements of program outcomes and impacts. We collected data during two visits to each of the sixteen study programs in 1992 and 1993. The first visit lasted one to two days; the second, three to four. Field researchers used lengthy, structured interview guides to collect comparable information from all the programs, and they met with program directors, employers (including executives and students' workplace supervisors), leaders of business intermediary organizations (chambers of commerce, trade associations, and organizations of local business leaders), school administrators, teachers, and students in every site. At five programs, an additional day of interviews was conducted with employers. Focus group discussions with students and parents were held to learn about their perspectives on the programs. Data collection was greatly aided by the efforts of local program directors, who gathered relevant documents, helped schedule the numerous interviews and the focus groups, and administered a brief survey to collect basic information on first-year students in their programs.

All of the data and information included here are accurate as of the 1992–93 school year, unless otherwise stated. However, as we discuss later, many school-to-work initiatives are continually undergoing development and refinement as more is learned about how these new educational approaches work best.

Like any study, ours has both strengths and limitations. Its strength is that it provides policy makers and practitioners with new knowledge about the experiences of sixteen innovative school-to-work programs at a time when relatively little is known about such initiatives in the United States. This descriptive program information can answer the crucial first-order question about whether it is feasible for educators and employers to change their long-established practices to help students learn about the world of work in new ways. It can also highlight the implementation challenges that the new school-to-work programs face. This information can inform

Table 1.2. Characteristics of Sixteen School-to-Work Programs (1992–1993).

Program and Location	Grades Served	Key School Features	Workplace Components	Students Targeted	Number of Students Participating
Career academies					
Baltimore finance academy, Baltimore, MD	9–12	School-within-a-school; two finance-related classes taken each semester; 9th-graders block-scheduled; plans for blocking in other grades. Planned integration of academic and finance courses.	Job shadowing, industry mentors. Internships in summer after grade 11.	Screened[a]; serves middle of Baltimore student population	200
Los Angeles medical magnet, Los Angeles, CA	10–12	Magnet school; college prep courses with health and science themes.	Work-based experiences one day a week. Students rotate through 10 positions in three years.	Open to all; located in disadvantaged area	220
Oakland health academy, Oakland, CA	9/10–12	School-within-a-school; science, English, social studies, math, and occupational courses thematically linked to health and bioscience careers.	Job shadowing, community service, industry mentors. Internships during summer after grade 11; optional during grade 12 school year.	Open to all; located in disadvantaged area	175
Socorro health academy, El Paso, TX	9–12	School-within-a-school; integration of academic and vocational curricula around health theme in blocked classes; postsecondary articulation agreement[b]; student leadership activities through Health Occupations Students of America.	Half-day co-op placements in health facilities in grade 12. Lengthy job shadowing planned in grade 11.	Open to all; high-poverty district	200

Occupational-academic cluster programs

Program	Grades	Description	Work-based learning	Type of school	Enrollment
Central Point cluster program, Central Point, OR	10–12	Three schools-within-a-school (business, social services, and ecology) and a work-based alternative program. Integrated English, math, science, and social studies instruction organized around the school's theme. Courses combine several grade levels.	Job shadowing, weekly half-day internships, group work-based projects.	Open to all	220
Dauphin County cluster program, Harrisburg, PA	9–12	Occupational clusters in grades 10–12 resemble schools-within-a-school tied to vocational shops. Academic classes use occupational examples. Ninth grade school-within-a-school emphasizes career exploration.	Co-op placements in grade 12.	Vocational high school: includes all students	800
Portland cluster program, Portland, OR[c]	9–12	Six occupational pathways with occupation-specific courses, application-based lessons, and some integration of academic instruction with occupational themes in grades 10–12. Career exploration and decision-making course in grade 9.	Job shadowing, work internships; youth apprenticeship (planned).	Comprehensive school, includes all students	275

Restructured vocational education programs

Program	Grades	Description	Work-based learning	Type of school	Enrollment
Cambridge vocational restructuring, Cambridge, MA	9–12	Vocational education emphasizing "all aspects of the industry"; integration of academic and vocational education; project-based activities; linkages to community development; school-based enterprises.	Youth apprenticeships in building maintenance and elementary education.	Vocational school, includes all students	250

Table 1.2. Characteristics of Sixteen School-to-Work Programs (1992–1993), Cont'd.

Program and Location	Grades Served	Key School Features	Workplace Components	Students Targeted	Number of Students Participating
Fort Collins restructured co-op, Fort Collins, CO	10–12	Career exploration and work-readiness course; seminar on workplace issues.	Work internships, job shadowing, community service.	Open to all	550
Tech prep programs					
Pickens County tech prep, Easley, SC	9–12	Applied academic courses in math, science, and English; industry-based examples; collaborative learning; career exploration. Post-secondary articulation agreement.[b]	None.	Open to all	2500[d]
Wayne Township tech prep, Indianapolis, IN	10–12	Fixed sequence of courses in English, math, science, manufacturing technology, and computer applications; application-based lessons, teamwork, competency-based assessments, student-teacher clusters. Post-secondary articulation agreement.[b]	Planned optional co-op placements in grade 12 or summer.	Open to all	89
Youth apprenticeship programs					
Fox Cities youth apprenticeship, Appleton, WI[c]	11–12	Academic and technical competency-based instruction at community college; integration of instruction. Planned third year for associate's degree.	Exposure to varied skills; trained industry mentors. Printing curriculum used in technical classroom and work-based instruction. Students at workplaces three days a week.	Screened[a]	7

Little Rock youth apprenticeship, Little Rock, AR[c]	11–12	Technical and work-readiness instruction at vocational high school. Nurse's aide state certification; credit towards BAT certification for heating/AC.	Training with heating/AC installers; nursing homes and hospitals.	Vocational high school, youth apprenticeships in two occupations	23
Pickens County youth apprenticeship, Easley, SC[c]	12–post-secondary	Applied academics in high school; electronics instruction at vocational center; computer-assisted modules. Articulation agreement[b], post-secondary tuition reimbursement.	Work-based instruction in specified competencies; 20hours/week; industry mentors.	Electronics vocational students	4
Tulsa youth apprenticeship, Tulsa, OK[c]	11–post-secondary	Academic and technical instruction at technology center; academics integrate themes relevant to metalworking; extended school day and year. Linkage with jr. college for associate's degree.	Work-based activities apply and extend skills taught in the classroom and develop firm-specific skills; industry mentors; work time increases each year.	Screened[a]	16
West Bend youth apprenticeship, West Bend, WI[c]	11–12	Academic and technical instruction for half-day in home high school. Dual credit arrangements planned with community college.	Exposure to varied skills. Printing curriculum used in technical classroom and work-based instruction. Students at worksites half-day every day.	Screened[a]	12

Source: MDRC field research.

Notes: [a]In "screened" programs, staff members select students from applicants based on criteria such as grades, test scores, recommendations, and attendance. Other programs do not screen students.

[b]Articulation agreements specify the conditions under which students can receive credit toward a college degree or training certificate based on the school-to-work courses they take in high school.

[c]The 1992–93 school year was the program's first year of operation. Planned grade levels are given; the number of students represents one grade level.

[d]The number represents the total enrollment in all tech prep courses in four high schools in 1992–93. Students enrolled in more than one tech prep class are counted more than once.

a broad policy audience as future, larger school-to-work initiatives are developed. It can also show what is possible for these programs—how they can be organized, what kinds of learning experiences they can provide for students in school and in workplaces, what types of students they can serve, and how schools and employers can carry out such programs. Because they are "proof of what is possible," our descriptions establish a realistic benchmark for policy makers and practitioners as they create the school-to-work programs of the future.

One possible limitation is that the programs described are not necessarily statistically representative of school-to-work programs now operating in the United States. However, we explicitly sought out programs that would enable us to answer key questions about the feasibility of including low-achieving students in school-to-work programs, and the experiences of programs that made major changes in traditional high school and job training practices. Therefore, we chose programs whose main features are still relatively rare, such as tech prep programs that provide work-based learning and youth apprenticeship programs that serve a broad range of students, including some low-achieving students. These programs provide revealing evidence on the strategic choices that face all school-to-work programs.

A more substantial limitation is that it is not possible to assess reliably and fully the effectiveness of the programs in this study, for two reasons. First, some programs have begun operation relatively recently and there has not been enough time for students to progress through them and graduate. Second, many of the programs studied have not systematically collected information on students' graduation rates, postsecondary enrollment rates, and other outcomes (although a few programs do have outcome data; see Chapter Four).

The programs we studied were created before a national school-to-work system was on the horizon; they focused on meeting intensely felt local needs. Consequently, while their experiences provide the best available information on the likely future challenges for a national school-to-work system, there are some important differences between these pioneering programs and those that a national system will spawn. The establishment of a national system will change both the incentives and disincentives facing schools, employers, and students. For example, when very large numbers of employers are recruited to provide work experience positions for students, the fear that nonparticipating employers will take advantage of the costly training supplied by participating employers—without incurring any of its expenses—will diminish. Also, the startup costs facing schools and employers may be reduced when information based on the experiences of pioneering programs and other technical assistance becomes widely available. And if a national system provides students with recognized credentials for their work-related competencies, young people will have a strong incentive to enroll and work hard in school-to-work programs.

The Diversity of Real-World School-to-Work Programs

The kinds of experiences that we investigated in existing U.S. school-to-work programs ought to be a particularly valuable source of information for policy makers, who currently have very little information to draw on as they work to build a national school-to-work system. Our field research found that school-to-work programs are strikingly diverse, even those that represent the same model. The sixteen programs vary considerably in their features, the kinds of students they serve, their relationship to the regular high school, and the services they provide. Their diversity is significant because it reveals the importance of adapting school-to-work programs to local circumstances and shows concretely how these adaptations have led to including a broad range of students, fostered school restructuring, and qualitatively changed students' experiences.

Hybrid Programs

Important differences exist between theoretical models proposed
by advocates of school-to-work programs and the actual design of
real-world programs. When we compare the five generic models
described in Table 1.1 with the features of the actual programs
shown in Table 1.2, three conclusions emerge. First, programs using
the same school-to-work approach differ in the particular features
they contain. Second, the programs generally contain all of the *key*
elements associated with the model that they represent. Third, they
often contain additional features that are associated with other
approaches, becoming "hybrid" programs.

Striking differences exist between the theoretical models proposed by advocates of school-to-work programs and the actual
design of real-world programs. For example, the federal legislation
defining the tech prep approach does not require work-based learning, but the Pickens County and Wayne Township tech prep programs include this learning method. The career academy model
usually is not seen as having links to postsecondary education, but
the Oakland and Socorro health academies have established ties to
local community colleges. The Oakland academy is also changing
its work-based learning program into a youth apprenticeship-style
training activity. Efforts to restructure cooperative education are
generally not portrayed as changing the school curriculum or the
traditional vocational education student population, but the Fort
Collins co-op program is based on a new course that uses distinctive instructional approaches and attracts a larger, more diverse
group of students than previously participated in vocational or co-
op activities. The developers of these hybrid programs have decided
that the best method for creating new ways to learn about work is
to draw on activities from a wide range of school-to-work models;
they are more concerned about helping students learn than about
the labels on their programs.

In designing the programs described here, local school officials
and employers made choices that reflected their own circumstances,

resources, priorities, and ability to form partnerships with collaborators. The resulting hybrid programs are tailored to the interests of people in each locality. For example, the career academies differ in the number of school-within-a-school (that is, academy only) courses they offer, and some do not have a mentoring component. In contrast to the model, some tech prep programs have minimal linkages to postsecondary programs. Thus, even among programs using the same general school-to-work approach there are significant differences. In order to understand a particular program, it is not enough to know the label that it carries, because the staff of different programs have adapted and implemented models in quite divergent ways.

This consistent pattern of programmatic variability demonstrates that program operators have deliberately decided to mix and match the components in their educational package. They generally have the ability to tailor their educational methods to a specific school and to improve them over time. These mix-and-match programs enable staff to respond to specific local needs and to take advantage of locally available resources, including employer contributions of various kinds. They can also take account of student interests, the distinctive organizational structure of the school or its curriculum, and the requirements of nearby postsecondary institutions. A sense of local ownership of the program and a commitment to it are additional benefits of the mix-and-match process.

Program hybridization occurs for several reasons, according to staff members. As staff acquire experience with their programs and students, they recognize unmet needs and problems that limit the program's success, and they often respond by adding new program elements. Programs also outgrow the circumstances that shaped their initial choices; programs that adopted a particular approach because of the availability of state funding for it, or because their knowledge of programs was limited to that approach, gain greater flexibility when their original funding ends or when they learn about other approaches.

For example, Wayne Township used its initial state pilot grant to create a tech prep program in grades 11 and 12 with new courses in English, math, and science. When the pilot grant ended, the program began working with tenth-grade students too, and added new required technology and computer-applications courses, an optional work internship, and optional vocational training courses. For Wayne Township teachers and administrators, the original narrow tech prep approach, lasting only two years and including only six courses, was not adequate to engage students, so they created a more intensive hybrid program that resembles the occupational-academic cluster and career academy approaches. Other programs have undergone a similar process over time, adding high-quality work-based learning experiences, new curricula and instructional methods, industry mentors, preemployment preparation, and other features.

The fact that many school-to-work programs do not conform exactly to their models has an important implication for policy makers. Although the models serve a useful purpose by enabling policy makers to consider clearly defined alternatives, program staff will inevitably be more concerned about identifying the educational and workplace activities that meet local needs than they will be about conforming to a model. As policy makers and program staff move toward creating a national school-to-work system, it may be more productive for them to think less about prescribing models and more about supporting combinations of activities drawn from several approaches.

Nevertheless, while most of the programs studied were hybrids that drew elements from several approaches, school staff and employers did often find it useful to have a particular approach in mind as they developed their program. As Chapter Two will show, there were several benefits of using a preestablished program model, including a reduction in program development costs.

Students Served

Designers of school-to-work programs differ on the question of which segments of the student population should participate, and there is no national consensus on whether disadvantaged students can be served adequately. We sought to determine whether programs that include disadvantaged and low-achieving students can operate effectively; therefore, all of the programs we chose enroll at least a few such students. We did not, however, attempt to select *only* programs with a particular student selection policy.

The programs vary considerably in the characteristics of the students served, reflecting differing approaches, local populations, and circumstances. Significantly, the case study programs were found to work with many relatively low-achieving and disadvantaged students, showing the feasibility of including a wide variety of students in school-to-work programs. A detailed discussion of this important issue is presented in Chapter Three.

School Restructuring

While the five generic school-to-work models call for particular program activities, they do not specifically require major changes in the broad principles and structures that are the basis of the comprehensive high school. However, our field research determined that considerable school restructuring occurred in programs using each of the approaches. Moreover, the sixteen programs we studied fell naturally into three categories with respect to the degree of school restructuring they caused in the host high school: schoolwide restructuring, partial school restructuring, and only limited restructuring.

In *the schoolwide restructuring interventions*, the school-to-work transition is the organizing principle for *all* students' learning in school and the workplace. The Dauphin County and Portland cluster programs, Cambridge's restructured vocational education program, and the Los Angeles medical magnet program demonstrate that high schools can use occupation-related instruction to engage students in a wide range of learning opportunities that are academically demanding yet very different from those in large comprehensive high schools, which lack a central organizing theme. In order to restructure the school and include all students in the program, some schools have had to deemphasize or sacrifice certain activities, for example intensive workplace components.

Some school-to-work programs have resulted in *partial school restructuring,* in which a substantial proportion of the school's students and teachers change their approach to learning and teaching, while other classes and activities in the school are relatively unaffected. The school-within-a-school programs are examples of this kind of intervention, including the Oakland, Baltimore, and Socorro academies, the Central Point cluster program, both tech prep programs, and the Little Rock youth apprenticeship program.

Limited school restructuring means that there were few changes in the host secondary school. Examples include the youth apprenticeship programs in Fox Cities, West Bend, and Tulsa, which operate separately from the regular high school, and the Fort Collins co-op program, which increases the number and diversity of students' co-op experiences in workplaces and adds a new elective course to the school's offerings without changing any other courses or activities. The fact that these programs make few changes in students' *school* experience does not prevent them from providing high-intensity *workplace* learning experiences. In some youth apprenticeship programs, workplaces provide such demanding and innovative learning experiences that program administrators have little reason to change the school experience.

Our programs show that schools and employers have a choice about whether to use the school-to-work initiative to change the regular high school structure. At one extreme, the regular high school can be transformed to provide a new approach to secondary education for all students; at the other extreme, program activities can be concentrated outside of the high school—in workplaces and community colleges—without directly affecting the high school itself.

Concern about the overall quality of the public secondary education system—prompted by low high school graduation rates, weak academic achievement, and students' lack of work-related skills—has led many schools and communities to consider restructuring their high school programs, although most hesitate to institute schoolwide restructuring. School-to-work programs provide one way for them to pursue that goal, and the variety and flexibility of such initiatives mean that they can be appropriate for schools with different goals and circumstances. Communities that are basically satisfied with the quality of their high school program for most students, but that want to add high-quality preparation for work to the school's menu of offerings, may want to consider a school-to-work program that involves limited or partial school restructuring, such as a youth apprenticeship or restructured vocational education program. If community members are uncertain about the need for school restructuring but wish to try a new approach to see how it works, they too may want to choose a program that involves partial or limited restructuring. Successful programs may lead such communities to move toward more extensive restructuring. For communities that are deeply dissatisfied with the way the comprehensive high school serves its students, one of the schoolwide restructuring approaches may be an attractive option.

Qualitatively Different Learning Experiences

U.S. public schools are constantly pressured to respond to the latest rhetoric of the education policy debate, and many districts and schools have learned how to be up-to-date without substantially altering their basic activities. This defense mechanism has led Seymour Sarason (1982) to observe that for most schools an old proverb applies: "The more things change, the more they remain the same." As an example of this phenomenon, Sarason points out that in the 1960s many schools announced that they had adopted the "new math," when in fact they had done little more than purchase new math textbooks; teachers' instruction and emphasis on memorization and drills did not change. Similarly, in the 1970s elementary schools felt pressured to adopt the open classroom approach; in response, many teachers set up one or two learning centers but rarely used them.

Now that interest in school-to-work programs is burgeoning, it seems likely that some schools will respond by establishing programs that involve few changes in teachers' or students' daily experiences—in other words, programs that cannot be expected to make much of a difference for students. Others will succeed in making major changes in established school practices, in the hope that they can substantially improve student outcomes.

The programs included here provide early evidence on the feasibility of school-to-work programs that are qualitatively different from the offerings of most comprehensive high schools. These programs significantly change the daily educational experiences of participating students by replacing existing instructional methods with substantially different, innovative methods; by using new kinds of learning activities; and by radically changing the context of students' learning, from a school setting to a workplace setting. They also provide students with several years of innovative learning experiences. The case studies show that it is feasible for a wide variety of schools and communities to create school-to-work programs that substantially change students' daily experiences. (A detailed analysis of the programs' school and workplace methods is presented in Chapters Four and Five.)

Students' experiences can also be changed without school restructuring. For example, some youth apprenticeship programs are essentially separate from the host school, and therefore require few changes in the school's operations, yet the programs drastically alter students' experiences through powerful work-based learning activities. Moreover, some of the schools that experienced schoolwide restructuring created programs that provide only one or two new courses in each grade level—a modest change in students' learning experiences, despite the aura of innovation that surrounds the concept of school restructuring.

Programs that emphasize school changes and those that emphasize workplace changes both have important strengths. A workplace emphasis enables students to receive training and preparation for high-skills jobs that are difficult for schools to provide. School-based programs can upgrade student achievement in a wide range of academic, occupational, and higher-order thinking and problem-solving skills that apply to many fields of endeavor.

Most of the school-to-work programs examined here apparently induce their students to take more science, math, and technical courses than are required for graduation, and more of these courses than they would be likely to take if they were not enrolled in the school-to-work program. For example, the Socorro health academy requires students to take algebra and science courses earlier than many of their regular high school peers, and pushes them to take additional math and science courses thereafter. The Los Angeles medical magnet school limits students' electives and requires them to take all of the courses required for admission to college. In these and other programs, many students who are attracted to the program because of an interest in its occupational theme wind up taking more advanced courses than they would have chosen by themselves. This more demanding collection of courses is one of the important ways in which school-to-work programs can be qualitatively different from the average school experience.

Many of the programs have made significant changes in their operations or instruction since they began in order to help students succeed in the program, and such student support is another important qualitative difference. In several cases, tech prep, cluster, and academy programs that were originally designed for eleventh- and twelfth-graders have been altered so that they start in the ninth or tenth grade, thereby reaching at-risk students before they disengage from school and providing adequate time and opportunities for them to learn a substantial amount of demanding material. These examples demonstrate that program operators can upgrade their program and add needed instructional elements over time. This ability suggests that state and federal funding could be used to lever- age improvements in local programs, perhaps by supporting pro- grams that have some, but not all, of the components that policy makers want to encourage and by requiring that program operators use the additional funds to add the missing components.

When we were working to identify potential case study pro- grams, we found that many schools recommended to us had made only a few modest changes in students' daily experiences. For exam- ple, some programs differed from regular high school only in that they offered a small number of elective courses. Others consisted simply of supplementary activities in one or two existing courses that were otherwise largely unchanged. These types of programs were not included in our study, but they may be quite common, and it is likely that greater state and federal funding for school-to-work initiatives will increase their number. However, if policy makers want to foster programs that significantly improve students' school and workplace experiences, they should design incentives to stim- ulate the creation of programs that can qualitatively change high school experiences.

Conclusion

The practical lessons provided by the sixteen programs in this study are a source of important counsel as this country begins to build its own school-to-work transition system. While other nations have school-to-work systems that are centrally designed and adminis- tered, such an approach is not likely to take root in the United States, because of the varied goals and circumstances of different communities and the deeply rooted tradition of local school gover- nance. Thus, Americans have the opportunity to make decisions about the instructional components, inclusiveness, and structure of school-to-work programs that will best meet the needs of their com- munities, drawing from various approaches as appropriate.

In the following pages, we will look closely at the ways in which qualitatively different school-to-work programs get started, recruit students, succeed in changing students' experiences in school, connect with local employers to provide students with work-based learning experiences, and meet specific implementation challenges.

Chapter Two

Planning and Developing School-to-Work Programs

History shows that how an educational reform gets started strongly shapes its evolution and accomplishments (Sarason, 1988). While it is far too early in the life of the school-to-work programs to write their history, it is not too soon to examine the circumstances that led to their creation. By examining the beginnings of these initiatives, policy makers, educators, and businesspeople can learn about the journey that they, too, will make as they plan and implement new programs.

Our case studies reveal that new school-to-work programs are created in response to needs that both schools and employers see as critical to their future success. Responding to these needs appears to require three things: leaders with a vision of a new approach to linking school and work; crucial resources with which to build the program; and the cultivation of broad-based support to sustain the program from its earliest days.

The Vision and the Visionaries: The Origins of Sixteen School-to-Work Programs

Perhaps the most important shared characteristic of the sixteen programs studied here is that they were begun by local people who had a vision of change and who were responding to needs of recognized importance in their community. None of these programs was created simply in response to a mandate; they are all programs that their communities wanted. Thus, as policy makers work to build a national school-to-work system, they will face an important challenge in finding ways to stimulate communities to base programs on their own local visions of change.

Students' Need for More Than Their School Offered

In all sixteen programs, the idea of connecting schooling with workplace learning was present from the beginning. Although the programs' eventual form was influenced by many local factors and participants—and thus the sixteen programs vary on many dimensions—in the beginning, the program developers had a common motivation: they recognized that their secondary school systems were failing to meet the needs of their communities. Table 2.1 lists the principal reasons for the creation of each program. From most to least frequent, these reasons were: the recognition of the need to improve students' school performance, the labor market's need for better-prepared workers, a desire to improve the quality of vocational education, and the incentives provided by a new state initiative.

The importance of meeting students' needs appears to drive the mix-and-match approach to program design used by the communities in our study; they chose features from several distinct models and combined them to form programs that would fulfill the education and job training needs of their students. For example, Wayne Township started with the state-suggested tech prep model but increased the length of the program because the state model did not allow sufficient time for students to reach the district's achievement goals. A required set of courses, provided in a school-within-a-school format, was added to the Wayne Township program. It seems likely that many communities across the nation will alter and adapt program models in response to their students' needs, resulting in a proliferation of hybrid school-to-work programs.

Leaders in the Program Development Process

The individuals and organizations leading the development of school-to-work programs can include business executives, teachers,

Table 2.1. Primary Reasons for Program Development.

Program	To Respond to Dissatisfaction with Students' Performance	To Better Meet Local Labor Market Needs	To Enhance Vocational Education	In Response to a State Initiative or Funding
Career academies				
Baltimore finance academy	yes	no	no	no
Los Angeles medical magnet	no	yes	no	no
Oakland health academy	no	yes	no	yes
Socorro health academy	yes	yes	yes	no
Occupational-academic cluster programs				
Central Point cluster program	yes	no	no	no
Dauphin County cluster program	yes	no	yes	no
Portland cluster program	yes	no	no	no
Restructured vocational education programs				
Cambridge vocational restructuring	yes	no	yes	no
Fort Collins restructured co-op	no	no	yes	no
Tech prep programs				
Pickens County tech prep	yes	yes	no	no
Wayne Township tech prep	yes	no	no	yes
Youth apprenticeship programs				
Fox Cities youth apprenticeship	no	yes	no	yes
Little Rock youth apprenticeship	no	no	no	yes
Pickens County youth apprenticeship	no	yes	yes	no
Tulsa youth apprenticeship	no	yes	no	no
West Bend youth apprenticeship	no	yes	no	yes

Source: MDRC field research.

school administrators, school district officials, community colleges, and business intermediary organizations. Table 2.2 shows the specific types of leaders who played central roles in the development of the sixteen programs. Most commonly, leaders were administrators or teachers at the school where the program began, followed (in order of decreasing frequency) by school district officials, business intermediary organizations, employers, and community college staff. As the table shows, many programs were the result of collaboration among several groups.

All of the programs were created in response to one or more needs that were either widely recognized already or could be clearly demonstrated to others. Most of the programs were initiated by school administrators or teachers who realized that the current educational approach was failing to meet students' needs in some way. For example, at Socorro High School, seniors were often unable to take advantage of occupational training courses and co-op placements because they had to make up academic credits for failed courses in order to graduate. The need for earlier intervention to support students' academic progress and to connect school performance with future opportunities, combined with the local labor market's strong demand for health-occupations workers, was the main reason for the creation of the four-year Socorro health academy.

In several sites, school staff recognized that college preparation instruction was not serving the needs of students unlikely to enroll in four-year colleges; these students needed more preparation for alternative postsecondary programs and good-paying jobs. At Roosevelt High School in Portland, Oregon, where only 15 percent of the graduating seniors went on to a four-year college in a typical year, a survey of the faculty found that 85 percent felt that the school was not meeting the students' needs, and 70 percent disagreed or strongly disagreed with the idea that the status quo at the high school was acceptable. The Portland occupational-academic cluster program was begun in response to the faculty's dissatisfac-

Table 2.2. Leaders in Initial Program Development.

	School Administrators and/or Teachers	School District Officials	Business Intermediary Organizations	Employers	Community Colleges	Other[a]
Career academies						
Baltimore finance academy	yes	yes	yes	no	no	no
Los Angeles medical magnet	no	no	no	yes	no	yes
Oakland health academy	yes	no	yes	no	no	no
Socorro health academy	yes	yes	no	no	no	no
Occupational-academic cluster programs						
Central Point cluster program	yes	no	no	no	no	no
Dauphin County cluster program	yes	no	no	no	no	no
Portland cluster program	yes	yes	yes	no	no	yes
Restructured vocational education programs						
Cambridge vocational restructuring	yes	no	no	no	no	no
Fort Collins restructured co-op	yes	yes	yes	yes	no	no
Tech prep programs						
Pickens County tech prep	no	yes	yes	no	yes	no
Wayne Township tech prep	yes	yes	no	no	yes	no
Youth apprenticeship programs						
Fox Cities youth apprenticeship	no	yes	yes	yes	yes	no
Little Rock youth apprenticeship	yes	no	no	yes	no	no
Pickens County youth apprenticeship	yes	yes	no	yes	yes	no
Tulsa youth apprenticeship	no	no	yes	yes	no	no
West Bend youth apprenticeship	yes	no	no	yes	no	no

Source: MDRC field research

Note: [a]Includes state officials and community organizations.

tion. The Pickens County tech prep initiative seeks to prepare students for viable careers that do not require baccalaureate degrees in a district where only one-third of the students go on to four-year colleges and where the local economy is shifting toward higher-skilled jobs.

The programs that emphasize instruction in the workplace were typically initiated by a local employer who approached the school system in an effort to improve the pool of skilled labor in its industry. For example, the Tulsa youth apprenticeship program was initiated by Hilti Corporation's vice president for human resources in response to his assessment of workers' performance at Hilti's Tulsa facility and the need for new training and recruitment strategies. The driving force behind Wisconsin's youth apprenticeships in printing was employers who had a strong interest in education and their community, and who recognized the need for finding new ways to attract skilled labor in a fast-growing industry that is undergoing major technological changes.

Not surprisingly, the programs that involved schoolwide restructuring were usually initiated within the school or by district-level officials, although the task of reforming an entire school had to have leadership from within the school and not just at higher administrative levels. For example, the Portland cluster program was originally conceived as a more limited intervention by a state official. Early on, he obtained the support of the district supervisor and the school principal, but the initiative became schoolwide in scope only after teachers became involved in shaping the reform effort.

Programs that entailed little school restructuring were usually initiated by employers, business intermediaries, and district staff, who designed programs that could be implemented without altering the school's operation in a major way. An exception is the Fort Collins co-op program, which was initially conceived by two high school vocational teachers. However, it was then developed in collaboration with the local chamber of commerce and with significant district support.

It is notable that program staff reported that business intermediary organizations were key leaders in developing seven of the sixteen programs, bringing schools and employers together and facilitating program development. This role appears to have been especially valuable when the initial program concept came from outside the school or when it involved more than one school. Intermediary organizations (such as chambers of commerce, trade associations, and other organizations of businesspeople) often have a broad base of involved members who can build support for a new initiative; these organizations have relationships with local businesses and community colleges, and can sometimes dedicate staff to the program development effort. In contrast, school staff and employers typically must continue doing their regular job while working on the initiative. In addition, intermediaries act as a broker between schools and employers that do not have an established, cooperative relationship.

Business intermediary organizations can be especially valuable in four areas:

1. *"Translating" between employers and the school system.* Schools and employers have very different modes of operation. Many employers are not prepared for the slow pace at which schools and school districts often make decisions or for the decentralized operating methods of school systems. Some employers discovered that talking to the school district equivalent of a CEO (the superintendent) did not lead to much progress without the support and interest of building-level administrators and teachers. Teachers and employers have sometimes been frustrated with each other's lack of understanding of their schedule constraints. Teachers cannot be routinely pulled out of classes to meet with businesspeople, and their work day ends earlier, so that the time available for planning and consultation is limited. Teachers are used to working independently and are not accustomed to working in teams or running meetings with a fast-paced, bottom-line orientation. Intermediaries,

especially those with a foot in both the employer and school worlds, can help explain each side to the other and align expectations so that productive relationships can develop. An example is the Business Youth Exchange, a close affiliate of the Portland Chamber of Commerce, which was created expressly to forge cooperative efforts between the business community and the Portland public schools to build a better-educated entry-level workforce.

2. *Recruiting employers to develop school-to-work programs.* Business intermediaries such as chambers of commerce have been instrumental in bringing together employers to help design school-to-work initiatives. Examples include the Tulsa Chamber of Commerce, which worked to identify, recruit, and support the employers who designed the Tulsa youth apprenticeship program, and the Fort Collins Chamber of Commerce, which organized a group of local businesses to contribute ideas for the co-op program's career development course to prepare students for workplace experiences.

3. *Contributing to program design and curricula.* In some of the case study sites, intermediary organizations with expertise in education reform led the effort to develop curricula and other parts of the program. For example, the Oakland Alliance helped teachers at Oakland Technical High School implement the academy model; the National Academy Foundation provided the framework and curriculum for the Baltimore finance academy; and the Partnership for Academic and Career Education developed the curriculum and articulation agreements for the Pickens County tech prep program.

4. *Building multischool initiatives.* Intermediaries have been instrumental in spearheading initiatives that involve multiple schools and school districts. They provided a "home base" for the program and contributed program elements that were then shared by all participating schools and employers. Examples include the Fox Valley Education for Employment Council, which sponsors the Fox Cities youth apprenticeship program, and the Partnership for

Academic and Career Education, which facilitated the development of tech prep programs in six other districts as well as the Pickens County district. Part of the strength of intermediary organizations is their insight into the needs of diverse groups that have not previously communicated with each other. Their position enables them to see opportunities for progress that are often invisible to others.

The various roles that an intermediary can play are illustrated by two organizations, one in eastern Wisconsin and one in the northwestern corner of South Carolina.

The Fox Valley Education for Employment Council provides the organizational home for the Fox Cities printing youth apprenticeship program, which serves eleven small and medium-sized Wisconsin school districts. The council's members are school administrators and business leaders, and it is closely linked with the local chamber of commerce.

In 1985, the Wisconsin state legislature called on school districts to recognize the key role schools play in job preparation and economic development, and the eleven Fox Cities districts decided to work together, creating the council in 1988. The Menasha school district and the Banta Corporation, a large printing and publishing organization, did much of the early planning for the youth apprenticeship program. However, it soon became evident that the program would require broader participation, and the Education for Employment Council was then asked to sponsor and oversee the program.

Program development benefited from relationships established by the council among the school districts and several business partners. The council's director of business–education partnerships (who is an employee of the local chamber of commerce) recruited employers as partners and facilitated coordination among all the partners. She acts as staff director for the council and is paid by participating school districts. She has successfully used the chamber of commerce's reputation and contacts to recruit employers for a wide range of school–business initiatives.

The council has also worked effectively with participating school districts to develop a course outline for the youth apprenticeship program, and to create and implement joint decisions taking into account each district's policies on such critical issues as waivers of graduation requirements, credits for nontraditional courses, and the creation of a program curriculum.

The Partnership for Academic and Career Education (PACE) in Pickens County, South Carolina, was created through discussions initiated by the president of Tri-County Technical College with local business and education leaders. PACE members focused on the tech prep approach as a way to meet increasing local demand for skilled workers, the lack of technical graduates to meet this demand, and rising concern about school dropouts. PACE is affiliated with and largely supported by the technical college; its goal is to expand the educational and career opportunities available to students in the three counties served by the college through the establishment of tech prep programs.

The Pickens County school district's efforts to build a tech prep program have been supported by PACE in several ways: PACE has developed materials, identified and trained staff to implement tech prep, helped schools and districts to share resources, and generally supported school staff's efforts to move the initiative forward. PACE's committee structure enables people to meet together regularly and to follow through on their ideas with PACE's guidance. PACE staff have also eased communication between educators and business people. An employer who works with the organization noted that PACE staff know how to run a good meeting and define a specific activity to be accomplished, and they keep their work focused on students.

PACE promotes the development and implementation of tech prep through the following activities:

- Investigating and purchasing applied academic course materials for use and modification by the participating schools (PACE also supports teachers' efforts to develop new teaching materials).
- Developing supplementary instructional materials using examples from local industries.
- Training teachers in cooperative learning methods and new instructional materials to help them shift away from lecture-style teaching.
- Supporting the development of articulation agreements between Tri-County Technical College and the seven participating school districts, with approximately forty high school courses now accepted for college credit in fourteen course areas.
- Helping to formulate workplace competency training plans and developing a mentoring guide for Pickens County's youth apprenticeship program.
- Through career counseling brochures and meetings, increasing the awareness of students, parents, teachers, and guidance counselors of the range of available occupations and the link between students' education levels and earning potential.
- Developing a list of volunteer speakers to enable teachers to bring business representatives into the classroom, and arranging summer internships for teachers in local businesses.

The Fox Valley and PACE intermediaries are two examples of organizations that were created to build school-to-work programs. Existing organizations can fill this role, too. In several programs, the local chamber of commerce took on the tasks of recruiting and organizing local employers for the school-to-work program; in others, a local trade association arranged for training positions and helped design the program's curriculum. Some intermediaries have members representing both employers and educators, while others are organizations of business people. Local traditions and local needs will determine which approach best meets the needs of a particular community.

Leadership Builds on Local Opportunities

Our field research found that the vision of each program was influenced by opportunities that were already present and easily accessible in the community. Table 2.3 highlights the major opportunities that contributed to program development in each locality. These include the ability to use a program model from another location, to build on an existing local program, and to take advantage of an existing relationship between local institutions; the availability of support from the state government; the presence of strong community support for starting a program; and the recognition by school staff of the need for a new educational approach. Emphasizing local involvement over the use of particular program elements led program developers to avoid narrow approaches and to respond to local needs.

In almost half of the sites, leaders imported a program model and then modified it to fit local circumstances, adding features from other approaches or changing key components. While program staff recognized that it is rarely feasible to import a program model without extensive adaptation, they said that they benefited from opportunities to observe the model in operation elsewhere and in some cases to obtain a curriculum, implementation suggestions, and technical assistance to reduce their development costs.

Five of the case studies used existing local programs—vocational courses and co-op programs—as the foundation for more intensive school-to-work initiatives. The leaders changed the existing programs to create a stronger linkage between academic courses and the world of work by developing applied academic courses, putting more academic instruction in vocational courses, linking

Table 2.3. Local Opportunities Contributing to Program Development.

Program	Program Model Available to Follow	Existing Local Program on Which to Build	Existing Relationship Between Local Institutions	State Support[a]	Community Support	Recognition of Need for Change Among District/School Staff
Career academies						
Baltimore finance academy	yes	no	yes	no	yes	no
Los Angeles medical magnet	no	no	no	no	yes	no
Oakland health academy	yes	no	no	no	no	no
Socorro health academy	no	yes	yes	no	no	no
Occupational-academic cluster programs						
Central Point cluster program	no	no	no	yes	no	yes
Dauphin County cluster program	no	yes	no	no	no	yes
Portland cluster program	no	no	no	yes	yes	yes
Restructured vocational education programs						
Cambridge vocational restructuring	no	yes	no	no	no	no
Fort Collins restructured co-op	no	yes	yes	yes	yes	yes
Tech prep programs						
Pickens County tech prep	yes	no	yes	no	no	no
Wayne Township tech prep	yes	no	no	no	yes	yes
Youth apprenticeship programs						
Fox Cities youth apprenticeship	yes	no	yes	yes	no	no
Little Rock youth apprenticeship	no	yes	no	yes	no	no
Pickens County youth apprenticeship	yes	no	yes	no	no	yes
Tulsa youth apprenticeship	yes	no	yes	no	yes	no
West Bend youth apprenticeship	yes	no	no	yes	no	no

Source: MDRC field research.

Note: [a]State support refers to political support, guidance, and encouragement, not financial support.

experiences on the job with instruction in school, creating a school-within-a-school, and giving students more time in the program by starting it in an earlier grade.

Examples of other local opportunities leaders can look for include the presence of intermediary organizations, which often stimulated broad-based community support and drew on their existing relationships with local leaders, and the interest of state officials, who provided valuable political support and technical assistance for several programs. Some states, including Wisconsin, have worked to develop curricula for school-to-work programs, which lifts a significant burden off local program staff. In some instances, the political support of state officials has been instrumental in securing the involvement of key employers and in persuading school districts to approve innovative educational approaches and waivers of graduation requirements.

Time and Money for Planning: The Resources Needed to Develop School-to-Work Programs

Policy makers should recognize that starting new school-to-work programs will require communities to find significant resources of time and money. In particular, our field research found that money and time for planning were essential to the development of the programs in our study. The experiences of the case study sites strongly suggest that the development of school-to-work programs is heavily subsidized by participating organizations that release staff from their regular duties for the development period, and by committed individuals who contribute large amounts of free time. It is also evident that the availability of financial resources is a major factor shaping the nature, scope, and length of the program development process. Table 2.4 shows, for each program, the extra funding sources that were used and the length of time spent developing the program before it began serving students.

There appeared to be several reasons for the crucial role of the resources of money and time for planning.

• There are limits to the amount of time that school staff and employers can take away from their regular jobs to work on developing the program. Even the most committed individuals can burn out, and many people resent the presumption that they will indefinitely carry the effort of moving the program forward in addition to doing their regular jobs. This feeling was most common at sites that lacked released time and development money. It appears that programs that rely solely or primarily on donated time are likely to be more limited in scope and size and may be less likely to become institutionalized than programs that can compensate people for some of their time.

• Program staff members repeatedly told the field researchers that a program coordinator is essential to the development of a good program. The program coordinator develops and maintains relationships with employers and other contributing partners. Because they are released from all or most teaching, coordinators have the flexibility to meet with partners on their own schedules and to troubleshoot at work sites when students have problems there. Without this program coordinator role, the development effort can stall because it is not clearly the responsibility of anyone to move the effort forward if staff are all essentially volunteers.

• Money for visits to other programs and for meeting and planning time can be critical to building support for the program.

As Table 2.4 illustrates, all but one of the case study sites obtained special funding to support their program development costs. These resources came from the school district (often from vocational education dollars), special state funding for demonstration efforts, federal demonstration funding, contributions from business partners, and grants from foundations. State and district funding sources were most frequently used. Programs used these

Table 2.4. Money and Planning for Program Development.

Program	Special School District Funding	Special State Funding	Special Federal Funding	Business Contributions	Foundation Grants	Length of Preimplementation Planning and Program Start Date[a]
Career academies						
Baltimore finance academy	yes	no	no	yes	yes	1 year, fall 1987
Los Angeles medical magnet	yes	no	no	no	yes	1 year, fall 1982
Oakland health academy	no	yes	no	no	yes	½ year, fall 1985
Socorro health academy	yes	no	no	no	no	½ year, fall 1991
Occupational-academic cluster programs						
Central Point cluster program	no	yes	no	no	no	2 years, fall 1991
Dauphin County cluster program	yes	no	no	no	no	3 years, fall 1985
Portland cluster program	no	yes	yes	yes	no	2½ years, fall 1992
Restructured vocational education programs						
Cambridge vocational restructuring	no	no	no	no	yes	¾ year, fall 1991
Fort Collins restructured co-op	yes	no	no	no	no	2 years, fall 1990

Program					Duration[a]
Tech prep programs					
Pickens County tech prep	yes	yes	no	yes	3 years, fall 1992
Wayne Township tech prep	yes	yes	no	no	2 years, fall 1989
Youth apprenticeship programs					
Fox Cities youth apprenticeship	no	no	no	no	½ year, fall 1992
Little Rock youth apprenticeship	no	yes	no	no	½ year, fall 1992
Pickens County youth apprenticeship	yes	no	no	no	1 year, summer 1992
Tulsa youth apprenticeship	no	no	yes	no	2½ years, fall 1992
West Bend youth apprenticeship	yes	yes	no	no	½ year, fall 1992

Source: MDRC field research.

Notes: All programs relied on contributions of staff time by participating school, college, employer, and intermediary organizations and the reallocation of existing resources to support program development. This table indicates new funds used for development efforts.

For the purposes of this table, additional Carl Perkins funding is noted as special district funding rather than special federal funding (which refers only to special demonstration initiatives).

[a]The program start date is when the program started to serve students. Since new programs often phase in one grade level per year, planning typically continues after program startup.

resources for staff development and information collection activities, to purchase curricula and new equipment, to pay teachers for curriculum development and planning, and to pay for a program coordinator. Case study sites that received only modest special funding tended to have shorter planning, fewer participants, and a smaller number of employers and occupational sectors.

Most of the sixteen sites used significant amounts of time for planning and consensus building. The planning process usually lasted a year or more, and two years of preproject planning was not uncommon. Even with this advance work, many programs began with course sequences and curriculum for only the first semester or year planned. Program revisions typically continue for the first three to five years. The initiatives that used less planning time include those with state or federal demonstration funding, which provided extra resources to jump-start the development process, and initiatives that built on preexisting programs. However, not all of these programs developed quickly.

The initiatives' scale and occupational scope also affected the time required to start operations. Schoolwide restructuring efforts typically take the most planning time and involve the most students. For example, for the Portland cluster program, a two-year process of discussion and planning preceded the program's implementation for 225 of the ninth-grade students. Additional restructuring innovations are being planned each year for the next year of this student cohort's progress through high school. At the other extreme are the two youth apprenticeship programs in Wisconsin, which began with seven and twelve students after only six months of planning time. This timetable was made possible by the state's role in developing curriculum and providing political support, and by the determination and leadership of two influential employers. However, the programs started with only one semester of plans completed and a focus on only one occupational area. Extensive work is continuing to develop the curriculum, recruit additional employers so that more students can participate, and plan for expansion into other occupational sectors.

As states and local communities move toward building a national system of school-to-work programs, it may be possible to reduce startup costs by sharing curriculum and by coordinating employer recruitment efforts at the state level. Yet significant costs in time and money are likely to remain. The field research found that extra funding appeared to play a powerful leveraging role in starting up the programs. Moreover, employers and school staff must determine how to fit the new initiative into their existing activities; they must build relationships among people who have little history of collaboration; they must participate in a planning process to give them a sense of program ownership; and they must work to anticipate the challenges of altering their established operating procedures. Most of all, they need to learn about the new methods of teaching and working that the initiatives require. These activities and the role of the local program coordinator will be just as important when a national system is established as they are in pilot programs, and they will always take time and money.

The Support Base: Laying the Groundwork for Survival and Growth

At a minimum, school-to-work programs need the support and involvement of schools and employers and the full spectrum of staff within both—the school district superintendent, principals, and teachers, and the employers' CEOs, senior managers, and floor supervisors. Without this strong support, school-to-work initiatives are difficult to implement and operate because they require many changes in traditional school practices and curricula and the introduction of a whole new range of responsibilities and experiences for employers. The case study programs used several strategies to build an effective support base across the constituencies of schools, employers, and postsecondary institutions.

Obtaining School and District Administrative Support

School and district administrative support is essential because administrators control money, time, personnel, and schedules (Odden, 1991). Their support is needed to permit innovative scheduling of both students' and teachers' time; to obtain waivers of graduation requirements; to allow teachers time to plan together, learn about other programs, and develop curricula; and to provide resources for ongoing program operations. These logistical changes are not always welcomed by school administrators, who may not see the value of "special treatment" for students in the program.

Administrators can also cultivate the support of teachers in a host school who are not part of the school-to-work program and can, when necessary, authorize exceptions to standard operating procedures. Over the years, teachers have seen many innovations come and go without affecting their day-to-day life in the classroom. It is school administrators who can communicate that changes will really be made. For example, after a year of planning for restructuring the Dauphin County vocational education program, the school's administrators abolished the academic departments and assigned academic teachers to the four occupational clusters. These actions were intended to signal that the restructuring plan would indeed be implemented. The administrator responsible for the Cambridge program used his position to close undersubscribed training programs and reallocate their resources and to build a meeting area for teachers and students, who designed and carried out the attractive renovations.

District support is also needed, even when programs have strong school-level support. The Portland cluster program, for example, encountered district-level and teacher union resistance to changing the scheduling and the amount of time for each class period. Conversely, district financial support has enabled Wayne Township's tech prep program to expand. For Dauphin County school leaders, the support of their board was critical; as soon as the academic departments were abolished, grievances were filed by three faculty members who objected to the cluster approach, but the board's support enabled the reform effort to continue.

In some of the case study sites, district-level support compensated for weak school-level support. The two teachers who conceived of the Fort Collins co-op program secured district support, which enabled them to investigate other programs and develop a program design. The first year they tried to implement the program, they encountered a great deal of resistance from both vocational and academic teachers. The district's administration pushed for program changes and a more inclusive planning process; the redesigned program has been successfully implemented in all three of the district's high schools. The Socorro career academy began when the district vocational director asked two teachers to develop plans for expanding the health-occupations program into a comprehensive school-to-work transition program; other school staff joined the program shortly before it began operating.

Administrative support is needed in each school building. For example, the Pickens County tech prep initiative has a high enrollment in one high school where the school principal is excited about the new approach, but at another high school, which emphasizes college preparation, the principal and faculty have been slow to implement the district's tech prep plans and few students have enrolled. Other administrative barriers have included scheduling problems, difficulty arranging for committed teachers to be assigned to the program, and problems obtaining needed resources.

In a leading analysis of systemic school reform, Smith and O'Day (1991) point out that school staff cannot assume that their reforms will receive support from the district, which must juggle competing priorities and demands for resources. Time and effort are required if the leaders of school-to-work initiatives are to cultivate and sustain administrative support from their districts and schools.

The case study experiences suggest several strategies that program developers can use to persuade school administrators to support the program:

- *Obtain information on similar initiatives.* By collecting evidence on other programs that use similar approaches, program developers can provide administrators with success stories and concrete information on the implementation process.
- *Respond to administrators' concerns.* School-to-work program leaders should make sure that the program is closely tied to administrators' educational goals, such as maintaining opportunities for students to attend college and support for low-achieving students.
- *Cultivate support among the faculty.* As discussed in the next section, program developers and operators need to cultivate the support of teachers in the host school. Doing so avoids conflicts and helps the program recruit students, who often depend on their teachers for information and advice about the program.
- *Obtain startup funding.* With special funding to support program development, the program can get underway more quickly.
- *Seek program publicity that reflects favorably on the district and school.* School administrators are responsible to school boards and depend on public approval. Good publicity for a school-to-work program makes both school and district look good, and administrators appreciate this. For example, the Portland cluster program's school benefited from hosting the swearing-in ceremony for the city's new mayor, who had previously authored Oregon's school reform legislation. President George Bush visited the Fox Cities youth apprenticeship program before the end of his term. Other programs have arranged for coverage on radio talk shows and in newspapers.
- *Develop community support.* Programs that have broad community support are attractive to school administrators. For example, leaders of the Tulsa youth apprenticeship program obtained the support of the chamber of commerce and the mayor before approaching the district superintendent. The Portland cluster pro-

gram has relied upon its strong relationship with state officials and employer networks to help persuade school and district administrators to approve changes in standard school procedures. These examples show how program staff can build strong links with school administrators. Without these links, the institutionalization, and even the survival, of the program is unlikely.

Cultivating Teacher and Guidance Counselor Support

Teachers play critical roles in developing and implementing school-to-work programs. They are typically among the key program developers and are usually responsible for developing or modifying the curriculum for the program. In addition, the programs will falter without broad support from teachers and guidance counselors, for it is they who provide eligible students with information and advice that determine whether they apply. Program staff said that without the knowledgeable support of counselors and teachers, students are likely to believe that the program will harm their chances for further education and success in the job market. Equally important, teachers and counselors can identify and recruit students whose inertia and apathy would otherwise keep them from seeking entrance to the program. Students' trust in their teachers, and their dependence on the suggestions and advice of their counselor, means that these people function as gatekeepers for the school-to-work program.

Many initiatives ask program teachers to work more hours and to carry out a wider range of activities than regular high school teachers. They often require teachers to work with peers in new ways, incorporate concepts that are outside the discipline with which they are most familiar, function as advocates for the program, work to get and keep employers actively involved, develop personalized relationships with students, adopt new pedagogical styles, work outside of school and school hours, and spend time developing curriculum materials.

Teams of teachers are often asked to integrate the curricula of courses from several academic and vocational departments. This is a dramatic departure from the experience of most teachers; in conventional high schools, teachers rarely collaborate. What teacher interaction there is occurs within a department; there are few opportunities for teachers in English and social studies, or math and science, to work together, and alliances between academic and vocational instructors are even more rare.

The support of teachers and counselors who must make these changes and do this work is rarely won by directives from the district or school or through payments for extra work on the project. Instead, program staff found that the following strategies were effective for cultivating teacher buy-in:

• *Educate teachers throughout the school about the goals and methods of school-to-work programs.* The cultivation process should help teachers understand the desirability and feasibility of creating a connection between school and the world of work. This includes increasing their awareness of the range of careers available to students, the employment opportunities in the community, and the ways teachers can help students prepare for their careers. Academic teachers often have limited exposure to the business world and are not directly familiar with the range of occupations and how skills are used in work settings. The case study sites educated teachers by providing information on employment opportunities in particular occupational sectors, sponsoring meetings with business people and teachers to discuss skills needed in the workplace, using staff development days to inform nonparticipating teachers about the program, arranging teacher field trips to local industries, and offering opportunities for summer externships in which teachers work in local businesses.

• *Connect the initiative to problems the teachers have identified.* When explaining a new approach to teachers, it is important to show them how it responds to the problems of school operation and student performance that they already recognize. Several of the case study sites found that early, positive testimony from students can persuade reluctant teachers of the desirability of the new approach.

• *Arrange for teachers to visit other programs and workplaces.* Visits to school-to-work programs at other schools enable teachers to see how new instructional methods work, to collect curriculum ideas, to talk to fellow teachers with experience in the program, and to see students applying their skills in workplaces. Dauphin County teachers emphasized the importance of seeing new methods in action. At the time of their development effort, there were no nearby programs to observe and it was difficult for them to envision what they were trying to put into place. Their program and experience are now a resource for other schools. So is the Wayne Township tech prep program, which is visited by teachers from many central Indiana schools. The Portland cluster program sends its teachers to visit other programs and to attend conferences.

• *Make it clear that "business as usual" is changing.* It is important for school faculty to understand that the new initiative will not go away. Clearly explained expectations for changes in teaching and the curriculum are necessary.

• *Bring teachers and guidance counselors into the program design process.* Teachers will not have a stake in the school-to-work initiative if they are not involved in its development. Some programs that were not initiated by teachers subsequently gave them the responsibility of designing the program. For example, the Central Point cluster program's principal challenged the school's faculty to come up with a way to improve students' learning, and they subsequently designed the program.

In other schools, teachers have developed new applied courses that were the cornerstone for the initiative. For example, the plans for the Wayne Township tech prep program were created by teams, each of which included a vocational education instructor, an academic instructor, a postsecondary instructor or administrator, and a business representative. Starting from scratch, the teams decided what should be taught in tech prep. Discussions continued for a year and a half, and the program's focus on applications-based instruction emerged only after a year of discussion. The summer before the program started, high school teachers worked to assess available materials, plan as a team, and develop lessons and competency checklists; and during the school year they worked together to refine their plans. These new responsibilities (for which they were paid) resulted in a strong sense of ownership among the teachers.

Guidance counselors can also contribute to the development process because, as the manager of the Wayne Township tech prep program pointed out, they are usually former teachers who combine an understanding of classrooms with keen insights into students' decisions to apply to a program and their ability to succeed once they have enrolled. Counselors' participation in program development will also facilitate their understanding of the program's goals, thereby encouraging them to identify and recruit appropriate students.

• *Recruit innovative teachers who can be leaders among their peers.* Several of the case study developers chose teachers with a reputation for being willing to try something new, putting in extra effort, and getting other teachers excited. With such teachers on board, other teachers can see that the program recognizes teachers' contributions, and a team can be built around the leading teachers.

• *Encourage and support teachers' efforts to use new approaches.* To help teachers put the new programs into practice, the study sites used varied techniques, including training in new teaching techniques and supporting teachers during the difficult process of change. The director of the Dauphin County program found that staff need to understand the reasons for changing the ways they worked, and they need support during the stressful transition process. He used consultants to keep teachers motivated and to prepare them for change. The director of the Cambridge vocational restructuring effort pointed to the need to provide teachers with support and respect and to get barriers out of their way. The Pickens County tech prep initiative provided teachers with training in using cooperative learning and new course materials before they started teaching applied academic courses that used those methods and materials. (Cooperative learning is a method of instruction in which students work together in small groups to accomplish a shared project; one of its goals is to teach students how to help each other and how to learn from peers with skills and knowledge different from their own. Cooperative learning is to be distinguished from cooperative education, which involves school-supervised work experiences.)

• *Arrange for teachers to have significant amounts of time to meet and plan with each other.* Group meeting time for teachers is difficult to obtain because teachers are in classes with students most of the day. However, if teachers are to participate in program development and to work in teams, arrangements must be made for meeting time. Moreover, program developers cannot assume that teachers will be willing or able to donate their time. The case study programs often paid for teachers' release time, after-school work (particularly for part-time staff), and curriculum development (which often occurs over the summer). One program gave teachers compensatory time for after-school meetings during the intensive early planning efforts, which helped gain the involvement of teachers who were initially less interested in the program. Including planning and coordination time in teachers' schedules once the program is operating is also critically important (see Chapter Six).

Several of these techniques for cultivating teacher buy-in and participation can be seen in the involvement of teachers in the planning for Renaissance 2000, Roosevelt High School's occupational-academic cluster program in Portland, Oregon. The initial planning involved more employers and administrators than teachers. As teachers became more involved in the design process, the focus shifted from technical education and youth apprenticeship to a schoolwide reform effort.

The project coordinator began recruiting teachers in individual meetings after school. Teachers were initially reluctant to get involved because "ideas come and go quickly," and they believed that the school administration would not support reform efforts. By brokering between the administration and the faculty, the program coordinator overcame these concerns, building teacher participation with several activities:

- A federal grant funded teachers' trips to other schools and conferences to learn about innovative educational approaches. Teachers learned about career pathway approaches and academic-occupational integration, and began to change the direction of their school's initiative. Consultants came to the school to talk with the faculty.
- Local businesses paid for eight-week summer externships for ten teachers.
- Several teachers agreed to develop and teach the Freshman Focus course, the first new course created by the initiative, working with local employers to choose jobs and industries to be studied and skills to be taught. Their involvement encouraged other teachers to participate.
- Teachers visited local industries. For many, it was the first time they had visited an industrial workplace.

In the fall before students entered the program, four one-day retreats were held, each involving one-quarter of the school's teachers, along with some business representatives and parents. Small groups were asked to envision the school in two years, after it had achieved recognition for its innovations; the groups then were asked to create a model that would make their vision a reality. Following the retreats, ten teachers summarized the proposals and developed a plan. The faculty then met to review and modify the plan.

This process of teacher involvement created the design for Roosevelt's cluster program. The next step was the creation of teams to develop six career pathways. These teams initially included teachers and support staff; business advisory groups were later added. Another round of retreats was held in the spring for each of the pathway teams to plan its work together. Teachers visited local industries related to their pathways, and summer externships were again provided for teachers. The program began by serving ninth graders, and development efforts for the remainder of the program continue.

Building School-Employer Relationships
Early in Program Development

Employers, too, play a critical role in developing school-to-work programs, particularly in shaping students' experiences in workplaces (see Chapter Five and the companion document to this book, *Learning Through Work* [Jobs for the Future, 1994]). We found that employer support provided needed resources, strengthened school commitment to sustaining their programs, and attracted students. Unfortunately, most schools have a limited relationship with the employer community prior to the school-to-work program's development, and the case studies show that it takes time to involve employers in a program. However, the case studies also show that involving employers at an early stage of development can increase their level of participation and the number participating. Programs that seek employer participation after the design decisions have been made run the risk of reducing employers' sense of ownership and commitment to the program. Participating employers frequently complained that they were not brought into the discussions early enough.

When employers are involved from the beginning of the program, they are often willing to donate considerable time to it and to participate in design efforts and general program management. The early involvement of employers gains the broad support of the business community and assures that the program is adequately preparing students for the targeted industry. For example, Fort Collins school officials worked with a committee of local businesses and the chamber of commerce to develop a career development course. Because of their early involvement, participating employers know that the program responds to their needs, and they appear to feel a special connection to it. More than 400 employers participate in the program, and many of them testify to the importance of community support for the schools and their own responsibility to help students understand the link between school and work.

To cite another example, employers in Wisconsin have been heavily involved in the design, curriculum development, and management of the youth apprenticeship programs. The state-developed curriculum (which covers both classroom and work-based instruction) is based on a curriculum provided by Printing Industries of America and on the skill and knowledge requirements identified by Wisconsin printing employers.

Without employers to provide work experience for students and technical support, most programs would have difficulty distinguishing themselves from other course sequences. Therefore, by making sure that employers are part of the program's support base, program staff can create opportunities that are available from no other source.

Establishing Relationships with Postsecondary Institutions

Most of the sixteen school-to-work programs seek to increase students' opportunities to pursue postsecondary education. This means that program leaders must work with colleges to ensure that their innovative, applied classes and work-based experiences will not harm students' prospects for admission to two-year and four-year colleges (see Chapter Six).

Some of the programs that work with colleges have arranged for a direct transition from high school to college. For example, the Tulsa youth apprenticeship program spans the last two years of high school and two years of college. Participating students can enter Tulsa Junior College with twenty-five credits for their work-based experiences and occupational classes. They then need to earn thirty more credits to get an associate's degree over two years, during which they combine school and work. In the Fox Cities youth apprenticeship program, participating eleventh and twelfth graders attend both academic and technical classes at the Fox Valley Technical College two days each week, with three days at their work site. It is anticipated that during the two-year program, students will earn the equivalent of one year of credits toward an associate's degree in printing. The college plans to offer a one-year program enabling students to continue the mixture of school and work-site training that they experienced in the youth apprenticeship program.

Other school-to-work programs have also arranged for students to take college courses while they are still in high school. However, programs that want their students to receive college credit for courses and training done in high school must begin to develop articulation agreements long before the first students complete the program. For many programs, this process took a year or more, and despite these efforts, the number of students using articulation credits is very low (see Chapter Six).

The case study experiences also show that postsecondary institutions can be a valuable source of ideas for program development and operations, and that college staff can play a key role in program development. This factor, too, argues for bringing community colleges and other postsecondary institutions into the development process at an early stage. Several of the case study programs—including the Portland cluster program, the Pickens County tech prep program, and the two Wisconsin youth apprenticeship programs—benefited from the involvement of community college and technical college staff in developing new curricula for the school-to-work initiatives.

College staff members' interest appears to reflect concern about students' lack of academic preparation for advanced occupational training. Many students entering community colleges need to take remedial courses before they can enter a degree program. These students take a long time to complete their degree, and many drop out before doing so. Indiana Vocational Technical College staff, collaborating on the Wayne Township tech prep initiative, persuaded the high school to require participating students to take a sequence of courses to prepare them for the college. El Paso Community College's health-occupations administrators, who are working with the Socorro health academy, see several benefits for their own program: better-prepared entering students who need less remediation; students who can make a more informed choice about the health-occupations area they want to pursue; more full-time students and degree completers, since better-prepared students who enter with articulation credits may be more motivated to complete the program quickly; and more students who obtain advanced certification.

Some colleges participate in school-to-work initiatives because they offer a way to attract qualified minority students. For example, Morgan State University, a historically black college, provides a free, three-credit introductory finance course for seniors in the Baltimore finance academy, whose students are African-American. The college hopes the class will help them recruit students. Lesley College's partnership with the Cambridge vocational restructuring initiative (providing a youth apprenticeship in elementary education) was shaped by the college's interest in attracting more minorities to become teachers.

Support from postsecondary institutions helps school-to-work programs show that they are not low-status, dead-end tracks for students of whom little is expected. As states and localities work to build a national school-to-work system, this message must be clearly communicated to employers, schools, students, and parents. Without the collaboration of colleges, it will be impossible for programs to communicate this message credibly.

Conclusion

School-to-work programs are started by visionaries to answer specific local needs. Beyond that vision lies a long period of planning and development, which requires detailed knowledge of schools and workplaces. Time, money, and a strong base of support are the critical ingredients needed to put together a program. Skimping on one of these ingredients is possible, but it increases the need for the others.

The visionaries who created our programs can be found in many kinds of organizations: schools, district offices, businesses, local employer associations, and community leadership groups. To bring about change, they depended on a shared local awareness that major changes were badly needed. But their support was not ready-made: it grew in response to vigorous and sustained efforts by the visionaries. Administrative support, along with the collaboration of employers and others in the community, can be home-grown, too.

Starting a school-to-work program also requires detailed knowledge about *students*—their needs, their interests, their goals for the future, and the ways that they think about the present—in order to motivate them to participate in a good school-to-work program. The pioneering programs we studied learned a great deal about attracting students, and the next chapter describes the lessons they learned.

Chapter Three

Targeting, Recruiting,
and Selecting Students

Currently, only a small proportion of high school students participate in innovative school-to-work programs, and it has been relatively easy for communities to fill the modest number of slots through ad hoc recruiting efforts. As programs expand, however, the debate about which students should be included in these programs will surely become louder, particularly as parents and students recognize that their access to the most attractive programs is constrained by resource limitations. In addition, as interest in school-to-work initiatives has grown, state and federal policy makers and program designers have often disagreed about which segments of the student population should participate. This disagreement is rooted in assumptions about the ability of low-achieving students to benefit from the programs and about the programs' effectiveness in meeting these students' needs.

The policy debate has spawned a wide range of answers to the critical question of which students should be served by school-to-work programs. Some people argue that all students would benefit from a high school program that connects their learning to work, through career exposure, work-relevant instruction, and work-based learning—the ingredients of innovative school-to-work programs. Some would target students who do not want to attend a four-year college, and some would target the middle 50 percent of high school students, which would exclude those likely to enter four-year colleges and those with below-average skill levels. Then there are people who see school-to-work programs as being particularly well-suited to the educational needs of low-achieving students;

these people want to make sure that low-achievers are served, along with other students. Others want to target students who are interested in and likely to pursue specific technical careers. Finally, some people want each student to be able to choose the high school program that is best suited to his or her interests and to have a wide variety from which to select, including school-to-work programs; this would enable students from all of the previously mentioned groups to participate if they wished.

Why the Target Group Matters

The debate about who should be served by school-to-work programs reflects three unresolved challenges facing policy makers and program staff: the current lack of information about the benefits of these programs for various kinds of students; the stigma associated with serving low-achieving and disadvantaged students; and conflict over access to desirable services and opportunities.

• *Uncertainty about what works for whom.* While there is tantalizing research (Stasz and others, 1993) on the benefits of instruction using work-related experiences—such as project-based assignments, applications-based instruction, hands-on experience, and work in teams—little is known about whether the new instructional methods are more effective for some kinds of high school students than for others. Some people have suggested that many students who do poorly in classes that use traditional instructional methods may benefit from the methods used in innovative school-to-work programs, but this hypothesis has not yet been carefully tested.

• *Stigmatization.* Teachers and school administrators often prefer working with high-achieving students, and schools with concentrations of low-achieving students often have difficulty recruiting and retaining qualified teachers. Parents know that vocational programs have sometimes been a dumping ground for low-achieving students; they also know that a college degree has historically been a ticket to high-status, high-salary jobs and are concerned that students in school-to-work programs may lose the chance to go to college.

• *Conflicts over access.* When school-to-work programs are seen as providing very desirable services, or helping students get attractive jobs or succeed in college, they are likely to become oversubscribed, forcing policy makers and program staff to make difficult choices about who will be admitted to the program. These selection decisions can be made in several different ways: by using a lottery; on a "first come, first served" basis; by admitting the highest-achieving or lowest-achieving students first; or according to some other criterion. In situations where the active collaboration of employers is central to the program, admission may be limited to students who seem able to meet employers' needs even before they enter the program. If school-to-work programs do a good job of preparing students for high-wage careers, then excluding low-achieving students who are capable of performing well in those careers will further widen the gap between educationally advantaged and disadvantaged students. The more attractive a program is, the more conflict can be expected over the best way to target its services.

Ultimately, policy makers and program staff must decide which groups they want to target and, once they have done so, they must design strategies for bringing those students into the program through marketing and selection processes. To shed light on this decision and the marketing processes that follow from it, this chapter assesses the experiences of the pioneering school-to-work programs that include disadvantaged and low-achieving students.

The three challenges of uncertain benefits, stigmatization, and conflict over access were faced by all of the programs in this study. Most responded to them by designing selection procedures that largely avoided the need to draw distinctions among students. This surprising finding shows that the need to build a broad base of support in the community led program staff to accept a wide range of students, particularly because labeling students as "acceptable" or "not acceptable" for the program could result in anger among community members. The overall results of these broadly inclusive policies suggest that it is feasible to include disadvantaged, low-achieving students in school-to-work programs without impeding program operation. The programs that include substantial numbers of disadvantaged and low-achieving students (along with other students) appear to function well, with few complaints from teachers, employers, or students.

Moreover, although some staff say they favor stricter screening criteria, none of the programs appears to be moving in that direction. In contrast, some of the programs with more restrictive targeting and selection procedures are under pressure to broaden access to include a wider range of students. This is the case in Baltimore, where discussions are underway on the need to serve a variety of students, including low achievers, in school-to-work programs, whose innovative methods may be of particular benefit to them. This does not mean that these school-to-work programs have no students who create problems for teachers, peers, and program operators. However, few of these students would have been screened out by selection criteria based on grades or attendance.

In addition, there is strong support for school-to-work programs among schools, employers, and communities, regardless of the programs' targeting methods and their inclusion of low-achieving students. This indicates that program support is not undermined by efforts to reach out to students who previously have not performed well in school, provided that programs do not focus exclusively on these easily stigmatized students. Finally, for practical reasons, program staff often chose a targeting strategy based on open eligibility, broad marketing, and self-nomination in order to gain acceptance for the program from students, parents, and teachers. Many program staff members report that narrower selection procedures would endanger their program. This suggests that while some people involved in designing and implementing school-to-work programs may hope for benefits from focusing on relatively high-achieving students, such an approach may not work in many schools and communities.

Therefore, at this early stage in the development of school-to-work programs, while there is no definitive answer to the question of who should be served by them, the evidence from the case studies clearly establishes that it is not necessary for a program to exclude disadvantaged and low-achieving students in order to flourish.

Targeting in Practice

Targeting activities can be divided into three key parts of the program intake process: eligibility rules; marketing to students, parents, teachers, and counselors; and the final screening criteria for selecting students for admission to the program. Table 3.1 describes these features for the sixteen school-to-work programs, along with the approximate proportion of low-achieving students they serve.

When we were choosing programs for our study, program staff were asked whether their program serves a broad range of students, including both disadvantaged and low-achieving as well as nondisadvantaged students. Programs that exclude low-achieving students were not selected for the study. However, our selection process did not require that programs use any particular methods for targeting or that they serve a specific proportion of low-achieving or disadvantaged students. Thus, while the case study programs are not statistically representative of all school-to-work programs in the United States, they do provide information on the feasibility of providing services to a varied group of students and on the range of methods used to target and serve diverse students.

It is striking to see in Table 3.1 that most programs in the study use similar targeting methods, with marketing aimed at a broad range of students, and that most serve a substantial proportion of

Table 3.1. Targeting for Eligibility, Marketing, and Screening.

Program	Grade Levels	Eligibility Criteria	Students Targeted for Marketing	School Screening Criteria	Employer Screening Criteria[a]	Proportion of Low Achievers Included[b]
Career academies						
Baltimore finance academy	9–12	Test scores, grades, attendance	All	Ranking	None	A few
Los Angeles medical magnet	10–12	Open to all	All	Self-nomination; if oversubscribed, district rules	None	Some
Oakland health academy	10–12 (a few in grade 9)	Open to all	All	Self-nomination, disadvantaged preferred	None	Most
Socorro health academy	9–12	Open; may review grades, ask for teacher recommendations	All	Self-nomination	None	Some
Occupational-academic cluster programs						
Central Point cluster program	10–12	Open to all	All	Self-nomination	None	Some
Dauphin County cluster program	9–12	Open to all	All	Self-nomination	None	Some
Portland cluster program	9–12	Universal coverage	All	None	None	Some
Restructured vocational education programs						
Cambridge vocational restructuring	9–12	Open to all	All	Self-nomination	None[c]	Some
Fort Collins restructured co-op	10–12	Open to all	All	Self-nomination and all alternative HS students	None	Some

Tech prep programs

Pickens County tech prep	9–12	Open to all	All	Self-nomination	None	Most
Wayne Township tech prep	10–12	Open to all; ask for counselors' recommendation	All	Self-nomination	None	Some

Youth apprenticeship programs

Fox Cities youth apprenticeship	11–12	Must be scheduled to graduate in two years; grades, attendance, level of interest	All	Competitive application process[d]	Employers choose students	A few
Little Rock youth apprenticeship	11–12	Review of grades, attendance[e]	All	Self-nomination[e]	None	Some
Pickens County youth apprenticeship	12-post-secondary	Grades, attendance, dexterity test	Electronics students	Competitive application process; maturity considered	Employers rank preference for apprentices	A few
Tulsa youth apprenticeship	11-post-secondary	Grades, test scores, statement of interest, interview	Broad	Competitive application process	Employers on selection panel	A few

Table 3.1. Targeting for Eligibility, Marketing, and Screening, Cont'd.

Program	Grade Levels	Eligibility Criteria	Students Targeted for Marketing	School Screening Criteria	Employer Screening Criteria [a]	Proportion of Low Achievers Included [b]
West Bend youth apprenticeship	11–12	Must be scheduled to graduate in two years; grades, attendance, level of interest	All	Competitive application process	Employers on selection panel	A few

Source: MDRC field research.

Note: [a]Refers only to employer's role in screening students for initial entrance into program. In most programs, employers do screen and select students placed at their workplace.

[b]Assessment of the proportion of low-achieving students in each program based on interviews with program staff. "Most" means more than half; "some" means one-fourth to one-half; "a few" means fewer than one-quarter.

[c]Employers on the selection panel for the grade 12 youth apprenticeship programs, but not involved in selecting grade 9 students for the vocational school.

[d]In the first year of the program, all applicants were accepted.

[e]Rules call for a 2.5 grade average in the most recent semester and no more than six unexcused absences. However, grade requirement is often waived.

low-achieving students: approximately one-quarter or more of their students enter with records of low achievement. The majority of the sixteen programs place few, if any, limitations on students' eligibility. Most rely heavily on students' self-nomination instead of screening students' records. However, many programs use some degree of screening before students enter the workplace (this usually occurs one or two years after students enter the program).

The consistency in targeting approaches used in the sixteen case studies suggests that open eligibility, broad marketing, and self-nomination to determine admission into the program are feasible and appropriate methods for targeting program services.

Open Eligibility

Eligibility rules are important because they tell students, parents, and teachers which students have a chance to be admitted to the program. They constitute the first hurdle that interested students must clear, and often provide the first message about the program that targeted students receive. The programs we studied display a strikingly consistent pattern of opening eligibility to all students. Ten of the sixteen impose virtually no restrictions on students' eligibility. Six programs use grades (and sometimes test scores) to determine eligibility, but all of them also admit some low-achieving students who do not meet the published eligibility criteria, and four of the six are quite small, serving fewer than fifteen students. One of these four, the Pickens County youth apprenticeship program, has decided to limit its admissions to students likely to be seen by employers as desirable, high-achieving, mature young people; however, since the program is marketed only to students in vocational electronics classes, the selection pool is not a "creamed" population and includes students with mixed records.

Program staff find several important benefits in open eligibility:

- The concerns of parents, students, and staff about possible discriminatory admissions are eliminated, and students' anxieties about failing to meet eligibility standards are greatly reduced.

- Staff are able to tell students that the program *wants* them, a positive message that improves the program's public image and students' attachment to the program.
- The stigma of programs for low-achieving, disadvantaged students is greatly reduced; instead, the program tends to be seen as including a broad range of students and as resembling the school as a whole.

When these messages are combined with a marketing approach that communicates the benefits that participants receive and the future high-wage careers that they can expect, the result is that the initial phase of the targeting process includes the broadest possible range of students. It makes the program a microcosm of the school as a whole, thereby strengthening the program's support within the school and community.

Broad Marketing

A program's marketing is its outreach effort to recruit students. Marketing assists the targeting process by getting information to those students whom program staff consider "right" for the program. The marketing efforts we examined vary in intensity, but most are modest, doing just enough to fill the available slots for entering students.

Almost all of the sixteen programs market themselves to *all* students at the appropriate grade level for program entrance. Of the two programs that market themselves more narrowly, Tulsa's small youth apprenticeship program relies on guidance counselors to identify appropriate applicants, including some low-achieving students, and the Pickens County youth apprenticeships are marketed only to students in vocational electronics classes. (However, Pickens County's tech prep program is marketed to all students.)

All the marketing efforts have two functions. First, they provide information that shapes the way the program is perceived by people in the host school, parents, and the community at large.

Consequently, a broad marketing campaign serves a public relations purpose, building support and rebutting stigmatizing perceptions. Effective program marketing can overcome people's predisposition to dismiss school-to-work programs as low-status dumping grounds for near-dropouts. Good marketing can also inform students, parents, and teachers about the goals of the program, the careers that participating students can enter, and the new instructional methods that the program uses in school and in workplaces. Program staff report that broad marketing efforts help them build support and attract students.

The second function of marketing is to create a pool of applicants for the student selection process. To generate interested applicants, marketing efforts must overcome the high level of inertia, and even apathy, of many high school students. Program staff find that many students who are eligible and appropriate for school-to-work programs simply make no plans for their high school years until their guidance counselor pushes them to agree to a list of courses that they will take in the next school year. Efforts to inform parents about their children's educational opportunities often fall on deaf ears as well. (However, a substantial minority of the students interviewed said that they chose the program because their parents pushed them to do so.) Many program staff thought that apathetic students are precisely the group that appears to benefit most from a good school-to-work program, but effective marketing is needed to get them to apply. These students have the potential to do well in school but are not interested in it and are therefore unlikely to apply for any school program without strong encouragement.

Widely inclusive marketing, then, is vital, since without it, the students who can benefit from a program may not apply to join it. Narrow marketing methods and marketing that emphasizes eligibility criteria undermine the program's ability to attract appropriate students, according to program staff. The marketing and recruiting strategies used by the sixteen case study programs are discussed in detail at the end of this chapter.

Self-Nomination by Interested Students

The third step in the targeting process is the selection of students for admission. The screening of applicants is often thought to be widely used to select students for school-to-work programs, but in fact most of the programs we studied use self-nomination, in which the people who volunteer are deemed acceptable by the program. The broad use of self-nomination is our most important and unexpected finding about student participation. Ten of the sixteen programs in this study use self-nomination (and another, the Portland cluster program, uses nonselective, universal coverage of all students in the high school). If more students seek entry to a program than it can accommodate, schools used several kinds of solutions: expanding the program (as in the Wayne Township tech prep program); using a lottery (as in the Central Point cluster program) or a first-come, first-served rule (as in the Dauphin County cluster program); or applying districtwide rules dealing with desegregation goals and school overcrowding (as in the Los Angeles medical magnet program).

Four programs use a process in which students are selected from the pool of applicants based on grades, test scores, attendance, and recommendations; this results in the selection of relatively higher-achieving students who have been successful in school and who are likely to be seen as desirable workers by employers. However, even in these programs a modest number of low-achieving students are selected, in most cases because there are not enough high-achieving applicants.

Student self-nomination has important benefits for school-to-work programs:

• Self-nominated students are interested in the program and its occupational theme, and are likely to be motivated to cooperate with teachers, employers, and classmates. While this may seem obvious, its great value lies in the fact that the disadvantaged and low-achieving students who nominate themselves for a school-to-work program are likely to be far more cooperative and motivated than similar students who do not volunteer for the program. Consequently, self-nomination is a powerful strategy for programs that wish to serve a broad range of students, including some low-achieving students, because it greatly reduces the problems of serving young people who do not want to be in school and therefore are difficult to teach.

• Self-nomination effectively rebuts the perception that school-to-work programs are undesirable dumping grounds for students who cannot function anywhere else. Of course, achieving this benefit depends on the program's ability to attract a broad range of students.

• It takes advantage of the important—and hard-to-get—information that students have about their own skills and needs, and matches students with programs that *they* perceive to be appropriate. Since there is little evidence that selection decisions made by program or school staff, no matter how thoughtful, will identify precisely the right students for the school-to-work program, self-nomination enables students to use their knowledge of their interests, strengths, and needs to choose an appropriate program, provided that they receive accurate information about their options.

• It is consistent with the growing movement for public school choice because of its strong accountability mechanism: If no one chooses a program, students and parents probably do not think it is beneficial or effective. (In public school choice plans, parents may select the public school in which they will enroll their children, whether or not they live within the school's attendance-zone boundaries. Schools participating in such plans typically offer distinctive programs designed to attract students; when a school has few applicants, district administrators push the staff to develop a more attractive program; see Witte, 1989.)

• Because no one is excluded, self-nomination avoids conflicts over demands for access by students and parents.

- Self-nomination reinforces the work ethic of school-to-work programs. When students choose programs with occupational themes they find interesting and valuable, they are likely to consider reasonable the programs' teachers and employers demands that they do the work necessary to succeed in those occupations. In a conventional high school program, many students see little reason to respond to demands that they work hard, since their courses often seem unrelated to their future plans, which are often vague. When students nominate themselves for a school-to-work program, they are likely to recognize the connection between their performance in the program and their career opportunities in the future.

- It treats high school students respectfully, as young adults. They are given the power to make important decisions about how they will spend their school and work time and how they will prepare for the future, within the context of a program that is designed to provide consistently high-quality education and work experiences.

Self-nomination also creates some potential challenges, but they are not without solutions. First, programs that rely on self-nomination may not reach some students who could benefit from the program but who are too apathetic to apply. For this reason, it is important for policy makers to support research aimed at determining which kinds of students are likely to benefit from school-to-work programs. Once this information is available, outreach activities can target the students who are most appropriate for the program.

Second, programs that use self-nomination are likely to recruit students with diverse achievement levels. Teachers and employers will need to adapt their instructional methods and training in response to these differences. In some cases, extra instruction will be required for students who enter the program with fewer skills than others.

Designing Student Selection Procedures to Support Program Operations

Student selection processes are closely tied to other key factors affecting the success of the programs. These factors include parents' support for the program; employer roles in the selection process; the use of entry criteria based on students' achievement of specific basic skills; and the program's federal and state policy context.

Parental Support

Some of the sixteen programs have learned through experience that the student selection process is the time when parents have the most concerns about the program. If the process does not respond to these concerns, conflicts can result, jeopardizing the program's survival.

Many school-to-work programs use the student selection process to try to gain the support of parents who know little about the program. They require that parents give their consent before a student's application can be accepted, and they provide information about the program to parents as part of the student selection process. Some programs go even further, holding evening and Saturday open-house meetings to explain the program, answer questions from parents and students, and provide testimonials from participating students. Tours of the program's facilities demonstrate new, high-tech equipment and show that the program has the financial and moral support of the school and district. Mailings to parents of eligible students are used by some programs; most have a telephone number that parents can call to get information and answers to their questions.

The perceived stigma of work-related programs is a central focus of these programs' relationships with parents. Some teachers and program managers confront the problem head on, with brochures whose theme is "tech prep isn't for dummies" and videos that answer such questions as: "Is the program easier than regular high school? Are there 'real' teachers in the program? Is it true that kids in the program are 'rowdy' and trouble-makers? Are there a lot of teen parents? What about drugs?" In Portland, the school district's plans to provide occupational cluster programs for most students triggered a protest by parents who were afraid that their children would be denied a chance to attend college; a series of meetings was held to put out the fires that had been ignited by misunderstandings about these plans.

Employer Roles

Program staff are well aware of the importance of involving employers in the school-to-work initiative (although, as Chapter Two showed, many programs seek employer support rather late in the implementation process). Employers are keenly sensitive to decisions about the selection of students for the program because these decisions determine the kinds of young people who will be entering their workplace.

Employer roles in the student selection process vary among the sixteen programs in the study. In some, employers seek to avoid the burden of interviewing many students because they lack experience in predicting which students will do well in workplace settings a year or more in the future. In these cases, employers rely on the decisions of school staff to select students.

In other programs, employers play a central role in choosing the students who will enroll. For example, in the Fox Cities youth apprenticeship program, applying students are interviewed by the employers who provide the program's work-based learning, and the employers decide which students will be admitted. The employers then negotiate with each other to allocate the students among the work sites, a process that balances the students' transportation needs and the employers' desire to have a share of the best-prepared students.

Another approach is used by programs that try to anticipate the preferences of employers without formally including them in the process of selecting students and assigning them to workplaces. For example, the Dauphin County cluster program uses criteria that prevent students whose attendance is below a certain level from receiving co-op placements, and the program's occupational teachers have broad authority to determine which students are deemed ready for co-op work opportunities. The goal of these procedures is to maintain the support of the employers that provide the placements by sending them the most able and reliable students; the competition from other programs for the modest number of good co-op positions strongly motivates school staff to anticipate the wishes of participating employers.

Some employers screen students after they are already in the program but before they are allowed to participate in work-based learning. Screening devices include job interviews, grades and attendance, and trial periods. The Baltimore finance academy screens students based on the number of internships made available by employers; lower-ranking students who would exceed the internship capacity are not admitted to the eleventh-grade academy program, even if their performance in grades 9 and 10 was acceptable. These screening procedures focus on employers' needs and give lower priority to students' interests.

The existence of very different strategies for involving employers in the student selection process raises an important question: What criteria accurately predict which students will do well in work-based learning activities? Research has not identified ways to forecast students' performance in these activities. Past school performance may not be a good predictor of success in the workplace, since students who have done badly in school may be stimulated to excel once they have hands-on opportunities as trainees. Success in the abstract learning and memorization tasks required by schools may not indicate how well a student will perform at work, and thus school staff may not be able to predict students' workplace performance accurately.

In the absence of reliable criteria that can accurately screen students for work-based learning activities, program staff may find it useful to send a wide range of students to work-based activities and to monitor their workplace experiences closely, to learn which students succeed in that environment. This approach will enable staff to avoid using questionable or unreliable screening criteria, and will allow both school staff and employers to learn more about the kinds of students who benefit from work-based activities.

Entry Criteria

Some analysts have argued that there is a strong case for requiring students to demonstrate that they have mastered specific basic skills before they are allowed to enter a school-to-work program. These "gateway" entry requirements could be based on an assessment or test, as proposed by proponents of the certificate of initial mastery (CIM), or on a student's completion of the tenth grade (which is the time suggested for most students to be assessed for the CIM). (The CIM would require that all students be examined by tenth grade on their mastery of reading, math, and other core knowledge, with high school graduation and entry into specialized high school courses conditioned on passing the examination. The goals are to ensure that all students possess the basic skills required in the workplace, to establish a credential that will be a reliable indicator to employers of students' mastery of these skills, and to give students an incentive to learn the skills, since the opportunity to receive work-related training will depend on passing the examination. See Commission on the Skills of the American Workforce, 1990.)

The evidence from the sixteen programs is that an entry requirement tied to students' assessment performance or completion of the tenth grade would substantially reduce the participation of disadvantaged and lower-achieving students, who are likely to be delayed or effectively barred by such requirements. Disadvantaged students have, on average, lower test scores and a higher incidence of grade retention than other students, and their high school dropout rate is higher. Consequently, using assessments and tenth-grade completion as hurdles that students must jump before they can enter a school-to-work program will screen out many of these students.

Moreover, many program staff want students to enter the school-to-work program well before the eleventh grade. Six of the sixteen programs start in the ninth grade, and five more start in the tenth grade (see Table 3.1). These programs have sought to include a broad range of students by beginning early in high school, before many students who are at risk of dropping out have become disengaged. Four of the eleven programs that start in the ninth or tenth grade have actually modified their programs from designs that began after the tenth grade; in all four cases, the change was made to include students while there is still time for them to make up for their academic and motivational problems. These programs (in Baltimore, Dauphin County, Socorro, and Wayne Township), all of which are located in areas with concentrations of disadvantaged students, report that the earlier start date has greatly improved students' success in school and at work.

This finding is extremely important, since policy discussions of school-to-work initiatives have largely assumed that programs should start in grade 11 or 12, after students have completed most of their graduation requirements. This assumption appears counter to the experiences of our school leaders and program staff, many of whom said that programs that do not start until grade 11 or 12 will encounter numerous problems with unprepared and unmotivated students; will miss the opportunity to include students who would normally drop out before reaching grade 11 or 12; and will forgo the benefits of using the powerful new work-related instructional methods in the early high school years. For students who have not benefited from traditional instructional methods, the early introduction of the innovative instructional methods used in many school-to-work programs may help them to succeed in school.

The apparent correlation of early-starting programs with those that serve a broad range of students (including some low-achieving students) supports the staff view that school-to-work programs that start before the eleventh grade can reach a larger number of disadvantaged students than programs that start later. In the United States, over one-third of sixteen- to twenty-four-year-old high school dropouts left school before completing the tenth grade (National Center for Educational Statistics, 1991, p. 20). Programs that start in the ninth or tenth grade can make contact with disadvantaged youths before they become discouraged, fall between the cracks, and stop attending school. In other words, these programs can have a dropout prevention effect.

The Portland and Central Point cluster programs demonstrate that students can work toward their certificate of initial mastery at the same time they participate in a school-to-work program. Oregon is moving to require the statewide adoption of the CIM; most students will take the CIM assessment at the end of tenth grade. Students in Portland's cluster program will have been in the school-to-work program for two years by the time they take the assessment, and those in Central Point's, one year. In these programs, the CIM will function as a requirement for graduation. Thus, while students who require extra time to achieve the CIM will not be denied entry into the school-to-work program, employers can still use it to identify graduates who have the skills needed to succeed on the job.

Based on the experiences of many of the pioneering school-to-work programs in our study, it appears that policy makers should reconsider the common assumption that programs should start in the eleventh or twelfth grade. Programs that start in earlier grades may have great advantages for many schools and employers, including better preparation of students for their work experiences and for postsecondary education, dropout prevention, and more opportunities for improving low-achieving students' performance. In addition, school-to-work programs that start early can expose students to a wide range of careers before they enter an expensive youth apprenticeship or other training program; students who understand the work requirements of a career are less likely to drop out of training programs later on.

State and Federal Policy Context

Many school-to-work programs depend on state and federal funding, which often include requirements that affect student selection. For example, several states have adopted legislation that limits program funding to certain grade levels. In California, state funding for academy programs is limited to grades 10 through 12, and in Arkansas and Indiana, state funding for tech prep pilot programs covers only grades 11 and 12. The Wayne Township tech prep program in Indiana originally included only eleventh and twelfth graders. When school and district staff decided that the program would be more effective if it started in tenth grade, they had to obtain local funds to expand it.

State policy also affects the number and kinds of students who participate in a program. Again, California provides a good example. The suggested size of its state-funded academies is fifty students per grade level, and each program receives the maximum level of state funding if thirty students per grade level meet three of four state-specified criteria related to disadvantagedness (low grades or other evidence of underachievement, irregular attendance, lack of interest in the regular school program, and economic disadvantagedness; see Stern, Raby, and Dayton, 1992). These funding rules have led many academies in California to include disadvantaged students and to aim for the suggested academy size of fifty new students each year. The California academy in our study, Oakland's health academy, serves a cross section of students in a highly disadvantaged community and easily qualifies for the maximum level of state funding.

Federal policies affect the participation of students in school-to-work programs as well. Some program staff disagree with the priorities for serving at-risk students stated in the 1990 Carl Perkins Vocational Education Act, preferring to recruit higher-achieving students for their programs. After the National Center for Research in Vocational Education held the 1992 Tech Prep Leadership Summit, it reported that "although the language of Perkins II includes students who are at-risk of dropping out of school, and early advocates of Tech Prep targeted the 'neglected majority,' the Summit participants believe we need to incorporate a wider student population into these programs. We need to focus on all students" (National Center for Research in Vocational Education, 1993, n.p.) Nevertheless, federal and state policies clearly have the power to shape local program decisions about which students they will target and serve. Using that power in ways that are sensitive to the diverse needs of local school-to-work programs will require careful thought on the part of state and federal policy makers and, ideally, consultation with representatives of students and parents, program staff, and employers.

Characteristics of Students in School-to-Work Programs

To learn more about the participating students, we asked program staff to administer a one-page background questionnaire to their first-year students. We wanted to collect information about the students who enter the programs before normal attrition changed the composition of the student body. Students completed the survey anonymously. We received information about students in twelve programs; four programs decided not to participate in the study survey, owing to logistical problems and reluctance to ask questions that some students might find intrusive. Table 3.2 summarizes the characteristics of students entering these twelve school-to-work programs. (While it would be desirable to compare the characteristics of these students to those of other U.S. high school students, comparable survey data are not available.)

Because the data are self-reported, it is likely that the students underreported the incidence of sensitive characteristics, including family welfare receipt, parents' limited education, students' low grades, and students' school behavior problems. The sensitivity of these items is suggested by the frequency of "don't know" responses; up to 20 percent of the students in some programs said that they did not know their parents' educational attainment, and up to 15 percent said that they did not know whether their family received welfare. Some of these responses were probably made by students who were reluctant to admit that a parent did not complete high school or that the family receives welfare. If this is the case, the data in the table can be viewed as understating the extent to which participating students are disadvantaged.

Also, because the programs do not all start in the same year of high school, the grade level of respondents differs. For example, the first-year participants in the Wisconsin youth apprenticeships are in the eleventh grade, while the first-year participants in Portland's cluster program are in the ninth grade. In two programs, Baltimore and Socorro, the respondents were eighth-grade students applying for entry into the academy.

Not surprisingly, the students' characteristics reflect differences among the programs' communities. For example, the high incidence of poverty in Socorro is reflected in the large number of parents without a high school diploma and the high AFDC and food stamps receipt rate.

The highest concentration of educationally disadvantaged students is found in the career academies and tech prep programs. Students entering these programs tend to have parents with relatively little education, and many reported that they receive low grades and have had behavior problems in school. The reported levels of

Table 3.2. Characteristics of Students Entering School-to-Work Programs.

Program	Minority (%)	Speaks Language Other Than English at Home (%)	Father Has No HS Diploma (%)	Father Has 4-Year College Degree (%)	Mother Has No HS Diploma (%)	Mother Has 4-Year College Degree (%)	Receives AFDC or Food Stamps (%)	English Grades Mostly C's or Lower (%)	Math Grades Mostly C's or Lower (%)	Absent 7 Times or More Previous Semester (%)	Student Sent to Office or Parent Warned (%)	Surveys Completed	Grade Level
Career academies													
Baltimore	97	6	21	8	25	12	18	34	31	11	53	96	8
Los Angeles	99	43	24	28	22	20	14	20	54	18	29	93	10
Socorro	96	90	72	1	64	1	48	16	33	7	25	104	8
Occupational-academic clusters													
Central Point	10	7	15	24	13	22	3	27	45	24	16	107	10-12
Dauphin County	9	5	24	6	15	9	4	53	41	32	34	98	10-12
Portland	40	28	22	13	26	10	6	40	36	39	46	98	9
Tech prep													
Pickens County	18	0	42	3	51	6	4	61	80	31	47	51	9-12
Wayne Township	25	8	42	5	55	5	17	57	33	17	25	24	10
Youth apprenticeships													
Fox Cities	0	0	0	14	0	29	0	33	57	0	17	7	11
Little Rock	18	0	40	0	36	0	9	73	45	18	10	11	11-12
Tulsa	18	6	20	13	25	19	0	19	29	6	18	17	11
West Bend	0	9	0	11	0	22	30	55	70	18	60	11	11

Source: Self-administered MDRC survey of first-year students, conducted in spring 1993; Baltimore and Socorro surveys were administered to applicants before their first year in the program.

Notes: Missing values were not used to calculate these results.

"Number of Surveys completed" represents the total number of surveys completed and returned. The number of respondents varies because of differences in program size.

"Grade level" indicates grade level of student respondents.

family welfare receipt are higher than those for students in other programs (although, again, underreporting is likely for students in all sites). In addition, the academy students are overwhelmingly members of minority groups and many come from families that speak a language other than English at home. Nationally, some career academies appear to serve a more advantaged population; the National Academy Foundation provides the curricula and program designs used in more than 100 academies, many of which target college-bound students (Stern, Raby, and Dayton, 1992). However, the academies in our study (along with the numerous academies funded by the state of California to serve mostly disadvantaged students, and many of Philadelphia's academies) show that it is possible to include substantial numbers of disadvantaged students in academy programs.

Nearly as disadvantaged are the students in the occupational-academic cluster programs. They reported notably high levels of absenteeism (24 to 39 percent reported seven or more absences in the previous semester), and a large proportion reported receiving low grades. Two of the youth apprenticeship programs appear to have fewer disadvantaged students than the other programs; however, the Little Rock and West Bend youth apprenticeship programs have a substantial proportion of such students.

The programs also include students with significant strengths. In the Los Angeles and Central Point programs, approximately one-quarter reported that their fathers have four-year college degrees, and two of the seven Fox Cities students said that their mothers have four-year college degrees. A substantial majority of the academy students reported receiving mostly A's or B's in English (however, the Baltimore and Socorro respondents were in the eighth grade, where higher grades may be more common than in high school). Also, both the academy and youth apprenticeship students reported a low incidence of absences.

Overall, the relatively high incidence of families in which a language other than English is spoken, low parental educational attainment, low grades, and school behavior problems strongly suggests that few of these programs are creaming—that is, recruiting the easiest-to-teach students. The survey results are consistent with program staff members' reports of disadvantaged, low-achieving students in their target populations and in their programs. From our data, it is reasonable to conclude that these school-to-work programs are serving a broad range of students and are not avoiding students who are difficult to teach.

Lessons in Recruiting and Marketing

To recruit students for a school-to-work program, it is necessary to provide them and their parents with clear and compelling information about the benefits that the program has to offer. Formulating such a message, and making sure that students and parents receive it, are new challenges for many programs. School staff tend to describe programs in terms of their educational goals and methods (which students and parents rarely find exciting), assuming that other benefits are clear without explicitly stating them. Employers, who may be more familiar with marketing methods, tend to lack experience dealing with students as a target group. When school-to-work programs begin recruiting students, they often have to try several strategies before discovering what works best, since the most effective strategies can differ from program to program. All the recruiting and marketing strategies used by the school-to-work programs are presented in Table 3.3, which shows the target group, the main messages, and the strategies used by seven representative programs.

Several lessons emerge from the programs' marketing experiences. It is crucial for program leaders to know how to locate potential students. Each district has its own distinctive ways of organizing students into classes, and program staff must learn how to use their district's organizational patterns to reach their target group, tailoring their recruiting efforts in response to the ways that students are distributed in classes.

Concentrations of students who are likely to be interested in a school-to-work program are sometimes found in a district's prealgebra classes, its first-year vocational shops, its alternative schools, or its general-track English classes. Some of the program's feeder junior high schools or middle schools may have more targeted students than others. In some districts, there may be no particular classes with concentrations of likely recruits, forcing the program to rely on broad marketing and referrals from knowledgeable guidance counselors.

The recruiting messages emphasize the benefits of high-skill, high-pay jobs and the need for students to prepare now in order to get those jobs in the future. Some also emphasize that program graduates can go on to college if they wish; this message refutes the negative stereotyping of many occupation-related programs.

However, despite these marketing efforts, we found that the programs are still affected by the stigma attached to work-preparation courses. The history of vocational education as a dumping ground for failing students, and the lack of college preparation in most vocational programs, have left a nearly indelible mark on all efforts to help students learn about careers. Future marketing efforts must continue to combat these views by offering convincing evidence on the college options and high-status work opportunities open to students in school-to-work programs.

Other marketing messages contain information about the support that students receive in the program and the positive atmosphere they will find. Communicating these points appears to respond to the major questions that many students have about the programs. Program staff also repeatedly described the value of personal contacts with students. They visited classes made up of eligible students, persuaded guidance counselors to talk with their students about the program, and arranged for public testimonials by students in the programs. These personal communication strategies raise student interest in the programs. Brochures and other printed materials, as well as videotapes, may be useful supplements to personal contacts, but their role appears to be secondary.

Table 3.3. Marketing and Recruitment Activities.

Program	Group Targeted for Recruitment	Marketing Messages	Strategies Used
Baltimore finance academy	All 8th graders in district; students are selected by composite ranking of grades, test scores, and attendance.	Opportunity to explore and prepare for banking, finance, accounting, and computer occupations. Special activities including work experience. Program for college-bound students. Greater support for succeeding in school.	Presentations made at all 26 middle schools. Efforts to seek support of middle school guidance counselors. Information provided in brochures and district guide. Citywide application process for all specialized high schools and programs.
Dauphin County cluster program	8th graders from six supporting districts.	An education students can immediately use in the labor market and that also prepares them for college. Possibility of greater student success in a school that was utilizing hands-on applications and links academics with occupational instruction. · Faculty cares about students. Vocational education not for "dummies."	Presentations to all 8th graders, using student testimonials, presentations, and an extensive tour of the school's 21 shops. Brochures and videos directly confronting stereotypes of vocational education.
Fort Collins restructured co-op	All high school students; students in alternative school required to participate.	Experiences link school and work. Firsthand knowledge of the world of work. Preparation for job seeking and help identifying career interests.	Information on program included in student information packages. Presentations to 9th grade civics classes and career development classes. Personal letters sent to prospective students and parents. Articles describing program placed in school and local newspaper.
Pickens County tech prep	All high school students in district, with early marketing to elementary and middle school students.	Workplace is changing and tech prep prepares students for good jobs and provides the education needed to get high wages. Students get solid academic skills in high school and get into the postsecondary training.	Outreach to entire local population through newspaper advertisements and brochures mailed home to all parents. Middle and elementary school activities, including presentations on tech prep and career exploration.

Program	Eligibility/Selection	Benefits to students	Outreach and recruitment
			Special training on tech prep for school counselors and administrators. Information on local wage levels and industry trends included in all high school guidance and course selection materials.
Tulsa youth apprenticeship	10th graders in Tulsa school district interested in metalworking field;[a] competitive application process that considers students' grades, scores on academic and mechanical tests, and performance during interview with selection committee.	Opportunity for work experience and training in reputable firms that may lead to good, permanent jobs. Intensive vocational training in a high-wage occupation. Direct linkage to junior college and opportunity to earn an associate's degree. Sizable stipends.	Presentations by employers to student assemblies at most high schools. Counselors identify and target potential applicants.
Wayne Township tech prep	9th graders in prealgebra and algebra classes; 9th and 10th graders not selecting college prep curriculum.	Students prepared for high-wage jobs. There are two doors to opportunity—college prep and tech prep—and both are valuable. High-quality program teaches valuable skills and information.	Guidance counselors included in program development to increase their knowledge of program. Counselors identify and target potential applicants. Presentations to 9th grade math classes. Presentations at parent meetings. Efforts to inform faculty about tech prep.
West Bend youth apprenticeship	Middle two quartiles of 10th grade; students with a good attendance record and GPA of 2.0 or higher.[b]	Opportunity to earn state-certified youth apprenticeship certificate of occupational proficiency. Skills provided so students can enter the workforce directly after high school graduation. Dual credit accepted by technical colleges; technical college or college can be pursued after high school. Credit earned for working; guaranteed summer job.	Presentations to all 10th grade English and introductory graphics classes. Brochure distributed to all staff and all 10th grade students and their parents. Open house for students, parents, staff, and the community at participating employer's facility. Newspaper and radio coverage of program development.

Source: MDRC field research.

Notes: [a]Program expanding to serve twelve school districts.
[b]Starting with second year of the program, the prerequisite of an introductory graphics course has been added; this requirement has been publicized in advance so that interested students can take the course during the semester they apply for the program.

U.S. public schools are financed in a variety of ways, and a school's financial structure can influence its marketing efforts. Two programs whose student selection processes are adversely affected by the financial interests of the high schools that refer entering students are the Dauphin County cluster program and the Little Rock youth apprenticeship program, which serve students who live in several school districts. These schools receive their funding from their students' referring high schools; that is, each student's home school district pays the costs of his or her participation in the school-to-work program. This creates financial incentives for the high schools to limit the number of students referred and to refer mostly students who would be expensive to educate in the regular high school program—especially in times of tight budgets. It is possible for the high schools to limit their referrals because students who want to apply to a program must submit a request to the high school's guidance counselor, and not all requests are approved.

The Dauphin County and Little Rock programs have responded to this situation by increasing their marketing to junior high school students. The local junior high schools do not face the same financial incentive as the referring high schools, because their eighth-grade students are all leaving to attend other schools; therefore, their funding is unaffected by the decisions of the departing eighth graders about where to attend high school. This shift in marketing efforts has substantially increased the flow of students to the Dauphin County program. (The Little Rock program is too new for changes in referrals to be measured.)

Dauphin County Technical School is also an example of a program that has created marketing materials that directly confront stereotypes of vocational education and its students. The program developed videos and brochures explaining that vocational education is not for "dummies" and that the school does not have major behavior or drug problems. These materials emphasize that a comprehensive vocational high school provides students with an education they can use—it promotes academic excellence, broad employability skills, and technical instruction, thereby preparing students for college or for immediate entry into the workforce. The materials underscore the fact that some students are more successful and interested in school when they learn through hands-on applications and can see how their studies relate to a career. Brochures are widely distributed to students and parents, and local video stores make the popular free video about the school available to a wide audience.

Presentations on the school are made to *all* eighth graders in the local junior high schools, not just to those identified as candidates by guidance counselors and teachers. Many of the junior high schools send their eighth graders to tour Dauphin Tech. These visits start with a group assembly in which Dauphin Tech students explain the benefits of attending a school that teaches skills that will help them get a good job. They emphasize the school's high expectations and describe the sense of community and support in the school. Students also describe efforts by some teachers and guidance counselors in their previous schools to talk them out of attending Dauphin Tech. During the assembly, prospective students can see two of the school's shops in action: communications students videotape the assembly and law enforcement students provide supervision and monitoring.

After the assembly, small groups of visiting eighth graders tour most of the school's twenty-one shops, with a ninth-grade Dauphin student as their guide. The teacher and students in each shop explain their vocational field, and students demonstrate skills they have learned. Some shops get prospective students involved in the demonstrations, making keychains in the metalworking shop and preparing fingerprints in the law enforcement shop.

Conclusion

In 1989, the National Assessment of Vocational Education found that disadvantaged and low-achieving students had less access to high-quality vocational programs than other students and tended to be relegated to low-quality programs (National Assessment of Vocational Education, 1989). The innovative school-to-work programs discussed here show that it is possible to operate ambitious programs that combine state-of-the-art instruction with workplace learning and to include a substantial number of disadvantaged and low-achieving students in them. They have adopted strategies to target a wide range of students; many of them have decided to open eligibility to virtually all students who desire to participate, and most recruit broadly, with messages that refute the traditional stigma of vocational education. Many programs emphasize the fact that students receive the necessary preparation for two-year and four-year colleges. They build support among guidance counselors and teachers who are not part of the program. In most programs, employers screen or select students for work experience positions but do not determine which students will be admitted into the program. Marketing efforts emphasize personal contacts and clear messages about the payoffs for students, both present (a supportive and positive school environment) and future (including college).

The evidence that it is feasible to include a broad range of students in school-to-work programs suggests that states and localities should strongly consider allowing program staff to recruit low-achieving students. This would mean *not* requiring a credential such as the certificate of initial mastery for program entry, although policies should encourage attainment of such credentials before high school graduation for all students in both regular high school and school-to-work programs. Also, states can help make the college option a reality by making sure that state-funded postsecondary programs do not use admission standards that exclude students in school-to-work programs.

Indeed, the ability of the programs in our study to serve low-achieving students without diminishing program quality suggests that a national school-to-work system should take steps to include many such students as part of a broad targeting strategy. Previous efforts to ensure that disadvantaged and low-achieving youths are served in education and training programs have shown how difficult this can be. For example, the experience of organizations in the Job Training Partnership Act system demonstrates the conflict between including low-achieving youths and meeting ambitious job placement goals, while keeping costs down (Kemple, Doolittle, and Wallace, 1993; U.S. General Accounting Office, 1990). The use of open eligibility and self-nomination may enable some programs to include disadvantaged students, but strong incentives for the programs to serve a broad range of students may be needed as well.

Policy makers should consider providing financial support and technical assistance for school-to-work programs that start in the ninth or tenth grade, rather than just for those that start in the eleventh or twelfth grade, since beginning a program in the first or second year of high school is seen by many program staff as an essential tool for motivating students, improving their achievement, preventing them from dropping out, and preparing them for success in the workplace.

Of course, providing students with access to a school-to-work program is only opening the door; what matters most are the experiences that can be found on the doorway's other side. In the next chapter, we examine the experiences that programs offered their students.

Chapter Four

How School-to-Work Programs Make a Difference

For school-to-work programs to succeed, they must make themselves into something different from what already exists in most high schools. They cannot simply provide more of what students are getting now. Simply put, school-to-work programs must substantially change students' learning experiences in high school and in workplaces.

Therefore, if we are to understand how these programs actually work, it is necessary to understand students' daily experiences in school and in workplaces. This chapter examines the ways the sixteen school-to-work programs shape students' learning activities, the new student support structures that the programs have created, and the nature of the students' experiences in the world of work—and thus reveals how it is possible to transform students' learning opportunities through school-to-work programs. We conclude with a description of student and parent views of the programs, and a summary of the available data on the programs' effectiveness over time that should be heartening to those who believe that school-to-work programs can provide many of today's students with both the short-term benefits that students tend to value and the longer-term gains that their parents, teachers, and employers seek.

School Learning Experiences

The distinctive curricular and instructional features of the school-to-work programs in our study are summarized in Table 4.1, which focuses on nine programs that together represent all of the strategies that were found.

We looked at the programs' school-based curricula and instructional methods, and whether they relied on elective courses or a specified set of required courses. We also performed a qualitative assessment of the intensity of the programs' school-based instruction. We found that the instructional activities appear to vary in four areas: the curricula of the academic courses, the use of new teaching and learning techniques, career exploration and work-readiness instruction, and expanded occupational training and exposure, all of which we explore here.

Academic Course Curricula

Teachers in the school-to-work programs consistently felt that regular academic courses do not successfully engage a considerable proportion of high school students at all achievement levels in the hard work of learning. Thus, the programs in our study have altered many academic courses to make learning more meaningful and valuable for these students. Some courses add examples and texts drawn from the world of adult occupations; some use an occupational theme to organize and present academic work in new ways; some integrate assignments with the curriculum being taught in courses in other departments; and still others introduce new applied academic courses that teach technical concepts that are not part of the traditional comprehensive high school curriculum.

Adding work-related examples to existing academic courses is the least difficult change for teachers to make, although some say they find it difficult to identify good examples to use in their classes; time and opportunities to visit workplaces are needed to create effective occupation-related examples. English teachers use short stories and novels with work-related themes (for example, Sinclair Lewis's novel *Arrowsmith*); math teachers recast word problems as measurement, stockroom, or logistics problems; science teachers use data and graphs from technical occupations; and computer-applications teachers use data from order forms and inventory spreadsheets. In all of these examples, the challenge for the teacher is to use the new material to stimulate greater interest, discussion, and sustained attention among students—a challenging task in any classroom.

In thematic curricula, covering material in a textbook is replaced by interrelated assignments that are directly relevant to students' career interests. Using an occupational theme to organize traditional academic course content is more difficult than simply adding work-related examples, but offers many opportunities to engage students in learning. Over an eight-year period, teachers in the Oakland health academy have developed a diversified thematic curriculum that gets students involved in their schoolwork for three reasons: students already have an interest in health occupations, making it easier for teachers to draw them into the field's demanding knowledge base; students share their interest in the health field with their classmates, making them want to discuss their schoolwork with those classmates, which motivates them to keep up with assignments; and the academy's thematic lessons build on each other cumulatively, sustaining student interest. For example, the academy's physiology course uses the health-occupations theme to build a logical sequence of lessons about blood pressure, beginning with observations of the blood flow in a goldfish's tail, then teaching how a heart functions, and finally describing heart surgery.

Integrating students' lessons and assignments with the courses they are taking in other departments represents an even bigger curriculum change, and can create problems with state and district course-content requirements. However, the benefits can be substantial for both teachers and students in school-to-work programs, because the skills taught in one course can be used in others. The Wayne Township tech prep program, for example, includes a required computer-applications course for first-year students. The course's word-processing and data-collection lessons are designed

Table 4.1. Changes in Students' Learning in School.

Program	School Curriculum	Instructional Methods	Electives or Set Courses?
Oakland health academy	Grades 10–12 (some 9): curriculum in science, English, and social studies integrated with biomedical themes, health occupations; career exposure trips; community college classes offered at high school.	Multidisciplinary projects and cooperative learning; portfolio assessments; reflective writing activities and seminars connected to work experience; laboratory and team methods in science.	Set courses
Central Point cluster program	Grades 10 or 11 through 12: schools-within-a-school, each with an occupational theme (ecology, business, social service), plus work-study school-within-a-school for at-risk students, used to restructure English, social studies, math, and an occupation-related course; these courses include career exposure, job shadowing, work-based activities.	Projects, cooperative learning, small student teams, and life skills problem solving linked to the occupational theme, which is integrated into academics; writing and discussion tied to students' internships; 4-hour block with flexible schedule; 3-teacher teams stay with students up to 3 years; some competency-based grading.	Set courses
Portland cluster program	Grades 9–12: after grade 9 course exposing students to 6 career pathways, they choose 1; each pathway will have 1–2 occupation-related courses per year, occupational themes will be integrated into some academic courses; preparation for certificate of initial mastery and advanced mastery exams; career exploration through job shadowing.	Hands-on and team projects, applied academics; evaluation through demonstration of skills; in grade 9 course, problem solving and decison making.	Set courses
Dauphin County cluster program	Grades 9–12: area vocational high school with exposure to 21 shops; career and life planning course and applied academics in grade 9; students choose a shop program for grades 10–12; academic courses use occupation-related examples.	Four clusters of English, social studies, math, and science teachers work with vocational teachers (divided into construction, services, communication/transportation, high technology) for collaboration, with a shared planning period; flexible schedules; some team teaching and projects; teachers stay with students for grades 10–12.	Set courses

			Set courses
Cambridge vocational restructuring	Grades 9–12: vocational and academic program within comprehensive high school; grade 9 linkage of 3 multidisciplinary courses: career exposure integrated with city exploration, social studies integrated with English, math integrated with science; students choose a vocational program in grades 11–12; plans for cross-shop projects and additional integrated academic courses in grade 10; planned school-based enterprises; emphasis on writing and communication skills; special grade 12 seminars for youth apprentices.	Hands-on, project-based instruction; team teaching and multidisciplinary learning; applied learning; cooperative learning; most academic courses in grades 10–12 taught conventionally in the comprehensive high school.	
Fort Collins restructured co-op	One-semester course on career exploration and work readiness, usually taken in grade 10; study of work-related personal strengths and weaknesses, career aptitudes and generic job skills, and finances; formulation of career plans, resume, portfolio of work; after earning a C or higher in this course, students may take paid or unpaid work experience for credit; during work experience, students take a weekly seminar on work issues and a related academic or vocational course; option to take a single vocational course, rather than multicourse training.	Demonstrations, self-assessments, career aptitude testing, practice interviews, projects, job shadowing, research project on two careers, and conventional instruction; grades partly based on portfolio and demonstration of work-related behaviors.	Electives
Pickens County tech prep	Grades 9–12: applied academic courses in math, English, and physics, with additional applied academic courses being planned; problem solving using occupation-related examples; all grade 8 students take 9-week "Introduction to Careers" and keyboarding classes.	Cooperative learning, multiple modes of teaching and learning, some projects and hands-on activities, some group grading of team projects.	Electives

Table 4.1. Changes in Students' Learning in School, Cont'd.

Program	School Curriculum	Instructional Methods	Electives or Set Courses?
Wayne Township tech prep	Grades 10–12: linked courses in English/communications, chemistry, physics, 2 years of math beyond algebra, technology, computer applications; vocational electives; some coordination of lessons across courses.	Predominantly applications-based instruction, with problem-solving assignments tied to a work application used to structure a large proportion of students' work; projects; hands-on assignments, cooperative learning; teacher clusters collaborate on planning.	Set courses
West Bend youth apprenticeship	Grades 11–12: technical course in graphics (linked to simultaneous workplace instruction) and a technical math course tailored to the apprenticeship; applied English and chemistry courses being developed.	Performance-based assessments and exams in graphics; applications-based instruction in math.	Set courses

Source: MDRC field research.

specifically to be used in other tech prep courses; the program's teachers know that all of their tech prep students have mastered certain computer skills and their English, science, and technology courses use these skills. Coordinating tech prep math instruction with science, technology, and occupational courses has achieved similar benefits. To achieve effective curriculum integration, teachers must work together, must coordinate their schedules, and—most important of all—must themselves learn material from outside their department and design lessons that will enable students to learn the material, too.

Applied academic courses that are new to a high school's curriculum represent a test of the school's willingness to deviate from tradition-laden curricula and course content. Applied academic courses are designed to focus on the technical principles that link academic disciplines to occupational tasks; examples of applied academics include courses on technical writing skills (including the creation of charts, graphs, and instruction manuals) and on the physics of engineering. However, offering applied academic courses as isolated electives produces only limited benefits for students and the school-to-work program, according to program teachers, because students in the elective courses find that most of their classmates in other courses are not aware of the ideas taught in the applied academic course; consequently, students do not use their applied academic lessons in these other courses, and their increased motivation and the new methods of applied learning are not reinforced. Conversely, if the skills taught in applied academic courses are used as the foundation for teaching and learning in other courses, such reinforcement can help students master higher-order thinking skills in the applications that they encounter in math, science, and occupational training. But small, stand-alone doses of these potentially powerful courses seem unlikely to produce such benefits.

Most of the sixteen school-to-work programs have made at least some changes in their academic courses. However, the extent and intensity of these changes vary considerably. When only one or two courses are changed, and when teachers attach low priority to the changes, there is little reason to expect that students' education will be improved.

New Teaching and Learning Techniques

Among the five generic school-to-work approaches, only the tech prep approach places dominant emphasis on changing the school's curriculum and instructional methods (see Table 1.1). However, programs using each of the five approaches made major changes in instructional techniques. Teachers say such changes are necessary in order to engage students who have not succeeded in school in the past, since conventional instruction simply does not work for many of them. Teachers in school-to-work programs use a variety of innovative instructional methods, including project-based assignments (such as learning about technology by designing a product-manufacturing sequence rather than memorizing information about manufacturing methods), hands-on tasks, team activities, instruction aimed at achieving competence in skills, multiple methods of presenting course material, an emphasis on teaching problem-solving and communication skills, and new kinds of assessment. Many students say that they are more interested and involved in these kinds of innovative assignments than in their other courses' assignments.

Competency-based instruction and assessment are used in several of the sixteen programs, particularly in the tech prep, occupational-academic cluster, and youth apprenticeship programs. These methods emphasize skills and performance rather than the ability to answer test questions correctly, which is often the goal of more traditional instruction. Teachers build their lessons around well-defined, specific skills or competencies, and provide students with assignments and projects that enable them to learn each competency. When a student can perform a new skill competently, the teacher certifies the student as having mastered the competency. Students who are unable to show that they have mastered a new skill receive more projects and assistance, and teachers are stimulated to try a wide variety of teaching techniques to find the right one for students who do not achieve a competency quickly.

A theme of much school-to-work instruction is applications-based learning, which is different from the applied academic courses described earlier. This method is based on using a carefully selected real-world task, or application, to teach a skill. Examples of application-based lessons include using mathematical formulas to determine the amounts of raw materials for producing a chemical, using an instruction manual to learn a skill that then is carried out by a team of students, writing a voters' guide based on information found in newspaper articles, programming a computer-assisted machine tool to cut plastic stock to specified dimensions, and doing a physics lab experiment measuring the energy required to operate an industrial lever system. When teachers design effective applications, teaching and learning can take on a remarkable intensity; students and teachers in the programs often cited applications-based lessons as the best part of their work.

Teachers in several programs also pointed to similarities between their instructional methods and the ways that adult workers are treated: workers are responsible for completing tasks and projects, rather than for responding to questions about memorized information; they are held accountable for work completed during the workday with less emphasis on work completed at home; they work in teams and are encouraged to learn from their colleagues; and they are evaluated on their skills and performances rather than on correctly answering test questions.

Cambridge's vocational restructuring program at the Rindge School of Technical Arts uses many of the new techniques. For example, the school has developed a unified vocational and community development course and two related academic courses for entering ninth graders. The three courses—CityWorks, CityLife, and CitySystems—use a range of innovative techniques that serve as the cornerstone of the school's instruction.

CityWorks is a hands-on, project-based course that uses the city of Cambridge as its classroom, teaches general skills needed in every job, and introduces students to a wide range of occupational areas. It starts with three months of projects investigating the city (such as mapping exercises and oral histories), with an emphasis on communication skills. Students then spend three months working on projects in the school's shops, exploring a wide range of crafts, skills, and occupations. During the last three months of the school year, students work on community development projects using skills from a number of occupational areas. The first CityWorks class planned and built models of four businesses, including an international café and a food court. They found a location for the businesses, drew plans, went to City Hall to complete the paperwork for regulations and construction approval, built models, planned menus and cooked the food, and developed marketing plans to advertise the businesses. Another class planned the development of a discovery museum for the city of Cambridge, responding to community interest.

CityWorks has broad goals: teaching problem-solving skills, teamwork, communication, understanding all aspects of an industry, the use of math on the job, an awareness of Cambridge's resources and needs, and the production of high-quality work. CityWorks students keep journals in which they describe and reflect on their learning experiences. They also develop portfolios containing writing samples and pieces or photographs of their work. Just as in the workplace, students are assigned group tasks and projects to learn to share responsibilities and figure out how to get things done. Vocational teachers are heavily involved in teaching the CityWorks course.

Two related academic classes are also part of the school's vocational focus: CitySystems (a combination of math and science) and CityLife (a combination of English and social studies) integrate academic and vocational knowledge using hands-on, project-based instruction. For example, CitySystems students study human and animal skeletal systems by examining the skeletal structure of buildings and erecting models. CityLife students study the history of the cities of their ancestors and then build models of these cities, drawing on the world history curriculum and CityWorks projects that mapped the city of Cambridge and studied its history. Participating academic and vocational teachers and the school's academic coordinator meet regularly to plan, coordinate, and share information on the new courses.

The changes in instruction that occurred in the sixteen programs were not achieved by teachers working alone—designing and implementing such changes is simply too demanding for a full-time teacher who is responsible for five classes a day. In all the programs studied, "teacher learning communities" enabled teachers to change their instructional methods. Recent research by McLaughlin and Talbert (1993) describes this kind of informal professional community as a collegial group that discusses ways to use new pedagogical methods and new materials in their teaching, while supporting each other's efforts to take risks and experiment. Having the support of their colleagues makes it easier for teachers to make major changes in the way they teach.

Some of the programs' teacher learning communities were created when teachers worked together during the summer on curriculum development or on panels designing their school's new school-to-work program. Others grew out of a teacher team in a school-within-a-school. Some benefited from a shared planning period for teachers in the school-to-work program, and a few programs had funding to give teachers an extra planning period to work together on developing new curriculum materials.

In all cases, the formation of teacher learning communities was preceded by a consensus-building process in which teachers took ownership of the school-to-work program and began to discuss with colleagues how to make it work. Program managers, many of them teachers or former teachers, strongly supported these collegial discussions and enabled them to flourish. However, it is important to note that the school-to-work programs did not cause the teacher learning communities to be created; the teachers created them because of their interest in working together on improving their instructional techniques.

The changes new instructional methods can bring to teachers' individual ways of planning and classroom teaching are exemplified by Crater High School in Central Point, Oregon, where teachers have created several schools-within-a-school with occupational themes that link school and work. Groups of teachers have worked together to develop and implement each school-within-a-school with new instructional approaches. Through sustained work and shared efforts to solve problems, they came to function as teacher learning communities, forming groups around specific vocational themes and soliciting other teachers to become part of the occupational-academic clusters. The groups were initiated by a core of members who wanted to work together or who had worked together in the past. Each group developed differently, building on the skills and talents of the founding members.

Planning activities occupied one school year and a summer. The teachers contributed many lunch and preparation periods, after-school hours, and time during the summer to meet and create new curricula and lesson plans. The biggest challenges were revising the curriculum to meet the needs of the restructured program and learning how to use a team-teaching approach. Teachers worked together to learn how to teach groups of students from different grade levels in the same class for lengthy blocks of time; together they planned and decided how to present their new lessons.

Participating teachers report that administrative support has been instrumental in their effort to work together. Administrators have encouraged them to do what they think is educationally sound for students, consistent with the goals of reducing the dropout rate and improving the connection between school and work. The principal and assistant principal provided teachers with ongoing support and information on other schools' initiatives. Administrators hope that the number of schools-within-a-school will grow and that other innovations will be created, and believe that these innovations must come from the teachers themselves.

Some programs use more formal training methods to help teachers learn new instructional methods; the two most common were workshops conducted by knowledgeable experts and conferences. Teachers found these experiences somewhat useful, but thought they required considerable adaptation to be applied in their classrooms. The limited value of teacher training that is based on the industrial model of showing workers exactly what to do in specified circumstances may come as a surprise to employers and some policy makers, who may assume that all training *should* be highly specific and prescriptive. However, teachers rarely benefit from training that is not directly tied to the needs of their own school and classroom, and to the particular instructional problems they face.

Teachers appear to benefit most from training that is flexible and from participation in teacher learning communities. These communities are analogous to industrial quality circles, in which groups of workers meet to study the way they perform a particular task, and use their detailed knowledge of the production process to design improvements that reduce defects, improve quality, and increase efficiency. Quality circles and adaptive staff development are based on detailed knowledge about a particular work setting, careful analysis of problems and new ideas, and discussions among skilled peers—methods that are particularly useful in pioneering organizations that face complex and uncertain tasks, such as new school-to-work programs.

Career Exploration and Work-Readiness Instruction

Many traditional vocational courses teach a job-specific set of skills, based on the assumption that the students have already decided what job they want to prepare for. Career-exposure activities question that assumption, and provide students with information that will help them to make informed career choices. Career exposure conducted in a classroom is of limited value for students who have never seen or experienced the work required in many careers, and so career-exposure activities often take students to workplaces. But before they visit workplaces, many students need to receive some basic instruction in how to behave there; thus, career exposure is often linked with work-readiness instruction. The Dauphin County cluster program, for example, provides all ninth graders with a week-long rotation in each of twenty vocational shops, enabling them to observe and experience the skills that are learned in each shop before they choose a vocational specialization.

The Fort Collins co-op program begins with a required work-readiness course called Career Development. Students are required to successfully complete the one-semester course before participating in a work-based learning experience. The course, usually taken during the tenth grade, emphasizes employability skills and career exploration; it combines topics covered previously in several courses, making instruction more easily available to a large number of students rather than only to those taking vocational classes. The course was developed with input from the local chamber of commerce, the Job Training Partnership Act agency, and the business community.

The career development course contains three curriculum units:

1. *Career analysis*. Students select and research several career fields, identifying the education and skill requirements, types of work, opportunities for advancement, and labor demand trends in each field. They complete several standardized career interest and aptitude inventories, learn job-seeking and job-keeping skills and their rights as employees, and create an individual career plan, assembling a portfolio of job preparation information including post–high school plans for additional education and starting a career.

2. *Personal growth*. Students conduct a self-assessment to identify their interests and abilities. They learn about time and stress
management and develop communication and leadership skills.
They discuss nontraditional careers for women and gender-equity
issues in the workplace.

3. *Resource management*. Students practice teamwork using
work tasks, problem-solving, communication, and decision-making
examples. They learn life skills, including keeping records of income
and expenses, preparing income tax returns, and assessing insurance
and benefit options. Students also receive an introduction to basic
economics and business competition.

Students in the career development course also explore careers
by visiting workplaces, and they are required to volunteer at least
four hours at a community agency. Many students devote more than
the required time and turn the volunteer assignments into internship opportunities. Students' volunteer experiences are used in class
to explore jobs and institutions that support their community.

Students study two or more careers, with at least one job-shadowing experience. They prepare a personal job portfolio that
includes a writing sample, letters of recommendation, and job application letters. After earning a grade of C or higher in the career
development course, students may continue their career exploration
for high school credit through work internships and community service positions. Students may choose to have more than one experience so they can explore several industries and careers, but there
is a maximum number of credits students can earn for each type of
experience.

Adolescence is a time of exploration and uncertainty, so it
should not be surprising that most teenagers do not know how they
want to spend their adult working lives. Yet career exposure has not
been a priority in many school-to-work programs. This may be
because neither school people nor employers have much experience
in providing students or workers with broad career exposure. Where
career exposure is offered, it is very popular among students, and

many make major changes in their career plans once they acquire some knowledge about their original career preference.

This suggests that expensive and high-intensity training programs, such as youth apprenticeships, might benefit from providing students with career exposure activities *before they enter the program*. This could be done by having students participate in a career academy or other program providing broad exposure to a range of occupations before they apply for an apprenticeship program. It seems likely that some students who planned to enter a youth apprenticeship will decide not to once they learn about the occupation and its work, and this would open up more slots for students who are likely to complete the apprenticeship and work in its field. The result would be savings of both public and employer funds, and a more efficient process of matching students with the scarce and expensive apprenticeship placements. California is working to make youth apprenticeships available to students nearing the end of a career academy program; this innovation will provide an early demonstration of this approach.

Expanded Occupational Training and Exposure

Career academies and occupational-academic cluster programs that focus on a particular industry have been strongly influenced by the Carl Perkins Vocational Education Act's goal of exposing students to "all aspects of the industry," according to program staff members. Although these single-industry explorations are narrower in scope than some of the career-exposure activities discussed above, they typically enable students to learn about and observe a wide range of jobs in a given industry, as the Perkins Act requires.

For example, the Socorro health academy replaced a program that focused exclusively on training nurses' aides with one that exposes students to numerous technical jobs in the health industry. The program head recognized that most of her students knew very little about the wide range of medical jobs—from physiotherapist and phlebotomist to surgical nurse, and from medical equipment salesperson to radiology machine operator—in a community with a very high labor-market demand for all such jobs; hence the ninth-grade course in the Socorro program that introduces students to the numerous health occupations. In subsequent years, students observe many hospital-based specializations. Also in response to the Perkins Act, the Dauphin County cluster program and the Cambridge vocational restructuring program have expanded their traditional shop training to include instruction in the financial, marketing, customer relations, and management aspects of businesses in each shop's industry.

Broad occupational courses are a central feature of career academies and cluster programs, and have been adopted by some other programs even though they are not part of those programs' basic approaches (reflecting the hybridization seen earlier among different school-to-work approaches). The Little Rock youth apprenticeship program provides both vocational and broad occupational courses, for example, and the Wayne Township tech prep program has a required first-year course introducing students to technology-related job skills.

School-to-work programs have also created new occupational training courses. Some are designed to introduce entering students to the program's occupational field, and others are designed to be taken at the end of a sequence of required academic and occupational courses. The latter tend to be more demanding than many vocational courses, because they build on the advanced content that students have already learned. The introductory courses help students decide what specific job they want to study in detail. Such new occupational training courses have been created by programs using each of the five school-to-work approaches; they are not limited to any one approach.

Finally, programs that have developed college credit agreements with postsecondary institutions follow a different sequence. Students start their occupational training in high school and then receive advanced technical training from a cooperating community college. However, currently only a few students take advantage of college credit agreements (see Chapter Six).

While there is considerable potential for students to benefit from career exploration and expanded occupational training, most of the programs we studied have placed more emphasis on new curricula and instructional techniques. The priority for these programs—perhaps a wise one—is helping students master intellectually demanding course content in the new curricular areas through high-quality teaching and learning experiences.

New Student Support Structures and Program Identity

In 1989, the Carnegie Council on Adolescent Development summarized what is known about the school needs of adolescents in its report, *Turning Points*:

> The onset of adolescence . . . involves drastic changes in the social environment. . . . These years are highly formative for behavior patterns in education. . . . Adolescence is typically characterized by exploratory behavior, much of which is developmentally appropriate and socially adaptive for most young people. . . . There is a crucial need to help adolescents at this early age to acquire durable self-esteem, flexible and inquiring habits of mind, reliable and relatively close human relationships, a sense of belonging in a valued group, and a sense of usefulness in some way beyond the self. They need to find constructive expression of their inherent curiosity and exploratory energy. . . .
>
> Most young adolescents attend massive, impersonal schools, learn from unconnected and seemingly irrelevant curricula, know well and trust few adults in school. . . . Millions of these young people fail to receive the guidance and attention they need to become healthy, thoughtful, and productive adults (pp. 12–13).

The Carnegie Council's report also presents compelling evidence of the importance of the in-school social environment for young people. In contrast, most analyses, legislation, and advocacy aimed at improving the school-to-work transition emphasize the instructional, curricular, training, and work-based experiences of students; little has been said about the role of school support structures for students, or about the value of a program-based identity and sense of belonging that students get from some school programs.

A striking finding of our study is the prominent role of distinctive student support structures in the sixteen school-to-work programs; these features may be far more important elements of school-to-work programs than previously thought. Teachers consider them essential tools for engaging students in the programs' demanding educational and work-related tasks.

Creating a More Supportive Environment for Students

School-to-work programs can create new ways of increasing the support that they provide to students by making changes in the schools' organizational structure and in the roles of teachers and other adults. Examples are given in Table 4.2, which presents the main features of student support structures in six representative programs: their organizational structure, the roles played by teachers, and other support mechanisms.

The organizational approaches that appeared to produce the most dramatic increases in support for students were the schools-within-a-school and the relatively small clusters of students in occupational-academic cluster programs. These methods of supporting students appear to work in many ways.

In some programs, students take classes with the same classmates for three or more courses each day. As a result, they know their classmates better, and their classmates are more likely to be aware of their contribution to a class, their completion of classwork and homework, and whether they are keeping up with school

Table 4.2. Changes in Student Support Structures.

Program	Organizational Structure	Teachers' Support Role	Other Supports
Baltimore finance academy	School within-a-school; students block-scheduled with same group of peers for most of their classes in grades 9–12.	Students have same team of occupational teachers for 4 years. Personal development seminars help students gain life and work-readiness skills. Program coordinator monitors students' progress, provides tutoring referrals, holds midsemester conferences with each student, and serves as liaison between students, teachers, and parents if corrective action is needed. Monitoring of student internships and job shadowing activities by school staff. After-school tutoring in math and English available. Teachers meet to discuss student progress and develop curriculum.	Ongoing contact with mentors through job shadowing component. Encouragement and support for college aspirations; workshops on PSAT/SAT preparation, college applications, financial aid. Outward Bound program helps students develop team-building skills. Student leadership skills developed through regional conferences for National Academy Foundation programs. Active parents organization.
Cambridge vocational restructuring	Vocational school within a large comprehensive school; academic courses are being incorporated into vocational school so that students will spend most of the day within the school with the same group of peers.	Students have same vocational instructor for 2–3 years once area of concentration is selected. Predominantly male staff provide role models for predominantly male students. Assistance with college and financial aid applications. Monitoring of students' activities at work sites. Academic and vocational teachers work together to integrate curriculum, coordinate instruction, support student progress.	Introductory course during first year of high school emphasizes teamwork and group projects, enabling students to develop close relationships with peers and staff during transition year. Guidance counselor assigned to school; regularly informs parents of students' progress. Attractive space created for physical "home" of school to promote group identity.

Program			
Central Point cluster program	Multiple schools-within-a-school; students spend 4 block-scheduled periods in their school with the same peers for 2–3 years; each school has its own faculty of 2–3 teachers; schools mix students of different grades and ability levels.	Students have same team of teachers for 2–3 years. Extensive individualized instruction. Work with students of varied abilities in groups to establish high expectations for all. Students encouraged to take leadership roles and determine focus of learning activities.	Group assignments and peer instruction promote supportive relationships among peers. Life skills instruction incorporated into varied activities. Promotion of involvement in community through projects and workplace assignments.
Dauphin County cluster program	Academic and vocational teachers grouped into 4 clusters by occupational areas; students have same vocational and academic instructors and group of peers for 3 years.	Teachers in each cluster confer with each other to develop strategies for students having difficulties. Emphasis on student-focused education in which each student performs up to his or her potential. Regular contact with parents during 9th grade program. Biweekly monitoring of students in work experience; counseling on adjustment to the workplace. Shop teachers help students establish contacts in their field.	Self-esteem and life skills instruction in 9th grade; special instruction for parents on communicating with their adolescent children. Varied support services for special needs students.
Socorro health academy	School-within-a-school; students will be block-scheduled with the same group of peers for most of their classes in grades 9–12.	Students have same team of vocational instructors for 4 years; same academic teachers for 2 years. Afterschool tutoring in math available. Close monitoring of students' activities in workplaces. Participating teachers meet regularly to discuss program operations, integration of curriculum, and student problems. Teachers follow up on repeated student absences, may call home to discuss absences with parents.	Students in co-op placements are mentored by hospital department supervisors and other professionals. Strong support for participation in Health Occupations Students of America activities that unify students and promote leadership. Bilingual presentations to parents to highlight student success and nurture parent support.

Table 4.2. Changes in Student Support Structures, Cont'd.

Program	Organizational Structure	Teachers' Support Role	Other Supports
West Bend youth apprenticeship	Apprentices mainstreamed with other students for academic classes half the day and receive technical instruction as a group.	High school and college technical instructors, program coordinator, and head mentor at primary employer make up a Youth Apprenticeship Support Team that oversees daily operations and monitors and supports participating students. Technical instructors work with head mentor to coordinate classroom and work-based instruction.	Head mentor oversees students' training and experience at the workplace. Students assigned individual mentors who provide overall guidance. Regular meetings for student, his or her parents, mentor, and program coordinator to review progress and any issues. Students assigned to work stations in pairs to support each other.

Source: MDRC field research.

assignments. Students are more likely to form friendships with class-mates who are in several of their courses and these friendships often involve discussions about shared school experiences. In contrast, when a group of teenage friends do not share any classes, it is diffi-cult for them to talk about the day's classroom events. Conse-quently, these friends are less likely and less able to support one another in their school experiences.

Spending several hours each day with the same group of people also gives students the opportunity to learn how to work together effectively and to trust one another. Team projects and cooperative learning, which are common in school-to-work programs, strengthen this opportunity. Students come to identify with the pro-gram because of the shared activities and time spent with the sta-ble group of students in the program. Moreover, students typically share an interest in the occupational field and future careers that are the program's theme, and these interests can stimulate addi-tional work on school projects.

Organizational structure also supports students when teachers in a school-within-a-school or cluster share the same students and can easily discuss students' needs with each other. Students know that their teachers are working together and that they can discuss a problem they are having in one class in the program with another teacher on the same cluster team. Some schools-within-a-school and clusters keep teachers and students together for several years of high school. For example, students in the Dauphin County cluster program have the same English, social studies, and vocational teachers for three years, and students in the Oakland health acad-emy and some other academies have the same English and science teachers for at least two years. In these programs, the teachers do not need to use the beginning of the school year to learn what stu-dents know and what instructional methods will be effective for them; consequently, teachers and students can get down to real work much sooner than in conventional high school courses.

Teachers and students also establish closer bonds over their years together, enabling teachers to demand more from students and building students' trust in their teachers. (Students who have an ongoing conflict with a particular teacher are typically assigned to another teacher at the end of the school year.) This increased involvement of teachers with students in a school-within-a-school may enable the teachers to perform some counseling and other services normally provided by other school staff. Also, to the extent that the increased stability of student peer groups reduces the incidence of behavior problems, the program itself functions as a substitute for some traditional school procedures for dealing with such problems. Consequently, the new student support structure can be a way to reduce costly school problem-solving activities.

In this manner, new organizational approaches can provide educational and social support to students in powerful ways that contrast sharply with the practices of most large comprehensive high schools. To a significant degree, these approaches resemble the middle school model that the Carnegie Council on Adolescent Development (1989) has proposed, and they share many characteristics with the small, special-purpose high schools with a strong sense of identity and mission described as "focus schools" by Hill, Foster, and Gendler (1990).

Program staff members told us that the students' social environment reinforces the program's educational demands for sustained attention, engagement in school tasks, and participation in team activities. In addition, the students receive a clear message that their classmates and teachers know them and value them, are concerned about them when they are absent, and want them to do well in school and in adult life. Of course, many teachers and students in comprehensive high schools also communicate these messages—but without the consistent reinforcement and daily physical evidence provided by the school-within-a-school and cluster settings, which constantly remind all students that they are recognized members of a stable and caring school community.

Even without the support provided by a school-within-a-school or a small cluster, there are other kinds of organizational changes that increase students' sense of program identity and support. Block scheduling, in which a particular group of students is scheduled to take two or more classes together in successive class periods, can reduce the flux and environmental changes that students experience; school-to-work programs can use the blocked time for field trips, speakers, and other special activities without interrupting other classes. In a less intensive approach, the weekly seminar that the Fort Collins co-op program uses for students to discuss their workplace experiences enables them to share problems and accomplishments and to build a sense of belonging to the program.

Students' feeling of program identity can also be facilitated by limiting program size. The Fox Cities youth apprenticeship program has seven students and the West Bend program has twelve; these students take the same classes, know their fellow program members well, and frequently discuss their shared program activities and schoolwork. They are also assigned to workplaces in pairs, enabling each student to draw support from a partner.

The new roles for teachers that we have described are central to the support that students receive from their school-to-work programs. Teachers meet regularly in most programs and discussions of students' needs are commonplace. Teachers also meet regularly with parents in some programs; in the West Bend youth apprenticeship program, parents have monthly meetings with teachers to discuss their children's progress in school and at work. Teachers in our case studies frequently handle student problems that are traditionally the responsibility of other high school staff: calling home when students are absent from school, setting up tutoring when students fall behind, conferring with parents to help solve school or home problems, helping students arrange for transportation to a workplace assignment, and counseling students on problems with workplace supervisors.

Having a teacher involved in solving students' noneducational problems appears to reduce the artificial compartmentalization of life that many students experience in large high schools. However, these activities require substantial amounts of time and energy and thus imply that teachers' normal job requirements must be changed to make the new roles possible. This can be done through reductions in class size or in the number of courses taught—both of which are costly.

Some programs place special priority on helping students gain access to postsecondary programs for training and further education. Teachers in these programs assume roles typically carried out by guidance counselors. They also provide assistance tailored to the educational needs of their students, by encouraging them to complete the prerequisites for postsecondary admission and helping them learn about the benefits of continuing their education and technical training. For example, teachers in the Oakland health academy use a newsletter and frequent personal contacts to remind students about college opportunities and requirements, and they have arranged for local community colleges to offer introductory college-level courses at the high school, so that students can try out college classes and gain confidence in their ability to succeed in college before they apply.

Some school-to-work programs also match students with adult mentors who work in one of the program's occupations. In the youth apprenticeship approach, the mentor is an adult employed at the student's workplace; in other programs, the mentor is recruited by the program's staff and meets with the student on a monthly or other occasional basis to discuss the student's interests in adult careers and the connections between schooling and those careers. Several academies and tech prep programs use mentors in this way.

The Oakland Health and Bioscience Academy exemplifies many of the ways to provide students with extra support and encouragement. Since the academy was established in 1985, its central goal has been to provide a high-quality academic, career-oriented program that prevents at-risk, disadvantaged students from dropping out. Many entering academy students have past records of failure, underachievement, or poor attendance. The academy's teachers recognize that these students need extra support.

The academy's most significant source of support for students is its school-within-a-school design. Unlike other students in the large comprehensive high school of which the academy is a part, academy students have the same classmates in most of their courses. As a result, they generally know one another better, are more likely to talk informally with each other about schoolwork, and give each other encouragement and reminders about assignments. The "specialness" of the program and the many shared activities it provides creates a sense of belonging among academy students that promotes pro-school attitudes and interest in school-related activities. Academy students have the same English and science teachers for several years, increasing their sense of attachment to adults who know them well and value their work and progress in school. The school-within-a-school creates the "reliable and relatively close human relationships, [and] a sense of belonging in a valued group" that the Carnegie Council on Adolescent Development recommends in its 1989 report, *Turning Points* (p. 12).

In addition to the structural benefits of the Oakland academy's design, its teachers have devised the following support features:

- Academy teachers call students' homes if they are absent from school for more than a day; they have found that family problems often underlie students' absences, and that resolving these problems can help students return to school before they have fallen far behind.

- Academy staff accompany students to their first meeting with an adult mentor who works in the health field, and to other activities outside of school; this reduces students' anxiety about these unfamiliar situations, enables staff to model professional behavior, and provides a clear message of the mentor's importance.

- During summer internships, academy staff frequently visit each workplace to check student attendance and work performance, to make sure that students and supervisors are communicating well, and to review training plans.

- University students are paid to tutor academy and other students during the lunch period and after school, and most academy courses have "in-class tutors" to help students with assignments. Tutors review and reteach science and math material, help with major projects, and assist students with homework.

- Academy teachers provide counseling and support related to problems with students' attendance, schoolwork, and non-school matters, making referrals to specialized staff when needed. Each teacher has an advisory group of students for which he or she assumes special responsibility. Teachers meet regularly to discuss the needs of individual students.

- Students congregate in the main academy classroom before school, at lunch, and after school to do homework, work on computers, and share meals.

Responses to the Added Support for Students

There appear to be both educational and social responses to the increased support that students receive from school-to-work programs, according to teachers and students. Educationally, students tend to become more engaged in their schoolwork in both their academic and occupation-related courses. Many students have improved attendance, spend more time and energy on schoolwork, and show greater interest in schoolwork. Students in school-within-a-school or small cluster programs talk about schoolwork with their friends—in most cases, something they say they did not do before entering the program. They become more adept at teamwork, team projects, and cooperative learning assignments than students outside the program. The stimulus and support for student interest in the work-related aspects of the program appear to increase their commitment to staying in the program and keeping up with its academic demands. Teachers' efforts to improve student access to postsecondary programs frequently pay off when students complete their prerequisite courses and submit college applications on time.

Students also respond in extraeducational ways to the distinctive social settings created by the school-to-work program. There appears to be increased interaction among students across the ethnic and racial lines that frequently divide high schools. In the Dauphin County cluster program and the Oakland health academy, students' friendships are more likely to grow out of being part of the same classes and having other shared interests than out of membership in an ethnic or racial group. In several other programs that draw students from a wide geographic area, such as the academy programs that recruit students from several middle or high schools, the tendency for students to form groups based on social class or family economic status seems to diminish. School-to-work programs give students a great many shared school-related experiences: field trips to work sites, visiting speakers, team projects, preparation for summer internships, and job interviews. Taken together, these experiences provide valuable opportunities for students to develop relationships with students in the program with whom they might otherwise appear to have little in common.

Students' sense of program identity and belonging is enhanced both through teachers' efforts to deal with students' attendance problems and other barriers to full participation in the program, and through the attachments that are formed with other students and between teachers and students. Students acquire a personal stake in their program that goes beyond the educational and work-preparation benefits and also reinforces them.

Students in several programs say they are treated more like adults than are their peers who are not part of the program. They refer in particular to their team assignments and other group activities, in which they work together on a shared goal; in contrast, most traditional high school assignments are completed by students working alone, and shared work is often regarded by teachers as socializing or cheating. Students' statements also reflect a sense of purpose in their daily school activities. Being part of a relatively intensive school-to-work program appears to show students that their schooling matters, for themselves and for their classmates and teachers, in ways that may be harder for students in conventional high schools to see in their daily experiences.

Most plans for new school-to-work initiatives have concentrated on curricular and work-based components and have failed to consider the role of student support structures. However, we found that when programs improved student support, there were important benefits, greatly increasing the apparent effectiveness of the programs and their ability to meet students' needs. Particularly notable is the broad use of the school-within-a-school as a way to foster the increased engagement of students with their schoolwork, teachers, and classmates (see Stern, Raby, and Dayton, 1992).

The ability of many students to succeed in these programs and in high school may be substantially affected by the extra support that they receive, and this may be particularly true for students who are at risk of dropping out of high school or of performing only at a minimal level. For them, a strong sense of adult involvement in their life at school, and close connections with a stable group of classmates who are seriously engaged in schoolwork, reinforces the program's message—that it is important to succeed in school because of the crucial preparation for a productive adult life that it provides and because the adults and young people in the program are trustworthy and caring.

When the program's organization and the conduct of its adults and students strike the same themes, they can sometimes gain the attention of students who would otherwise be distracted by problems at home or in their peer group. Therefore, policy makers may wish to facilitate the use of new student support structures in the national school-to-work system by providing technical assistance on this topic. In states that provide funding and other support for creating school-to-work programs, communities seeking state funding can be asked to include in their proposal a discussion of how they plan to provide needed support to students.

Workplace Learning Experiences

A critical part of many school-to-work programs is the workplace-based experience they provide for students. In recent years, researchers and practitioners have argued that many types of students can benefit from workplace experiences that are part of their high school education. They point to contextual learning as the core of these experiences.

Berryman and Bailey (1992), building on the well-known arguments of Resnick (1987) and others, summarize the research literature on contextual learning as follows: "School learning is so heavily symbol-based that connections to the things being symbolized are often lost. These symbolic activities tend to become detached from meaningful contexts, and school-like learning tends to become learning rules and saying or writing things according to rules. In non-school situations, people's mental activities are grounded in things and situations that make sense to them. Context turns out to be critical for understanding and thus for learning. . . . The importance of context lies in the meaning that it gives to learning" (p. 65).

Proponents of this view suggest that students can use workplace-based experiences as a powerful context to give meaning to the tasks that they perform there, and as an opportunity to learn ideas and skills *better* than they could in a traditional classroom setting. However, they also point out that many workplaces are inhospitable for learning because they provide little training and require the rote performance of a limited variety of low-skill tasks.

The widespread adoption of cooperative education programs in school districts throughout the United States has shown that it is feasible for students to participate in a school-related work experience. In co-op education, the experience usually consists of after-school work for pay in a local business that agrees to provide at least a limited amount of training and to be monitored by a co-op teacher. Students usually take related vocational courses before starting the work experience (see Stern, Stone, Hopkins, and McMillion, 1990, and U.S. General Accounting Office, 1991). However, not all work-experience programs provide opportunities for contextual learning.

We examined the workplace components of the sixteen school-to-work programs, described students' experiences in workplaces, and determined the extent to which students participated in contextual learning experiences. Our findings show that it is possible for school-to-work initiatives to go beyond simple work experience, giving students a wide range of contextual learning opportunities in workplaces and connecting these experiences to their schooling. Significant elements of contextual learning were found in all of the programs that have started their work-based activities (four of the study programs are in the startup phase and have not yet begun placing their students in workplaces).

Components of Contextual Learning in the Workplace

Contextual learning can take many forms, partly because students can learn many different kinds of lessons in workplaces and partly because the workplace settings and goals of participating employers vary enormously. Based on a review and assessment of the research literature on work-based learning and the underlying field observations, we identify four components of contextual learning in the workplace (see also Stern and Nakata, 1989):

1. *The work experience component.* Students in workplaces may learn how to use skills that they were taught in vocational courses and may have opportunities to apply their reading, writing, math,

and other academic skills to real-world tasks and problems. Work placements may show students the intrinsically interesting nature of tasks in a particular occupational field. Student attitudes, motivation, and behavior may be changed and improved through direct experience in an appropriate work placement. They may develop relationships with adult workers for the first time. Students can develop and apply problem-solving skills to their work tasks. In some programs, students have structured opportunities to reflect on what they are learning in their work experience through seminars, journal writing, or discussions with a mentor or teacher.

2. *The training-related component.* Many work sites provide entry-level training to students, which they are able to apply to their job tasks. In some work sites, students can receive advanced technical job skills training and can practice those skills under the supervision of seasoned workers. A few work placements rotate students among several jobs, providing them with training in a wide range of skills used in an industry, particularly in industries that need workers with the flexibility to perform several different kinds of skilled tasks.

3. *The career-exposure component.* Students may be able to observe and experience the daily activities of workers whose jobs they have only read about or seen on television, and may gain a new appreciation for the nature of the challenges faced in those occupations. Job shadowing and providing assistance to adult workers are common career exposure activities for students. In those work placements that rotate students through many different departments in a workplace, students are able to see many different kinds of technical specialties being practiced. As mentioned above, some programs use structured reflection activities such as journal keeping to help students examine and study the careers they see.

4. *The academic component.* In some school-to-work programs, schools and employers have arranged for students to learn through workplace activities some subjects that are normally taught in school. Students may study academic topics in science, English, and

other courses by gathering and organizing information from co-workers, supervisors, and the students' job tasks. Sometimes supervisors teach skills and lessons from students' school courses. In other cases, students carry out school assignments in the workplace.

The case studies contain examples of all four components of contextual learning experiences. Table 4.3 summarizes the components of contextual learning in workplaces and the main activities that can be used as part of each component. The next section uses the four components to describe the contextual learning opportunities in each of the sixteen programs; see Table 4.4.

In addition to the contextual learning opportunities that students in school-to-work programs receive, there are other benefits of work experience for some students. They may receive certification or licensure for skills that they master, gaining a valuable and portable credential that enhances their earning capacity. This benefit is still relatively rare, both because most programs provide students with limited amounts of training and because certification and licensing are available in only a limited number of occupations and states. However, federal and state efforts to set certification standards and establish testing procedures may make these opportunities more widely available.

Much more common benefits of work experience are the pay that many students receive for their work and the possibility of being hired as a permanent employee after completing the program-sponsored work experience. Some of the contextual learning activities described here are also part of traditional cooperative education programs. Co-op programs do typically include some elements of the work experience and training-related components but rarely provide advanced training or training in diverse industrywide skills, career exposure, or academic activities.

In our case studies, all of the contextual learning activities are chosen and managed by the participating employers. For example, some employers provide technical training as part of their contex-

Table 4.3. Components of Contextual Learning in Workplaces.

Work experience components
- Work uses special vocational skills
- Work uses reading, writing, math
- Work is intrinsically interesting
- Develops work ethic, prowork attitudes, and motivation
- Develops appropriate behaviors (punctuality, attendance, responsiveness to supervision)
- Develops relationships with adult workers
- Develops problem-solving skills applied to work tasks
- Provides structured reflection on work experience

Training components
- Entry-level job skills training
- Advanced job skills training
- Training in diverse industrywide skills

Career-exposure components
- Job shadowing
- Participation in diverse work settings and tasks
- Assisting adult workers
- Structured reflection on careers

Academic components
- Context-based instruction in disciplinary knowledge
- School-based assignments carried out in workplaces

Source: MDRC literature review.

tual learning activities, and others do not. The diversity of the activities listed earlier suggests that program staff, students, and employers will often face difficult tradeoffs as they decide which activities are best for them, since a student's decision to participate in one activity typically reduces the time and resources available for other activities.

Some programs that we did not study provide workplace learning through school-based enterprises, which are workplaces created by school staff and operated by students. A school-based enterprise can provide most of the contextual learning opportunities listed here, and students may be able to participate in designing and redesigning the organization of their work, which is simply not

Table 4.4. Workplace Contextual Learning Activities.

Program	Work Experience Components	Training Components	Career Exposure Components	Academic Components
Career academies				
Baltimore finance academy	Primary emphasis	Some provided	Primary emphasis	
Los Angeles medical magnet	Some provided	Some provided	Primary emphasis	Some provided
Oakland health academy	Primary emphasis	Planned	Some provided; Planned	
Socorro health academy	Some provided	Primary emphasis	primary emphasis	
Occupational-academic cluster programs				
Central Point cluster program	Some provided		Primary emphasis	
Dauphin County cluster program	Some provided	Primary emphasis		
Portland cluster program	Planned	Planned	Primary emphasis	
Restructured vocational education programs				
Cambridge vocational restructuring	Planned	Planned	Primary emphasis	Some provided
Fort Collins restructured co-op	Some provided	Some provided	Primary emphasis	Some provided
Tech prep programs				
Pickens County tech prep				
Wayne Township tech prep	Planned	Planned		
Youth apprenticeship programs				
Fox Cities youth apprenticeship	Some provided	Primary emphasis	Some provided	Some provided
Little Rock youth apprenticeship	Primary emphasis	Some provided		
Pickens County youth apprenticeship	Some provided	Primary emphasis		
Tulsa youth apprenticeship	Some provided	Primary emphasis	Primary emphasis	
West Bend youth apprenticeship	Some provided	Primary emphasis	Some provided	Some provided

Source: MDRC field research.

feasible in most workplaces. However, students in school-based enterprises do not develop relationships with adult workers, as they do in local firms.

Student Workplace Experiences

Table 4.4 shows the existing workplace-based activities in the twelve programs that offered these experiences at the time of the field research visits and the planned activities in the programs that were still in the process of setting up their workplace linkages. All but two of our sixteen programs provide or will provide training-related workplace experiences. Some programs provide advanced job skills training and training in diverse industrywide skills. All of the youth apprenticeship programs have established or plan to establish high-intensity training and intend to provide certification of job skills competencies. The use of the three other components of contextual learning varies among the programs. Numerous programs offer career exposure or academic activities in addition to their work experience component. The central focus of the programs' workplace activities is typically either the training component or the career-exposure component. This distinguishes these school-to-work programs from many cooperative education programs that emphasize work experience and provide only modest training and no career-exposure activities.

The widespread use of career exposure activities is particularly striking. Career academies, occupational-academic cluster programs, and restructured vocational programs have worked with employers to create career-exposure opportunities that appear to go far beyond those available to most high school students. There are numerous examples of these activities among the case studies. The co-op placements in Fort Collins include opportunities to participate in several community service activities for short periods so that students can try several different jobs. Job shadowing is used in the Los Angeles, Central Point, and Portland programs to enable students to observe the range of activities of an adult worker during a typical workday. The students participate in job shadowing several times in order to compare the tasks and responsibilities of different jobs. Some employers have developed summer internship programs that expose students to high-skill tasks that are normally reserved for senior employees; working with skilled staff members, Baltimore finance academy students help prepare reports on loan applications and Oakland health academy students have assisted in delivering babies. Borrowing the concept from medical training, some employers rotate students among all of their major production centers; for example, Socorro health academy students spend time in each of the main departments of the largest hospital in El Paso.

Students use journals to record and reflect on their workplace experiences in some school-to-work programs, including the Socorro health academy and the Cambridge vocational restructuring program, which also includes a seminar for students to discuss their workplace experiences and journal entries. Since many young people have virtually no knowledge about the world of work, these career-exposure activities can widen their horizons dramatically— a particular benefit for students who have no vision of a productive future life.

A few employers have agreed to provide instruction in topics that would normally be taught in classroom settings; this represents a major departure from the kinds of work experiences that most employers have traditionally provided to high school students. The Cambridge vocational program assigns projects that students carry out in the workplace. At the King-Drew Medical Magnet High School in Los Angeles, all students take a curriculum that includes work experience linking learning in school and at the workplace. Students learn biological, chemical, and physiological concepts, as well as methods and ideas of scientific research. Students work in ten different medical settings over the course of three years, selecting their placements from approximately ninety possible workplaces at the M. L. King Jr. Medical Center, the UCLA Medical Center, local clinics, medical offices, and veterinary hospitals. The work experience positions involve a combination of observation and hands-on activities.

Los Angeles program and hospital staff work together to create training plans that specify experiences and outcomes for each student placement. Close coordination between workplace supervisors and school staff maximizes learning opportunities at the workplace and their connection to classroom instruction. Workplace objectives are designed to help students understand scientific aspects of their work experience in the context of the division or department to which they are assigned. For example, during the rotation in gastroenterology, students learn the parts of the stomach and their functions, why biopsies are performed and how the results are used, and procedures for gastric analysis. Grade 11 and 12 students who select a research laboratory as a placement are expected to learn how to set up a scientific investigation, how to perform laboratory techniques and procedures, and the procedures for conducting a scientific investigation. Hospital staff prepare reports that students have learned specified topics.

Each semester, students in the Los Angeles program take a course related to their work experience; these courses include career exploration, health, hospital careers, and health occupations. As part of these courses, students must show that they have completed the learning objectives specified for their work placements; for example, students working in the trauma department are expected to demonstrate an understanding of how triage decisions are made and some of the principles of emergency first aid. Students are also given assignments that require research efforts at the workplace, and grade 12 students must write two research papers based on investigations completed at their workplaces; for example, students working in neonatology have written about birth defects. Students' academic courses also draw on their workplace experiences; for example, English assignments and vocabulary words draw on students' work-based experiences, and eleventh graders write a term paper related to their workplace as part of their history course. Teachers spend some of their planning periods at workplaces to gain a better understanding of students' experiences.

As part of the two Wisconsin youth apprenticeships in the printing industry, employers teach and certify students' mastery of technical knowledge, science, and math, much of which is usually taught in community college training programs. The technical curriculum is adapted in each community to reflect technologies used by local printing firms. The first semester of workplace instruction introduces students to all areas of printing. In West Bend's program, the second semester focuses on screen printing, used primarily by local employers; instruction in the second year covers prepress and offset methods.

West Bend's workplace instruction is designed to expose youth apprentices to many occupations and specialties in the printing industry. Youth apprentices are grouped in pairs and assigned to line-level trainers as they rotate through several divisions during the first semester. In subsequent semesters, students spend more time at each work station. The curriculum is made up of competencies that are broken down into specific steps that the student learns to perform. Examples of competencies that youth apprentices are expected to learn during the first semester include using job cost estimating software, performing basic electronic publishing operations, producing pasteup sheets, producing a diffusion transfer line print, producing a metal offset plate and an electrostatic plate, and performing a lithographic offset duplicator setup. Trainers are responsible for determining when students have achieved a specific competency and for rating overall performance. Students develop portfolios from their work-based experience that include checklists of their competencies, test results from training they have received, and samples of their work. Grades are determined jointly by classroom instructors and workplace staff.

Not all program-sponsored work experiences are of such high quality. Some programs have sought to provide work opportunities with relatively high pay (up to $10 an hour), but these jobs some-times involve little more than clerical work. Other programs, faced with a scarcity of positions in the program's occupational field, have placed students with employers who offer little training and low-skill work. Some work-experience positions do not provide oppor-tunities for students to observe and learn about a range of careers; for example, students who worked in stockrooms or medical offices complained that they saw little work other than their own, although they did gain considerable knowledge about their specific job. However, in most programs, problematic work placements affect only a fraction of students. When work placements are unsat-isfactory to students or program staff, efforts can be made to improve the quality of the work experience. For example, staff members of the Oakland health academy are working to upgrade their clerical placements and to incorporate elements of youth apprenticeship into students' summer internships.

Currently, a majority of high school students work in after-school jobs that are not connected to their schooling. Researchers have characterized these jobs as predominantly low-skill jobs that involve little contact with adults. Some analysts have pointed to evidence that these jobs may foster low motivation and the growth of antiwork attitudes (Stern and others, 1993). School-to-work pro-grams can place their students in work experiences that appear to be of considerably better quality, and with more opportunities for contextual learning, than the jobs that most students would be likely to get on their own.

Taken together, the workplace-based activities we researched are distinctive in several ways. Most do not emphasize narrow and specific preparation for a particular job. Instead, and with varying degrees of success, they aim for broad understanding of the careers in an industry. Most workplace experiences provide students with training, and most involve students in productive work for pay. Critically, most students appear to participate in broad contextual learning, and many employers have cooperated in making these contextual learning opportunities available, although their short-term self-interest might incline them to push for greater amounts of productive work from students. Many employers have cooperated with the school-to-work programs by asking students to use their vocational skills and their reading, writing, and math skills on the job, and by exposing students to the varied departments and jobs in their companies.

Interestingly, many school-to-work programs enable relatively young students to participate in workplace experiences; in more than half of the programs studied, some of the tenth- and eleventh-grade students visit workplaces, participate in rotations, and work in community service and other employment. This occurs in all of the career academies and restructured vocational programs and in two of the three occupational-academic cluster programs. By giving students an early and relatively intensive look at workplaces, these programs help students make more informed decisions about their future education, training, and career choices.

The feasibility of using workplaces for contextual learning activities as part of school-to-work programs is clearly shown by these programs. In all of the programs studied, hard work by program staff members and employers was required to create valuable workplace experiences for students and to link them to students' schooling. Desirable workplace learning opportunities are not restricted to any particular programmatic approach, underscoring the fact that school-to-work programs can develop workplace contextual learning opportunities in many different ways.

Workplace Experiences' Effect on Schooling

Secondary education in the United States typically takes place in schools, and for many students the classroom experience has little direct connection to learning experiences outside school. When school-to-work programs provide both instruction in school and contextual learning in workplaces, it is possible—but not necessary—that students' experiences in these two parts of the program will be connected. Even if the classroom and workplace components of a school-to-work program are essentially independent of each other, students may benefit from both. However, we suggest there are at least four potential benefits of having strong connections between school and workplace learning. Students' workplace experiences can

- Encourage them to complete high school and to pursue post-secondary education and training.
- Advance their academic instruction in school.
- Advance their vocational instruction in school.
- Improve their job performance and contextual learning in the workplace.

Determining the extent to which these benefits are produced by school-to-work programs would require outcomes data that were not available for our study. However, we can say that the programs with workplace-based components are attempting to achieve these benefits.

Encouraging students to complete high school and to pursue further education and training is an explicit goal of the career-exposure activities in workplaces. For example, the career academies and the occupational-academic cluster programs use work internships to show students that educational credentials are prerequisites for a desirable career. Students in the health academies learn about the wide range of health occupations, most of which require postsecondary training and credentials, and the occupational clusters that expose students to environmental careers also expose them to the specialized fields of knowledge used in those careers. Youth apprenticeship programs start in students' high school years and continue after their graduation, providing a clearly marked path to postsecondary training. Another kind of encouragement to complete high school is provided by employers who participate in a school-to-work program because they want to help students understand that success in school is a crucial first step toward success at work; their mentoring, advice, and friendships with students send a clear message about the importance of completing high school.

Improved academic instruction in school is an explicit goal of the programs that include academic components in the workplace (including the Los Angeles medical magnet, the Cambridge restructured vocational program, the Fort Collins restructured co-op program, and the two Wisconsin youth apprenticeships). Teachers in these programs build academic lessons on students' workplace experiences and are enthusiastic about the results. Some programs arrange for teachers to visit workplaces or to spend part of a summer working closely with employers to learn how new technologies shape the nature of work. In such programs, including the Wayne Township tech prep program, teachers have created classroom learning activities that build on their own workplace visits—for example, in projects on using math to control dynamic manufacturing processes with information from meters and gauges.

When Wayne Township began work on its tech prep program, teachers from the district's high school joined with faculty from the state technical college and local employers to design the curriculum. The employers and technical college faculty made important suggestions for the kinds of applied skills that tech prep should teach but had little to say about designing lessons. Not surprisingly, teachers had difficulty envisioning how they were to change their approach to instruction.

A crucial source of ideas for these teachers was a series of visits to local high-tech workplaces. Several large local employers undergoing downsizing were not able to provide workplace learning positions for students, but they were enthusiastic about inviting teachers to observe their operations and meet with workers and supervisors. The visits were lengthy and intensive: teachers spent a full day in each workplace, where they questioned workers and supervisors about the kinds of technical problems they confront on the job and skills they use to accomplish tasks. The workers told them about competitive pressures for high-quality, zero-defect work, the need for constant monitoring of the production process to avoid waste and to keep automated production speed high, and their reliance on technology for information on the overall process. While the teachers had heard these general themes before, they were difficult to grasp in the abstract. For many of the teachers, the experience of observing the workplace firsthand, talking to workers, and watching them apply their skills to real-world problems was a revelation.

Few high school teachers have the opportunity to visit each other's classes, making it difficult to compare notes based on shared experiences; but because the Wayne Township teachers had visited the workplaces *together*, they were able to discuss what they had seen and its implications for their teaching, discussions that turned workplace visits into a powerful professional development opportunity. Teachers reinforced each other's motivation to adopt new instructional methods; by focusing on the opportunities and benefits of doing so, they encouraged each other to "break out of the mold of how you were taught," in the words of one teacher. They discussed the relevance of the tech prep curriculum to the workplaces they had visited. They learned how to teach the organizational and interpersonal skills that workers must combine with technical skills to carry out assignments. They identified such crucial workplace skills as being able to explain a production process clearly, write a note about a production problem, calculate the amount of materials needed at a work station, and perform punctually and effectively as a member of a team; and they planned ways to teach these skills.

The teachers' visits to workplaces provided many ideas about the highest-priority topics for inclusion in the curriculum, new instructional methods, and applications-based lessons that went beyond the narrow work-related examples that many published curriculum guides include. In applications-based lessons, disciplinary knowledge is used to solve a concrete problem that workers might encounter; the problems are relatively brief, usually requiring one to five class hours for students to solve. For example, after seeing how high-tech workers use meters, gauges, and timers to control a production process, the teachers devised several applications-based lessons in which feedback information from a control panel is used to correct a problem in a dynamic manufacturing process.

Other applications-based lessons devised by the teachers include simulated job interviews for high-tech industries; the use of mathematical formulas in high-tech work situations; writing assignments in which students give clear directions for operating a piece of equipment, followed by an oral presentation to classmates who judge the clarity and effectiveness of the directions; using graphs and charts to solve a work problem; and controlling computer-assisted design and computer-aided manufacturing processes in the high school's technology lab. All of these applications were created and revised based on the teachers' visits to workplaces.

Using students' workplace experiences to improve their learning in vocational classes is a stated goal of the youth apprenticeship programs, where workplace activities and classroom lesson plans are linked. The school-to-work programs with strong cooperative education components—the Cambridge, Dauphin County, Fort Collins, Little Rock (particularly in its heating/air conditioning placements), and Socorro programs—have vocational classes that complement students' co-op placements. The Wayne Township tech prep program has been innovative in encouraging students to take vocational courses *after* their technical academic courses and work experience, an approach based on the idea that student interest in vocational courses can grow out of school and workplace experiences.

The programs try to improve student performance in the workplace by teaching them about the jobs, careers, and industries they will see in their work placements. Not surprisingly, these efforts are more advanced in some programs than in others. Some programs prepare students for their workplace experience by instructing them in relationships with supervisors, punctuality, and attendance, and by carefully monitoring their initial days on the job. School staff members have extensive practical knowledge about working with adolescents, and some have shared this knowledge with employers to help them work effectively with students. Many employers reported that this preparation helped students perform well at work.

The tradition of separating the academic world of school from the world of the workplace is a long one, and it has left schools and employers with limited knowledge of how to connect their two worlds. Integrating school and workplace learning is difficult for many reasons: Teachers have limited knowledge of many careers and workplaces; employers have little training or experience in the instructional methods and curricula used in high schools; teachers feel they have no time for workplace-related issues because they must cover the material required by the state curriculum frameworks; textbooks present abstract concepts rather than work-related, applications-based lessons; employers' production goals limit the time that they can allocate to instructing students; the accountability systems of schools, based on tests, and workplaces, based on production, differ greatly; and while teachers often work with students whose achievement levels vary greatly, employers have less experience dealing with diversity among employees. In sum, both schools and workplaces find it difficult to comprehend and respond to students' experiences in the other setting. The programs we describe are still learning about the most valuable and effective ways to connect workplace and in-school learning, but their early experiences are encouraging; they suggest that linkages between school and workplace learning can make both experiences more valuable for students.

Student and Parent Views

In brief interviews, students were asked to compare their experiences in the school-to-work program and the "regular" school program; their responses provide valuable insights into their perceptions of the programs. Although some students spoke about their schooling in terms of preparation for work and postsecondary education, almost all of their assessments reflected their concerns about the present and particularly about their experiences in school. This is not surprising, given the importance to adolescents of the immediate issues posed by their changing social relationships, their search for independence, and the unfolding changes in their bodies. Like many other teenagers, the students in school-to-work programs have a strong interest in having money to spend on clothes and social activities; future career plans are far down on their list of priorities. This affects their perceptions of school, work, and the school-to-work program. The students' views are a rich base for hypotheses about the ways that school-to-work programs affect students' daily experiences and about the aspects of the program to which they pay the most attention. When asked how their program differs from regular high school classes, students gave four kinds of responses:

1. In most cases they said that the program's classes are better and more interesting.

2. In more than half of the sixteen programs, they volunteered the view that their school-to-work classmates and teachers know each other better and provide more support than do students and teachers outside the program.

3. They like the hands-on activities that are part of most of the programs and feel that these experiences will help them in the world of work.

4. For most, daily interactions with other school-to-work students rather than workplace activities are the most prominent part of their program experience.

The underlying theme of the student descriptions of their experiences is one of incremental but noticeable shifts from traditional high school learning experiences toward interesting, often hands-on instruction and a familylike, supportive atmosphere. Many students value their new workplace activities, but see them as only a part of a high school experience that is defined mostly in school and by teachers and peers.

From the point of view of employers, teachers, and program staff, the key components of a school-to-work program can be seen in its instructional and substantive content, in both school and the workplace. In contrast, students appear to place more emphasis on the program's environment for learning and its supportive atmosphere than on its substantive focus. For example, in school-within-a-school and magnet programs, the students spoke emphatically about the importance of their close relationships with classmates and teachers, and they attributed their feelings of strong connection to the program to their bonds with teachers and other students, rather than to interest in the program's occupational theme. One Oakland health academy student said that he liked the academy because "it's like going to a different school—it's much easier to get to know people [in the academy]."

While a considerable number of students said that the program's occupational theme was a primary attraction for them, even more said that the occupational theme was not the most important reason they entered the program. Many wanted to sample several potential careers to learn which they liked best. This apparently widespread absence of a deep commitment to a particular vocational field is consistent with teenagers' orientation to the present. Many students enrolled in the school-to-work program because they had no other plans, because a friend recommended it, because it was a place where they could get extra help, or because they wanted to earn money while in school; few said that their parents had known about their decision to enroll in the program. Many described themselves as being relatively directionless when they entered the program and as valuing it more for the positive day-to-day experiences in school than for the long-term employment benefits. These perceptions underscore the importance of using a strong student support structure to keep these young people engaged in school, as the school-to-work programs in our study seem to have done.

In several schools, students complained that other students who are not part of their program see it as being for "dumber kids and dropouts who can't handle academics." One student said, "It's like they all think we're the stupid ones, and we're dropouts. And that we're only good for working, not for learning." These students pointed out that many of their program's graduates attend college, and students in more than half of the programs characterized their courses as more demanding than the regular high school courses. Nevertheless, they were aware that the stigma attached to programs with a workplace component or an occupational theme remains strong.

Some students—a very small minority—were dissatisfied with their program, usually because they had to give up elective courses, extracurricular activities, or time with friends, especially for the most time-consuming programs (including some of the youth apprenticeships and the programs with lengthy co-op placements). Other students enjoy the time they spend in their work placement.

To develop more detailed hypotheses about student views of school-to-work programs and the reputation of the programs, the research team conducted two focus-group discussions: with ten students in the Cambridge restructured vocational education program, and with nine Oakland ninth graders who were in classes targeted by the health academy's recruiting efforts (to obtain information on the reputation of the academy among its potential applicants). In both groups, the students were mostly minority-group members, were receiving mostly C's, and reported doing two hours of homework or less each week. Approximately half came from a home where a language other than English was spoken, and a few said that their families received welfare. Overall, they appeared to be moderately disadvantaged.

There were few differences among the views expressed by the two groups. When asked to describe their feelings about school,

they characterized regular high school classes as boring, discon-
nected from the rest of their lives, and lacking focus; they found little to like in school and believed that many of their teachers
disliked them. One student said, "School is mostly boring. You read
the chapter and then the teacher gives you a test at the end of the
week. Chapter and test over and over again." Another agreed,
adding, "You do the homework and you hand it in, but then they
don't return it to you or else they do it so long in the future that you
forget what it was about." The two benefits of school were that it
provides time to be with friends ("just hanging out, and seeing them
in the halls and at lunch") and access to college (necessary for
"most of the good jobs").

In contrast, the same students gave high ratings to the teachers
and the learning-oriented atmosphere of the school-to-work programs. (The students considering the Oakland academy had no
direct experience in the program but said that their views were
based on its reputation.) "It's a lot easier to learn when you are with
other students who want to learn," said one student. Another issue
was discussed by the Oakland students: "One of the problems in this
school is that you don't always feel safe. In the academy, things can
be more familiar and safer; you don't have to wander all over the
whole school." The Cambridge students specifically said that they
liked their collaborative projects with other students ("while you're
working on something, you get to know someone"), their good relationships with teachers, and their interesting assignments. The
Oakland ninth graders said that they had heard current academy
students talk about how much they enjoy their activities: "A lot of
us know students in the academy, and they like it; they like going
to the morgue and learning first aid and that kind of thing."

The focus-group students had not yet participated in workplace
activities. While they expressed modest interest in these activities,
the desire to connect school with work was not central to their
interest in the program. Once students have participated in a program-sponsored work experience, their views of the value of this

activity may change a great deal. Still, efforts to recruit students for a school-to-work program by advertising the program's work placements, and lessons aimed at motivating students by demonstrating the work relevance of certain skills, may fall on deaf ears—at least until students have had the opportunity to participate in the program's workplace-based activities.

The focus-group discussions suggest this hypothesis: many students perceive their classes in large, comprehensive high schools as uninteresting, unfocused, and cut off from their interests and their friends; teachers' efforts to get them to complete assignments are often seen as criticism and meanness. School-to-work programs are preferred if they can replace these experiences with a supportive, challenging, and friendly setting. Other benefits, including preparation for a desirable occupation, may be less important to many students than the immediate gains of a more desirable and involving school experience.

Focus groups were also held with ten parents of students in the Cambridge program and five parents of students who were being recruited for the Oakland health academy. The parents were blue-collar and clerical workers and also mostly members of minority groups.

As the parents discussed what they knew about the school-to-work program, they mostly focused on its reputation. One Cambridge parent explained: "When my child announced that he wanted to go to [the Cambridge restructured vocational program], I was a little taken aback, because my experience in vocational [education] had been that it was strictly vocational and was for the dumber kids. What I learned was not only do they get the vocational skills they need, but they get the academics that will prepare them to make a choice later in their school career as to whether they are going to college or whether they want to go directly to work. I understood that vocational was being addressed in a whole different way."

The parents candidly discussed their negative opinions of most vocational programs, but all said that the reputation of the school-to-work program in their children's school was good. They expected their children to graduate from high school and then to work while attending college, and they expressed no fears that the school-to-work program would harm their children's chances of going to college; instead, several parents thought that students would benefit academically from the school-to-work program and its small, school-within-a-school character. "One good thing about the academy will be to cut her off from some of those kids who are always getting into trouble," one parent said of a daughter. Others liked the attention that students received from teachers and guidance counselors in the program.

While the parents expressed approval of the program's work-related activities, they thought that the opportunity to learn about a wide range of occupations was even more valuable. Almost all of the parents had changed careers; several had gotten what they thought was a "dream job" and then found it lacking; they wanted their children to make more informed decisions about their careers than they did. One parent said, "I didn't have a chance to advance in my chosen field until I was a lot older. The academy gives kids these opportunities—to learn on the job, to meet the right people—much earlier. That's a great thing and that's why I fought to get my daughter in the program."

These parents knew little about school-to-work programs before their children became interested in them, and initially they had reservations about all vocationally oriented programs. However, they were quickly converted into supporters of the program by the combined emphasis on schooling and preparation for work, by the opportunities for career exploration, and by the program's reputation for having a small, familylike, supportive atmosphere. This suggests that school-to-work programs can build substantial support among parents if they clearly communicate what they do and how they do it. A package containing high-quality academic instruction, career exploration, work-based learning experiences, and a supportive atmosphere will be attractive to many parents.

Outcomes

Because the research team made only two visits to each of the case study school-to-work programs, it was not possible to gather the data needed for a reliable assessment of the programs' effectiveness. Such an assessment would require measuring how well students in the program performed compared to how they would have performed had they not been in the program, research that is prohibitively difficult for program staff who are working hard to create and maintain an ambitious school-to-work program. It is therefore not surprising that outcome studies have been completed for only two of the case study programs; four other programs are participating in ongoing, independent evaluations, and only fragmentary data are available for some other programs. This section summarizes the limited information available on the outcomes of the case study programs.

The two programs for which independent outcome studies have been completed are the Oakland health academy and the Wayne Township tech prep program. The findings are encouraging, although they should be treated cautiously because these studies compared students in school-to-work programs with students who may have systematically differed from them, raising questions about the accuracy of the assessments.

The Oakland health academy was included in a study of eleven California academy programs; results for individual academies were not given (Stern, Dayton, Paik, and Weisberg, 1989). Comparison students for each academy were chosen from the academy's school, and resembled the school's academy students in ethnicity, gender, attendance, grades, course credits, and test scores. The authors point out that "students were not randomly assigned to academy and comparison groups. The results therefore may contain unknown biases" (p. 406). Academy and comparison group students in each school were compared in each year; 270 outcome comparisons were made for attendance, credits earned, grades, courses failed, and leaving high school. Using the .05 statistical significance level, up to 14 positive and 14 negative results would be expected by chance in 270 comparisons. There were in fact 61 statistically significant positive results (defined as better attendance, more credits, higher grades, fewer courses failed, and fewer dropouts) and 11 statistically significant negative results. This large preponderance of statistically significant positive results shows that overall, the California academies in the study produced benefits for their students.

In studies of the Oakland health academy and other Oakland academies, the University-Oakland Metropolitan Forum (1991, 1992) found that grade 10 and 11 health academy students' test scores in reading, language, and math exceeded the school median for their grades in the spring of 1991; no statistical significance tests were reported. Of the thirty-nine students in the 1991 grade 12 cohort in the health academy, sixteen enrolled in a four-year college, seventeen enrolled in a two-year college, one was employed full time, and four did not graduate (there was no available data for one student).

The Wayne Township tech prep program was included in a study of Indiana's pilot tech prep programs (Wentling, Leach, and Galloway, 1990, 1991). Grade 11 students in the pilot year of the Wayne Township program were compared to a single control class (judged as having "similar capabilities" to the tech prep group) in the school's general education track. Forty students in each group were compared. The researchers used statistical techniques to control for differences between the tech prep and comparison students, and found statistically significant differences favoring tech prep students on a career maturity inventory and on attitudes toward technological careers; there were no statistically significant differences in eleventh grade achievement test scores, absenteeism, grades, and other attitude measures. When the researchers examined these outcomes over a two-year period they found statistically significant differences favoring tech prep students on grades, the career maturity inventory, and attitudes toward teachers, further education, and "questioning." Other attitudes and absenteeism showed no differences.

The Baltimore finance academy and the Socorro health academy are participating in an evaluation of academies currently being conducted by MDRC. Eligible students are randomly assigned to a group entering the academy or to a group entering the regular high school program. Information on outcomes for both groups will be gathered and compared, enabling the researchers to reliably measure the impacts of the academy experience on students; initial impact findings will be available in 1996. Independent studies are also underway for the Little Rock youth apprenticeship (part of a larger study of youth apprenticeships in Arkansas using pre- and post-testing of students) and for the Pickens County tech prep program (part of a study using surveys of students).

Fragmentary outcome information is available for several of the case study programs. Wayne Township tech prep program staff have collected data for tech prep students and a control group on attendance, grades, class rank, achievement test scores, credits earned, and graduation rate; all comparisons show that tech prep students had better outcomes than controls, although no tests of statistical significance were reported and sample sizes were small. The Dauphin County cluster program reports that 3 percent of its students drop out and an additional 3 percent transfer to another school. Fort Collins co-op program staff have collected data showing that its students' grades and attendance do not decline after they enter the program. The West Bend youth apprenticeship staff found that their students' grades improved by the end of the first semester in the program. Fox Cities youth apprenticeship staff report that their students made large gains in self-esteem, gains that were particularly notable for previously low-achieving students. High rates of enrollment in college were reported by two programs for which this is a major goal: Baltimore's finance academy reports sending 98 percent of its graduates to college (approximately half to two-year colleges and half to four-year colleges); the Los Angeles medical magnet reports that almost all of its graduates plan to attend college (mostly four-year colleges).

Programs that were in their first or second year of operation typically had little available outcome data. These programs included the Central Point cluster program, the Cambridge vocational restructuring program, the Pickens County youth apprenticeship, the Portland cluster program, and the Tulsa youth apprenticeship.

Conclusion

The evidence on the outcomes of the school-to-work programs in this study should not be overstated; it is not possible to draw broad conclusions about the effectiveness of these programs at the present time. However, the completed studies and other outcome data that are available underscore that these programs have considerable promise. Early indications suggest that these programs may be able to accomplish their goals of improving students' attendance, grades, course credits earned, high school graduation, and preparation for further education and for productive, high-wage employment. Studies that are currently underway will show whether this promise will be fulfilled. Our examination of the degree of difference experienced by students in the programs, the striking phenomenon of support mechanisms for students, and the generally positive views of parents and students underscore the significant transformation in students' learning opportunities that carefully planned and structured school-to-work experiences can produce.

Chapter Five

Expanding the Involvement of Local Employers

The school-to-work programs in this study offer students the opportunity to participate in workplace learning experiences that are provided by local employers. These employers also helped conceive and manage the programs, develop their curricula, and recruit students and other employers. These contributions convincingly demonstrate that it is feasible for school-to-work programs to draw on local employers' expertise and resources to improve the programs' ability to teach and train high school students. However, a crucial question facing policy makers and practitioners concerns the scale of workplace learning opportunities. Can employers provide enough workplace learning positions so that a substantial number of students can participate? This chapter begins by describing the scale of the workplace learning activities in the case study programs, and then examines how employers came to participate in the programs. It examines employers' diverse contributions (including the kinds of jobs they provide for students), along with the roles of business-related intermediary organizations and the use of financial subsidies to increase employers' willingness to provide workplace learning positions.

Our most important finding is that employers are providing a substantial number of positions for students that go beyond simple work experience, enabling students to have a wide range of contextual learning opportunities in workplaces. However, persuading employers to provide these positions requires extensive work by program staff and by leading employers. Because employers and schools have different priorities, getting employers to participate in school-to-work programs requires showing them how their firms will benefit, how workers' and union concerns can be addressed, and how workplace supervisors can be trained to deal effectively with adolescents.

Scale of Work-Based Activities

School-to-work programs depend on local employers to provide workplace learning opportunities. If local employers are not able or willing to create enough positions for all of the programs' students, the program will be undermined.

Local employers provided workplace learning experiences for all eligible students in eleven of the sixteen case study programs (see Table 5.1). The number of students participating varies from 4 to 550, reflecting differences in the programs' size. For students in three of the programs—the Dauphin County cluster program, Wayne Township's tech prep program, and Little Rock's youth apprenticeships—cooperative education jobs are optional, and school staff are able to find co-op jobs for virtually all students who want to participate, except for those students in the Dauphin County program whose occupational fields have minimum age requirements (criminal justice) or licensing limitations (cosmetology). Portland's cluster program has not yet started its workplace learning activities, and workplace learning is not part of the Pickens County tech prep program.

In some programs, the staff obtained local employers' commitments to provide a specified number of positions for students, and this number determined how many students could enroll in the program. This approach was used in most of the youth apprenticeship programs and in the Baltimore finance academy. In the other programs, staff sought out workplace learning positions after students were enrolled. These programs sometimes needed to place students in positions that offered only limited training opportunities, because higher-quality positions could not always be found.

In six of the programs, more than thirty students participate in workplace learning. The programs that are currently serving fewer students are making plans to expand in the near future; for example, the Fox Cities and Pickens County youth apprenticeships plan to offer more positions for students and will recruit more students to fill the available positions. Although their expansion goals are not precisely defined, most programs must grow in order to reduce their per-student costs and their reliance on special sources of funding.

Most of the participating employers are providing three or fewer job slots for students. However, three programs—Los Angeles, Central Point, and Fort Collins—were able to recruit from nine to thirty employers that offered more than three work-based learning positions each. In several programs, a single large employer provides jobs for many of the students (Serigraph in West Bend, Polaroid in Cambridge, and M. L. King Jr. Medical Center in Los Angeles). Participating employers generally had more than fifty adult employees, suggesting that some of these firms have the capacity to expand their participation. In only three of the programs are most of the jobs provided by employers with fewer than fifty employees.

To serve a large number of students, at least two of the programs have placed students in jobs that provide only limited technical training and career-exposure opportunities. This suggests that there may be a tradeoff between the quality of workplace learning and the ability to provide workplace learning for a large number of students. However, even in positions with limited training and career exposure, students may benefit from a work experience that develops skills and behaviors they need to succeed on the job.

Overall, our data indicated that in order to increase their scale of operation, school-to-work programs must persuade participating employers to provide more positions, recruit new employers to participate, or both. Recruiting employers and coordinating the programs with employers requires a great deal of staff time and energy. Obviously, the kinds of employers that must be recruited will also affect the program in several ways.

Table 5.1. Scale of Work-Based Activities.

Program	When Work Activities Occur	Do All Students Have Jobs?	Total Number of Slots in 1992–93 School Year	Total Number of Employers	Number of Employers Providing More Than 3 Slots
Career academies					
Baltimore finance academy	Summer after 11th grade	yes	44	30	4
Los Angeles medical magnet	10th–12th grades	yes	220	13	9
Oakland health academy	Summer after 11th grade, some during 12th grade	All in summer of 11th grade; some in 12th grade	70	15	5
Socorro health academy	12th grade	yes	25	9	3
Occupational-academic cluster programs					
Central Point cluster program	10th–12th grades	yes	190	70	20
Dauphin County cluster program	12th grade	no	118	73	2
Portland cluster program[a]	Not yet defined				
Restructured vocational education programs					
Cambridge vocational restructuring[b]	11th or 12th grade	yes	12	1	1
Fort Collins restructured co-op	11th–12th grades	yes	550	400	30

Tech prep programs					
Pickens County tech prep	No work-based learning				
Wayne Township tech prep[a]	12th grade	no	n/a	n/a	n/a
Youth apprenticeship programs					
Fox Cities youth apprenticeship	11th–12th grades	yes	7	5	0
Little Rock youth apprenticeship	12th grade	no	12	5	0
Pickens County youth apprenticeship	12th grade and postsecondary	yes	4	4	0
Tulsa youth apprenticeship	Each summer, 12th grade, and postsecondary	yes	16	6	2
West Bend youth apprenticeship	11th–12th grades	yes	12	1	1

Source: MDRC field research.

Notes: [a]Work-based activities not yet initiated.
[b]Information is for the youth apprenticeship program in building trades.

Choosing Specific Industries or Diversity

Many school-to-work programs are tied to particular industries or occupational fields, such as health occupations, high-tech printing, or computer electronics. When these programs were designed, a decision was made to target a particular industry, and the program's success depends on the soundness of this decision. Other programs do not target a particular industry, aiming instead to prepare students for varied occupations.

Eleven of the sixteen school-to-work programs in our study focus on a particular industry or related group of occupations (see Table 5.3). Among our programs, only the occupational-academic cluster programs, the restructured co-op program, and one tech prep program seek to prepare students for careers in varied industries; career academies, youth apprenticeships, and many tech prep programs are designed to emphasize a specific industry. These programs' initial choice of an industry sometimes resulted from a decision by the state education agency or the state economic development agency to target that industry. Wisconsin state officials targeted the printing sector as the focus of a youth apprenticeship program because of its relatively large size and fast growth: The state's printing and publishing sector grew by 6,500 employees from 1987 to 1991, exceeding the job growth of any other manufacturing sector in the state. In addition, two large printing firms whose officers served on state planning committees pushed for the focus on printing. In other cases, particular local employers pushed for a program related to their need for skilled workers. In still other instances, program staff or teachers selected the industries, based on their review of the local labor market.

A key factor in local programs' decisions to target a particular industry was the interest of local employers. In eight programs, employers helped conceive and push forward the program idea. Other programs were initiated by school staff, who sought early support from local employers in the targeted industry. For instance, the teachers who created the Socorro health academy contacted top officials of several local health institutions and gained their support soon after beginning work on the academy.

Some programs focused on narrow industrial sectors have had small numbers of student applicants. This may reflect the fact that these programs are new; student interest may increase when the programs become better known. However, the supply of students interested in narrowly specified industries may fluctuate substantially in response to changes in other employment opportunities in the community, unless compensation and security in the targeted industry are very high. Because of this and other risks, at least six of the programs have expanded or plan to expand the range of industries they include, to serve more students and to respond to changes in the demand for workers.

Soon after Tulsa's Craftsmanship 2000 was created, the local demand for machinists declined substantially because of defense cutbacks, the contraction of American Airlines (the largest local employer), and the recession. Craftsmanship 2000 responded by expanding the scope of its training to include welding and by recruiting firms with welding operations. By redefining itself in this way, the program obtained enough training positions for entering students. However, programs with a narrow industrial focus will always run the risk that the targeted sector will contract, offering fewer workplace learning opportunities (and, later, jobs) for students.

Five of the case study programs aim to provide students with workplace learning opportunities drawn from a large number of industries and occupations. These diversified programs—the cluster programs in Central Point, Dauphin County, and Portland; the restructured co-op program in Fort Collins; and the Wayne Township tech prep program—serve a large number of students with a wide variety of interests. While these programs' fortunes are less subject to industry vagaries, this diversity does affect program structure. These programs do not have the close linkages between the school-based curriculum and students' workplace experiences that characterize some programs with a narrower occupational focus. Instead, students' workplace experiences in the diversified programs (and in some of the more narrowly focused programs, too) emphasize general performance measures such as absenteeism, teamwork, and appearance rather than competencies in specific job skills.

Whether diversified or targeted, school-to-work programs need to build a strong relationship with local employers, based on a clear understanding of the prospects and problems of their industrial sectors.

Recruiting Employers

Employers agreed to participate in the school-to-work programs because they were contacted by knowledgeable and persuasive advocates (Table 5.2 shows the key recruiters for each program). In most programs, more than one type of recruiter was influential.

Intermediary organizations served as effective recruiters in seven programs. Their networks of local employer contacts, and their credibility in discussing issues affecting employers, make them persuasive recruiters.

Not surprisingly, some students who are interested in working in a particular industry have useful contacts in that field, and several programs took advantage of students' and parents' personal networks. In Los Angeles, Little Rock, Central Point, and Fort Collins, students or parents found employers who were willing to offer employment and training to students. School staff then met with the firms' supervisors to make sure that the work was appropriate for students and to solidify the firms' relationship with the program. In Fort Collins, students who had already found jobs by themselves enrolled in the restructured co-op program to obtain course credit for their work; the program's teachers then recruited these employers to provide jobs for other students, too.

While no avenue of recruitment should be ignored, and while intermediary organizations, students, and parents are vital resources,

Table 5.2. Key Recruiters of Employers.

Program	Intermediaries	Participating Firms or Firms On Advisory Board	Students or Parents	School Staff
Career academies				
Baltimore finance academy	x	x		x
Los Angeles medical magnet		x	x	x
Oakland health academy		x		x
Socorro health academy	x	x		x
Occupational-academic cluster programs				
Central Point cluster program		x	x	x
Dauphin County cluster program		x		x
Portland cluster program	x	x		x
Restructured vocational education programs				
Cambridge vocational restructuring				x
Fort Collins restructured co-op	x	x	x	x
Tech prep programs				
Pickens County tech prep[a]				
Wayne Township tech prep				x
Youth apprenticeship programs				
Fox Cities youth apprenticeship	x	x		x
Little Rock youth apprenticeship		x	x	x
Pickens County apprenticeship	x	x		x
Tulsa youth apprenticeship	x	x		x
West Bend youth apprenticeship		x		

Source: MDRC field research.
Note: [a]No work-based activities.

policy makers and practitioners should be aware that the most common recruiters are school staff and companies that are already participating or that serve on the program's advisory board. Employers invited to serve on an advisory committee subsequently contributed workplace learning positions, and some functioned as recruiters themselves, persuading other organizations in their network to participate. When employers' senior managers served on advisory boards that had real decision-making authority and were strongly motivated to help the schools, they often made substantial commitments of their time and energy to recruit other employers. Conversely, in two programs, employers who sat on advisory committees said that they felt that their time was being wasted or their views ignored, and this may have undermined their interest in contributing to the programs.

Most of the case study programs relied on school staff members' efforts to recruit employers. Employers that provide lengthy high-tech training or large numbers of positions for students were often recruited by school staff making direct contact with the chief executive officer or other top manager. The experience of the Socorro High School for the Health Professions (SHSHP) is a compelling example.

While senior staff of local hospitals had encouraged the creation of the program, few were willing to provide paid work experience slots for its students. To recruit employers, a small group of health co-op teachers approached the El Paso Hospital Council, which represents the top administrators of the local hospitals. In her presentation to the council, SHSHP's lead teacher persuaded several hospital administrators that they could expand the pool of people entering health professions with labor shortages by introducing high school students to these fields. Moreover, she argued, the hospital that provided students with their first job opportunities would have a competitive advantage over other local health employers, since students would establish a bond with their first employer that would persist while they were completing the postsecondary training needed for permanent employment. Soon after this presentation, several of the administrators invited the teachers to speak at their hospitals. In addition, the teachers wrote a supporting article that was published in the *El Paso Physician,* a local medical journal. Soon after, the top administrator of El Paso's Thomason Hospital persuaded several of his department heads to participate in Socorro's program, providing many desirable co-op positions.

However, a few key hospital staff remained skeptical, including some who managed departments (such as pediatrics) that are of particular interest to students. To create co-op positions in pediatrics, Socorro's lead teacher suggested that a capable co-op student serve as the department director's personal assistant; the pediatrics director agreed to this arrangement and quickly grew to trust the student. The director soon increased the student's responsibilities, assigning her to manage the playroom and to market a home safety video to parents, two tasks that the department had had difficulty staffing in the past. After this experience, the pediatrics director decided to offer jobs to other SHSHP co-op students.

This example suggests several arguments that can be used to win over employers. Program staff who recruited local employers identified seven factors that were most important in influencing them to participate. In order of importance (averaged for all programs), these factors were:

1. Interest in helping the students and the local community.
2. Interest in helping the industry.
3. Dissatisfaction with the number of job applicants possessing adequate technical skills for specific jobs.
4. Interest in maintaining a good image with local customers, residents, community leaders, and employees.
5. Dissatisfaction with job applicants' academic and general work-readiness skills.
6. Desire for opportunities to identify and assess good job applicants.
7. Interest in using students as part-time workers.

Employers from different industries varied considerably in the factors that were most salient to them. Hospitals were more likely to want to help students and the health care sector in general and were concerned about maintaining a positive image in their community. In contrast, many of the participating manufacturing firms wanted to train and hire full-time workers with good basic and technical skills. This factor was particularly important to manufacturing firms participating in the youth apprenticeship programs.

Employers' reasons for participating were not consistently related to the number of positions they provided. Some of those providing the largest number of student positions said that they wanted to improve the skills of entry-level workers; others said that they wanted to help students and the community. Employers that provided smaller numbers of student positions had a similar mix of reasons.

Program design affects the kinds of benefits the program can offer to employers, and thus the kinds of employers who agree to participate. Programs that emphasize technical skills can attract employers that are looking for well-trained employees; for example, the youth apprenticeship programs, Socorro's health academy, and Dauphin County's cluster program supply employers with students who have specialized technical skills. Programs that emphasize career exposure and provide little technical training, such as the Fort Collins restructured co-op program and the Los Angeles medical magnet, attract employers who want to help students and their industry as a whole, and are willing to offer brief workplace learning experiences rather than specialized training.

Once a firm participates in a school-to-work program, its view may change. For example, the Dauphin County cluster program's co-op education teacher reported that most participating employers initially want to use the students' workplace experience as a way to identify good permanent employees for their firms. Later, many employers see how much students are learning and become more interested in helping the students. In contrast, those employers whose goal is to use students as inexpensive part-time workers tend to leave the program.

The firms that continue to participate are also willing to make larger contributions by accepting less qualified students and providing more training. In Socorro, the health academy initially recruited some hospitals by gaining top officials' support; although some department heads feared that students would not be effective workers, they found that students could perform moderately sophisticated tasks and could reduce the work loads of other staff. These experiences led them to become enthusiastic supporters of the program.

Several employers thought their adult workers benefited from working with students: some improved their supervisory skills, and others were motivated to learn new technical skills or to become supervisors.

Variation in Work-Based Activities

The workplace learning opportunities that employers offer students vary greatly in their technical focus. This variation makes it difficult for program staff to build a unified work-based curriculum and to specify competencies for students to acquire in the workplace.

Table 5.3 shows the types of jobs that various industries have provided students. It is clear that many of the jobs introduce students to meaningful and responsible work. Students removed stitches from hospital patients in Socorro, counseled middle school students in Central Point, prepared plans for kitchen countertops in Dauphin County, and helped assess bank loan applications in Baltimore.

The diversity of the students' jobs reflects both the variation in employers' labor force needs and the programs' efforts to serve students with diverse interests. Even a single employer can sometimes provide quite diverse jobs. For example, Thomason Hospital provides Socorro health academy students with jobs as medical lab

Table 5.3. Examples of Student Job Titles and Tasks.

Program	Industries Targeted	Examples of Job Titles	Examples of Tasks
Career academies			
Baltimore finance academy	Finance	Loan officer assistant Account assistant	Help prescreen loans. Work on computer spreadsheets.
Los Angeles medical magnet	Health	Varied hospital rotations	Observe radiation therapist's work, assist in taking vital signs, assist in applying fetal monitors.
Oakland health academy	Health and biological sciences	Respiratory therapy aide	Obtain oximetry results, perform EKGs.
		Pathology lab aide	Centrifuge specimens, set up and record cell studies.
Socorro health academy	Health	Central supply aide	Stock supplies, prepare medical carts, pick up supplies. Help remove stitches.
		Medical assistant Medical lab aides	Rotate chemicals, draw blood from patients.
Occupational-academic cluster programs			
Central Point cluster program	Varied	Middle school peer counselor	Counsel individual students and groups of students.
		Loan officer assistant Soil conservation assistant Radio ad manager assistant	Help prescreen loans. Match soil photos with soil slides. Observe and assist radio ad manager.
		Hardware store clerk	Inventory/sales clerk, customer service.
Dauphin County cluster program	Varied	Metalworking operator	Blacken parts, weld food-quality equipment.
		Nurse's aide Drafting assistant	Assist patients, take vital signs. Prepare plans, sketches, and drawings.

Program	Occupational area	Job title	Work-based activities
Portland cluster program[a]	Varied	Not yet defined	
Restructured vocational education programs			
Cambridge vocational restructuring[a]	Education, building trades	Building maintenance assistant Elementary teacher's aide	Repair plumbing, air conditioning, electrical equipment. Tutoring; lead groups of children in projects.
Fort Collins restructured co-op	Varied	Financial analyst assistant Computer assistant Plumber's apprentice	Reconcile accounts. Install PC software and hardware. Maintain inventory and fill orders.
Tech prep programs			
Pickens County tech prep	No work-based activities		
Wayne Township tech prep[b]	Manufacturing technology, health, business (planned)		
Youth apprenticeship programs			
Fox Cities youth apprenticeship	Printing	Printing assistant	Perform pre-press, press, binding, scanning; estimate cost of jobs.
Little Rock youth apprenticeship	Heating, ventilation and air conditioning; health	HVAC workers Hospital tray line worker Nurse's aide	Move supplies, install ducts. Serve food onto patients' trays. Assist patients, take vital signs.
Pickens County youth apprenticeship	Electronics	Meter repair Production worker	Repair meters used by electric utility. Maintain electrical machinery under supervision.
Tulsa youth apprenticeship[b]	Metalworking	Machining assistant (planned)	Machine parts, detail blueprints.
West Bend youth apprenticeship	Printing	Printing assistant	Perform screen printing, pre-press, and offset.

Source: MDRC field research.
Notes: [a]Refers to the youth apprenticeship part of the Cambridge vocational restructuring initiative.
[b]Work-based activities not yet implemented.

technicians and as central supply aides; the aide jobs offer less training but greater opportunities for full-time employment. Many jobs also combine low-skill, routine work with other tasks that provide more learning opportunities.

School-to-work programs vary in their emphasis on providing students with career exposure or production-line experience, in training students in a single cluster of skills or in varied skills, and in whether students gain specific job competencies. These program design differences are reflected in the jobs that each program provides, as shown in Table 5.4.

Most of the youth apprenticeship programs focus on providing students with the training needed for skilled high-tech jobs in the targeted industry. Employers also evaluate students' job skill competencies in four of the five youth apprenticeship programs. These competencies involve several occupations in the targeted industries, requiring employers to cross train workers. For example, in the two Wisconsin programs, students learn prepress, printing, offset, and finishing skills; this prepares them for a broad range of printing trades. In the Tulsa metalworking youth apprenticeship, students learn standard and computer numerically controlled milling and turning methods, blueprint reading, and machine maintenance. The goal of cross training is to produce flexible, multiskilled workers who can carry out many tasks, solve problems readily, and communicate effectively with staff in other jobs. In addition, cross training prepares students for a wide range of jobs in their industry.

Cross training is also used in programs that emphasize career exposure. For example, students in the Los Angeles medical magnet rotate through ten positions in local hospitals and medical offices during their three-year program. They observe medical workers and write journal entries about the workers' jobs; many students also contribute to the tasks they observe.

Some workplace learning experiences emphasize productive work in a single job. Some production jobs develop only limited technical skills (placing food on trays for hospital patients), while other jobs develop high-tech skills and perfect the skills students

Table 5.4. Characteristics of Student Jobs.

Program	Production or Nonproduction Jobs or Both[a]	Cross Training Emphasized	Sector-Specific Competencies Evaluated
Career academies			
Baltimore finance academy	Production	No	Sometimes
Los Angeles medical magnet	Both	Yes	Yes
Oakland health academy	Both	Sometimes	Sometimes
Socorro health academy	Production	No	Sometimes
Occupational-academic cluster programs			
Central Point cluster program	Both	No	No
Dauphin County cluster program	Production	Sometimes	No
Portland cluster program[b]	Not yet determined		
Restructured vocational education programs			
Cambridge vocational restructuring[c]	Production	No	No
Fort Collins restructured co-op	Both	No	Sometimes
Tech prep programs			
Pickens County tech prep	No work-based component		
Wayne Township tech prep[b]	Both	No	Sometimes
Youth apprenticeship programs			
Fox Cities youth apprenticeship	Both	Yes	Yes
Little Rock youth apprenticeship	Production	No	No
Pickens County youth apprenticeship	Both	Yes	Sometimes
Tulsa youth apprenticeship[b]	Nonproduction until postsecondary	Yes	Yes
West Bend youth apprenticeship	Both	Yes	Yes

Source: MDRC field research.

Notes: [a]A production job is one in which most of the student's workplace time is spent in work activities that directly benefit the firm (as opposed to observing co-workers, receiving training, or making products that are ultimately discarded).

[b]Work-based activities not yet implemented.

[c]Refers to the youth apprenticeship part of the Cambridge restructuring initiative.

have learned in the classroom (installing insulation and ducts in homes). In production jobs, students' work can contribute to employers' financial success (encouraging the employer to maintain participation in the program), but only if the students have been carefully trained; otherwise, they are likely to damage equipment and products or alienate customers.

The Baltimore finance academy's summer work internship focuses on career exposure but emphasizes actual work experience in a single job rather than cross training. The academy's students participate in a nine-week, paid summer internship after completing the eleventh grade. By this time, they have taken at least five courses in finance-related topics and have learned about a range of careers through class activities, workshops, field trips, job shadowing, and meetings with mentors. They have also participated in seminars on work-readiness topics, including interview skills, resume writing, punctuality, business attire, and communication skills.

For most students, the internship is their first job in a corporate setting. Several features of the Baltimore finance academy's internship component make it distinctive. More than thirty participating employers span the financial services sector, including brokerage houses, Big Six accounting firms, the Federal Reserve Bank, commercial banks, and finance-related divisions of major consumer products and service firms. Peer-group discussions help students learn about employers. Many positions require financial skills and knowledge and entail considerable responsibility. For example, students may assist loan officers in prescreening commercial loans under $10,000, construct international wire transfers, and help coordinate a company's annual report. While not all positions are this advanced, each student has the opportunity to make tangible contributions to a firm's bottom line. Other internships include computer data base management and administrative support positions.

Baltimore students are matched with employers through an

interview process. In the spring, the academy director distributes descriptions of available internships and students indicate their preferences; each student then is matched with three potential positions that appear to be a good fit, and interviews with those firms are scheduled. Three students interview for each position; the employer chooses among the candidates, and the students accept their best offer. A written job description is prepared by the employer and academy director, describing the nature of the position, necessary qualifications, and types of skills and experiences the student is expected to have. Daily activities are managed by an internship supervisor in each firm who works in the student's department. In addition, an internship coordinator, usually someone from the firm's human resources department, meets with the student periodically to provide exposure to other segments of the firm and industry and to serve as a troubleshooter. Academy staff visit the workplace twice during the summer and maintain close contact with the internship coordinators and supervisors.

As part of their internship, students are evaluated on work-related competencies and write a research paper on their experience. During the summer, three half-day seminars give the interns an opportunity to reflect on their work experiences and future goals and learn about current industry trends. Recent seminar topics included financial planning, current economic conditions, and establishing and maintaining credit.

More Than Jobs

In all the programs, employers contributed more than workplace learning positions for students. They helped conceive and manage programs, developed curricula, provided career-exploration activities, recruited other employers, and recruited and screened students (see Table 5.5), participating in a wide range of activities that complemented students' work-based activities. (Their role in screening students for program entry is discussed in Chapter Six.)

Table 5.5. Employer Contributions to School-to-Work Programs.

Program	One of the Principal Initiators of the Program	Co-Manage Program[a]	Provide Curriculum Input	Provide Job Shadowing or Career-Exploration Activities	Help Recruit Other Employers	Help Recruit and Screen Students for School Program	Provide Work-Based Learning Jobs
Career academies							
Baltimore finance academy	x	x	x	x	x		x
Los Angeles medical magnet	x		x	x	x		x
Oakland health academy	x		x	x		x	x
Socorro health academy				x	x		x
Occupational-academic cluster programs							
Central Point cluster program			x	x	x		x
Dauphin County cluster program			x		x		x
Portland cluster program			x	x	x		x[b]
Restructured vocational education programs							
Cambridge vocational restructuring[c]	x	x				x	x
Fort Collins restructured co-op	x		x	x	x		x

Tech prep programs

Pickens County tech prep			x	x
Wayne Township tech prep		x	x	x[b]

Youth apprenticeship programs

Fox Cities youth apprenticeship	x	x	x	x
Little Rock youth apprenticeship		x	x	x
Pickens County youth apprenticeship		x	x	x
Tulsa youth apprenticeship	x	x	x	x
West Bend youth apprenticeship	x	x	x	x

Source: MDRC field research.

Notes: [a]Employers exercise some executive policy-making authority.
[b]Planned.
[c]Refers to the youth apprenticeship part of the Cambridge restructuring initiative.

The history of the West Bend printing youth apprenticeship program shows the variety of roles that a single employer can play in developing a new program. The chief executive officer of Serigraph, a large specialized printing firm, served on Wisconsin's Commission for a Quality Workforce, which advocated the creation of youth apprenticeship programs throughout the state. He then called for the creation of a printing youth apprenticeship in his firm's community, West Bend, to operate under the auspices of the state's initiative. His firm helped to organize a state conference in which eight printing firms defined the competencies that students will learn in their workplaces. Serigraph provided all of the training positions for the program's first year, and has helped recruit additional printing employers to join in the program. Serigraph and the other participating firms also serve on the decision-making body for the West Bend program, the Youth Apprenticeship Consortium.

In eight of the case study programs, employers played an important role in helping to initiate the program by working on its original design and marshaling support for the program. They formed partnerships with the public schools enabling both parties to respond quickly and effectively to issues as they arose. In five of the eight programs, employers also play an active role in helping to manage both the school-based and work-based activities, and they share in the administration of the programs. In particular, employers have been involved in both initiating and managing three programs with lengthy, high-tech workplace training (Tulsa, Fox Cities, and West Bend), a finding that reflects employers' need for assurance that they can shape a training program to which they will contribute substantial resources.

In some cases employers conceive the programs that are now managed by the local school district, which maintains close communication with the employers. For instance, the Los Angeles medical magnet was conceived and developed by staff members of the Charles Drew Medical College (a medical school affiliated with UCLA and the M. L. King Jr. Medical Center) during a summer program they ran for eleventh graders. Medical school staff and community leaders persuaded the Los Angeles Unified School District to create the magnet program in collaboration with the medical school's staff. The magnet school is part of the school district, and its principal reports to the district's senior high school division and the high school magnet program office.

Employers have contributed to curriculum development in almost all the programs, defining the competencies that students learn and becoming active shapers of the programs' curricula, not rubber stamps. For example, in the Tulsa metalworking youth apprenticeship, during an early planning meeting for Craftsmanship 2000 a local chamber of commerce staff member asked the six participating employers for their definition of a machinist. They gave six different answers. Formulating a shared, precise definition of a machinist required a year of meetings and discussions among the employers and the full-time work of a curriculum specialist. The program's competencies could not be fully defined and applied until the youth apprentices' supervisors received extensive training in deconstructing the tasks required for the job and specifying appropriate and measurable learner outcomes. The professionals who ran the training sessions found that supervisors needed a great deal of time to discuss and absorb these concepts—time that was often difficult to achieve, since many supervisors could not attend all the sessions.

Participating firms in Tulsa reached an agreement on a common core of competencies that all students are to be taught; they also agreed that each firm would decide on its own methods of evaluating students' skills. In some firms students will demonstrate lathe-turning skills as part of their work making that firm's products. In other firms, students will display the same skills in special projects unrelated to the firm's production. In addition, each firm identified its own particular skills that its youth apprentices will learn. At WEBCO, a metal tube manufacturer, students will learn specialized skills related to sharpening saw blades and measuring the dimensions of completed tubes; at Hilti, a manufacturer of fasteners, students will learn to maintain equipment and change tools used in the firm's cold-forming operations. One additional result of this process of defining competencies was that Craftsmanship 2000 broadened its occupational target group from machinist to metal-working craftsman, reflecting the broad range of skills that the employers want the students to learn.

Interestingly, program staff find few employers have pushed for a specialized curriculum customized to meet the needs of their particular firms. Instead, they want to hire workers with strong general skills, and several employers have pushed program staff to help students maintain broad and flexible career options.

In Little Rock, Oakland, and Tulsa, employers actively help recruit students for the school-to-work programs. In Little Rock, for example, the Arkansas Heat Pump Association hosted a dinner for the high school counselors who provide students with information about vocational programs, including the heating, ventilation, and air conditioning (HVAC) youth apprenticeship program. The HVAC program's other trade association sponsor, the Association of Building Contractors, contributed staff who met with students and teachers in several Little Rock high schools to describe the HVAC program. These contributions helped students make an informed decision about applying to the program.

Barriers to Employer Participation

Program directors and participating employers say that the most important reasons for nonparticipation or failure to provide more positions for students are the cost of supervising and training students and the cost of students' wages. Other barriers cited were fear of high student turnover, insurance costs, the low maturity and weak skills of some students, and federal or state regulations. These issues have significant implications for efforts to expand employer participation.

While some employers told program staff that insurance costs and federal or state regulations limited their ability to provide students with workplace learning positions, this appeared to affect few employers' decisions to participate. (Chapter Six discusses participating employers' responses to these and other regulatory issues.) Instead, the key barrier for many employers is the cost of staff time for planning the school-to-work program and for training and supervising students. This cost can be quite large, greater than the cost of student wages. When programs are new, participating employers bear the cost of general program development—planning the curriculum, defining competency goals for students, and devising schedules and training plans for students' work. After the first year of program operations, these costs decline, but supervision and training costs remain, and these will affect many firms' willingness to participate.

The cost of students' wages and fear of student turnover were obstacles to expansion in Tulsa's metalworking youth apprenticeship program, for example. The initial program design called for paying students for much of their time in school, and many interested employers told program staff that the high cost of student stipends deterred them from participating. In response, program staff cut the stipend by approximately 40 percent (to about $30,000 paid over four years) for the students entering the program in the fall of 1993. After some employers also expressed concerns about student turnover, fearing that participating firms with higher wage scales would hire the most skilled students after they received training from other firms, the higher-wage employers were willing to make an informal commitment not to recruit students trained by other firms. However, these employers were also concerned that it might be illegal for them to promise not to hire a particular student. Uncertainties about hiring and turnover will remain until programs and firms acquire several years' experience in hiring program graduates.

Employers' concerns about some students' immaturity and weak job skills understandably reflect their lack of experience with adolescent employees. Program staff are usually able to provide participating firms with useful guidance and training on methods of supervising student workers, thereby reducing the burden on employers. However, employers correctly point out the importance of providing adequate time for supervisors to work closely with students, and they note that this is a significant cost for the participating firms. Moreover, they also note (sometimes with surprise) that many students exceeded their supervisors' expectations and that the supervisors greatly enjoyed working with them.

Wage Subsidies and Tax Credits as Incentives for Employers

Efforts to design a national school-to-work initiative have included discussions of using wage subsidies or tax credits as incentives to increase employers' participation. These discussions are speculative, since little is known about the effects of these incentives in school-to-work programs. The available studies, which used a classical experimental design, examined financial incentives aimed at inducing employers to hire disadvantaged workers; the evidence suggests that these incentives stigmatize the workers, reducing employers' willingness to hire them (Burtless, 1985). However, since many school-to-work programs serve a broad student population, it is not possible to determine whether a stigma may attach to participating students.

The evidence from our data about the value of subsidies and tax credits is inconclusive. Wage subsidies were used in the Socorro and Oakland health academies as an employer incentive. Program staff said that without these incentives, some public hospitals and clinics could not afford to pay students and would not have participated. (Hospitals' reluctance to pay students may also reflect their access to postsecondary students who are seeking field experience, have some technical skills, and will work for low wages.) However, both the Socorro and Oakland programs also obtained some unsubsidized positions provided by local health employers.

Although Socorro program staff found that wage subsidies increased the supply of workplace learning positions, they also found that the rules imposed by the funding source, the Job Training Partnership Act (JTPA), created problems. Because JTPA funds were limited, students were paid only for six of the fifteen or more hours they worked each week. Hospital supervisors found that the performance evaluation forms required by the local JTPA agency did not measure key aspects of students' work, and the JTPA requirements for processing time cards (which had to be submitted by noon on Friday, even though many students worked that afternoon) were burdensome. Because of JTPA restrictions on wage subsidies paid to students working for private-sector firms, only nonprofit and public-sector employers participated. Finally, program staff had difficulty getting students to attend the Saturday remedial English and math classes required by the JTPA agency for students receiving wage subsidies. The Socorro teachers who taught this class were not allowed to contribute to the lesson plan and believed that the classes had few benefits for students.

In Oakland, wage subsidies for students' summer work internships were funded by local tax revenues and the JTPA agency, and were managed by the Mayor's Summer Youth Program. Work internships during students' senior year are funded by the Oakland Redevelopment Authority, HealthNet (a large health maintenance organization), and employers. Oakland program staff find that, when the program pays students for their internships, it is easier to make students aware of the educational aspects of their work experience. In addition, unions' concerns about the possible displacement of adult workers were reduced when students were paid by the school-to-work program rather than by the hospital. The participation of local hospitals in the Mayor's Summer Youth Program has a long history that predates the Oakland health academy. This helped the health academy persuade hospitals to provide summer internships for academy students, but it also meant that many hospital staff did not know which students were from the health academy until academy staff developed relationships with supervisors. These relationships inform the hospital staff about what students have studied, enabling the internship supervisors to build on the knowledge that these students have gained in school. Academy staff also reported that students' internship wages were sometimes delayed by several weeks, causing some students to consider seeking another job.

Some employers say they are unlikely to use wage subsidies or tax credits even when these incentives are available. One hospital supervisor said that the cost of the time required to process wage subsidies would exceed the benefits. Some program directors said that tax credits might be a useful tool, because some employers see tax credits as having less regulatory burden and red tape than wage subsidies such as those provided by JTPA. However, tax credits are not likely to be a useful incentive for nonprofit institutions (including many hospitals) or other entities that do not have tax liabilities.

The lack of evidence on the effects of wage subsidies and tax credits means that policy makers are operating in the dark and that the information they need to devise policies will come from local school-to-work program staff who are trying to persuade employers to pay students. If large numbers of employers refuse to pay students, experiments with subsidies and tax credits should be urgently pursued. Until then, the uncertainty surrounding the issue of pay for students will continue to cloud efforts to design programs that can provide work-based learning experiences to large numbers of students.

Role of Business-Related Intermediaries

Employers often make valuable contributions to local school-to-work programs through intermediary organizations. Because they are supported by many businesses in a locality, these organizations are able to spread the cost of participating in a school-to-work program more widely than is the case when only a few local employers donate their time and services. Thus, intermediary organizations offer an efficient vehicle for coordinating businesses' involvement in a program, devising and refining the list of competencies that students are taught, developing training plans for students, and serving as the communications link between businesses and the schools. When an intermediary carries out these functions, the burden on individual employers is reduced, and the program does not become overly dependent on a single employer. In addition, the intermediary's network of local employers enables it to draw on greater resources of information and contributions than a few employers can provide. Intermediaries can also organize and motivate employers, appealing to their interest in helping their industry and engaging them in the school-to-work program.

Our information on the activities of intermediary organizations that have substantial employer membership and control and that coordinate the relationships of employers and the sixteen school-to-work programs is summarized in Table 5.6. In two of the programs, the Fox Cities and Tulsa youth apprenticeships, the intermediaries performed all five of the major activities we identified and clearly made critical contributions to the development of the youth apprenticeship programs. They helped initiate and manage the programs, develop the curriculum, and recruit employers and students.

In Little Rock, local trade associations representing small firms in the heating and air conditioning installation business have made critical contributions to Little Rock's youth apprenticeship program. The trade associations were contacted by the program's heating and air conditioning teacher when he was developing lesson plans for the youth apprenticeships. The education director of the local affiliate of the Association of Building Contractors (ABC), a national organization, not only suggested that the program could use an

Table 5.6. Roles of Business-Related Intermediaries.

Intermediary	Program	Help Initiate Program	Co-Manage Program[a]	Develop Curriculum	Recruit Employers	Recruit Students
American Association of Subcontractors (Harrisburg, Penn.)	Dauphin County cluster program					
Association of Building Contractors Arkansas Heat Pump Association	Little Rock youth apprenticeship			x	x	x
Fort Collins Chamber of Commerce; Larimer County Private Industry Council	Fort Collins restructured co-op	x		x	x	
Fox Cities Education for Employment Council	Fox Cities youth apprenticeship	x	x	x	x	x
Greater Baltimore Committee	Baltimore finance academy	x			x	
Portland Business-Youth Exchange	Portland cluster program				x	
Printing Industries of America	Fox Cities and West Bend apprenticeships			x		
Texas Health Association	Socorro health academy				x	
Tulsa Chamber of Commerce	Tulsa youth apprenticeship	x	x	x	x	x

Source: MDRC field research.

Note: [a]Employers exercise some executive policy-making authority.

ABC textbook developed for the industry's four-year adult apprenticeship program, but also identified the most relevant chapters of
the textbook: trade math, human relations, safety, and tools of the
trade. ABC helped recruit local employers to train youth apprentices and donate equipment to the school. To recruit students to
join the youth apprenticeship program, ABC staff met with students
and teachers in several Little Rock high schools to describe the program and the career opportunities in their industry. Representatives
from another trade association, the Arkansas Heat Pump Association, sponsored a dinner for high school guidance counselors, providing them with information about both the heating and air
conditioning industry and the youth apprenticeship program. The
experience of the Little Rock youth apprenticeship program
demonstrates how trade associations can spread some of the program development costs among the firms that are likely to benefit
from the program.

As was described earlier, some program staff members and participating employers express concern that nonparticipating employers can avoid the cost of supporting the school-to-work program
while benefiting from it by hiring students who are trained by the
program and thus there is an incentive for employers to rely on their
competitors to support the program. This "free rider" problem may
undermine the ability of programs and intermediaries to persuade
individual businesses to participate, resulting in inadequate levels
of employer participation, from the perspective of both the industry and society as a whole. Even if a national school-to-work initiative greatly increases the scale of employers' participation, there
will still be incentives for firms to economize by choosing not to
participate.

In response to this situation, intermediaries have attempted to
spread the costs of training students and supporting programs widely
among employers (keeping the costs for each employer low) and to
offer benefits to participating employers that other employers do
not receive (such as the opportunity to influence the curriculum,

shape decisions on students' training and competencies, receive information about the training, and participate in hiring fairs for graduating students).

Some intermediaries' efforts to share costs are explicit, as in the case of trade associations and chambers of commerce whose staff salaries are financed by member businesses' dues. Other intermediaries share costs indirectly. For example, the Fox Cities Education for Employment Council, created in response to a 1985 Wisconsin law providing resources for job preparation and economic development, serves as the link between employers and schools in developing and implementing the Fox Cities printing youth apprenticeship program. The salary of the council's coordinator is paid by the participating school districts, and the council relies heavily on the chamber of commerce's staff, business network, and information resources.

In several school-to-work programs, program staff and community leaders have worked to increase intermediaries' participation in the program (see Chapter Two). In Tulsa, the mayor vigorously encouraged the chamber of commerce to expand its role in Craftsmanship 2000, enhancing the influence of chamber staff with employers. The chamber's influence was further increased when the U.S. Department of Labor awarded a demonstration grant to an organization affiliated with the chamber to manage the youth apprenticeship program. In the Fox Cities youth apprenticeship program, participating school districts pay the costs of the Education for Employment Council in order to foster this intermediary organization.

At the national level, the U.S. Department of Labor is currently funding a number of trade associations to develop occupational standards, and there are other precedents for involving trade associations in education and training programs (Osterman and Batt, 1993). For instance, several publicly funded training programs are administered through trade associations, such as the National Tooling and Machining Association. These intermediaries have great influence and credibility with their members, and they also have access to highly technical information about their industry's skill needs. It seems likely that these associations will be able to make important contributions to developing the curricula and competencies used by school-to-work programs.

A Possible Role for National Trade Associations

These national examples and our finding that local trade associations have played important roles in school-to-work programs raise an obvious question: Can national trade associations help build a nationwide school-to-work system?

Some preliminary answers come from our interviews with officials of four leading national trade associations representing banking, machine tooling, manufacturing, and printing. Some of them appear to be ready to play an active role in facilitating the expansion of school-to-work programs; others will play a more limited role.

Many trade associations exist in the United States, representing most industries. Some represent firms in a specific industry or profession, while others have member firms drawn from a broad range of related industries. One or two trade associations are dominant in most industrial sectors. For example, among the more than forty associations in the banking industry, the American Bankers Association (ABA) plays a central role; its 10,000 member banks represent more than 95 percent of the commercial banks in the United States.

The principal activities of most trade associations are conducting government relations, providing information to members on developments affecting the industry, and (usually at a somewhat lower level of priority) providing education and training for member firms. In most sectors, a few leading associations devote substantial resources to education activities to develop courses and curricula, accredit training programs, and provide professional certification.

Limiting Factors

The national trade association officials interviewed generally prefer that state and local affiliates take the lead in school-to-work activities, with national groups playing a supporting role. They are willing to make their instructional materials and labor market information available to school-to-work initiatives, promote awareness of these initiatives among their members through newsletters and conferences, and participate to a limited extent in meetings and other policy development activities. They pointed to cost as a factor limiting their ability to do more, since their members' dues are designated for other specified purposes. Funding from the federal government or other sources would be needed for the associations to become heavily involved in new school-to-work activities.

Association officials also stressed that they would carefully scrutinize their potential involvement in school-to-work activities for possible violations of industry regulations, antitrust laws, and other regulations. Other factors likely to affect a national trade association's involvement are the association's mission and expertise, the priorities and traditions of its industry, the attitudes of its members toward involvement in government programs, and the changing training needs of its industry.

Mission and Expertise. Trade associations whose highest priorities are government relations and information sharing, such as the National Association of Manufacturers (NAM), are positioned by their mission and expertise to participate in the national policy debate and to promote awareness and consensus building among their members. NAM has endorsed proposals for federal school-to-work legislation, and it plans to remain active in this field by holding forums for member firms' chief executive officers, publishing reports, and building coalitions with other organizations. The interest of NAM's members in education and training is growing, an interest on which NAM has continued to build.

Industry-specific information sharing and education are central to the mission of associations such as Printing Industries of America (PIA) and banking's ABA. PIA provides an accreditation process called PrintEd for the graphic arts programs of secondary and postsecondary schools in thirty-eight states; it rates programs on nine quality standards. ABA sponsors the American Institute of Banking, which provides course materials for entry-level and advanced jobs, accredits banker education programs, and develops and distributes instructional materials for workplace literacy in banking. ABA's Education Foundation provides course materials for elementary and secondary schools on personal finances, banking services, and careers in banking. PIA and ABA officials view their current activities as compatible with future involvement in disseminating information on school-to-work programs and on successful models to their members, and encouraging them to become involved at the state and local levels.

Some national trade associations' missions place a particular priority on training activities. The National Tooling and Machining Association (NTMA), for example, provides accreditation, curricula, and course materials in thirty states, and offers its own courses through contracts with thirty-five community colleges and fourteen schools operated by member firms. With funding from the U.S. Department of Labor, NTMA offers a twelve-week course that prepares disadvantaged youths and adults for apprenticeships in the machine tool industry, serving 550 people each year. NTMA officials expect to support school-to-work programs by continuing to develop and disseminate materials, curricula, and standards. In addition, they interpret their mission as supporting efforts to develop pilot school-to-work programs, build local coalitions of member firms to participate in school-to-work programs, and share information with member firms to build awareness of those programs.

Priorities and Traditions. Each industry association has a history of priorities and traditions that shapes its activities. For example, banking industry associations tend to focus on the impact of federal regulations on banking operations, a concern that tempers the willingness of the ABA to become involved with federally supported skill standards development and that may affect its future participation in school-to-work programs. In contrast, the printing industry's PIA is actively involved in developing skill standards and participates in several school-to-work programs. However, officials say that the future involvement and interest of PIA and its members in this field may be affected by changes in their highest-priority concerns: environmental, health and safety, and economic issues.

Members' Attitudes Toward Government Programs.   Trade association leaders believe that, on the whole, it is the responsibility of all levels of government to improve the performance of the public schools, which should in turn be held accountable for educating entry-level workers. Some trade associations' training programs were begun after the member firms became convinced that the public schools were not responsive to their needs and offers of assistance. Past experiences have led some members to question whether their involvement in school-to-work programs will have lasting results. They fear that even if they invest in developing curricula and skill standards these may not be widely used, and they suspect that the federal and state governments may lose interest in school-to-work initiatives. Such attitudes on the part of member firms are likely to result in a cautious approach to school-to-work programs by national associations.

Changing Training Needs.   An industry's labor needs change in response to new technologies, the reorganization of production, new distribution processes, and shifts in demand for products and services. Such changing labor needs force trade associations to rethink their training activities, curricula, and the ways in which training is delivered. Rapid changes in the manufacturing sector have prompted NAM and other associations to call on schools to upgrade students' academic skills and to provide additional instruction in computers, communication, management, and financial operations. These skills can then be connected with technical training provided by employers in the workplace.

In banking, the ABA-sponsored American Institute of Banking is changing its traditional lengthy sequence of required basic courses, electives, and advanced courses; currently it is working to shorten courses, tie them more closely to particular job tasks, and link them with on-the-job learning. This will require extensive revisions in course materials and curricula, reducing the amount of time and attention that association officials can devote to school-to-work programs in the near future. Thus, while new training needs will push some national trade associations to increase their involvement in school-to-work programs, this will not necessarily be a universal response.

Current Efforts and Words of Advice

Despite the various factors that appear likely to limit the involvement of national trade associations in school-to-work programs, there is evidence that some associations are increasing their involvement. The West Bend and Fox Cities youth apprenticeship programs in printing benefited from PIA's work with state officials on their printing curricula and course materials, and PIA helped recruit employers to participate. State officials in Wisconsin have also worked with the Wisconsin Bankers Association to develop a youth apprenticeship program in banking that will use course materials developed by the American Institute of Banking. In the machine tool industry, NTMA operates the federally funded training programs mentioned above and works with numerous state and local school-to-work initiatives. PIA and NTMA are participating in the federal government's effort to develop skill standards for their industries, as are many other national trade associations. Several of the case study programs use instructional materials developed by national trade associations.

Association officials caution that it may be difficult in particular for small firms to participate in school-to-work programs. They report that member firms are concerned about the costs of providing work-based learning for students and that financial incentives may be needed to persuade some firms to participate (although, as described earlier, financial incentives have their own drawbacks). They reiterate some firms' fear that their competitors will reduce costs by refusing to participate in school-to-work programs and then hire away students trained at considerable expense by the participating firms. Employers also want to avoid spending large amounts of time in meetings and constructing school-to-work programs from scratch.

National trade association officials offer this advice to state and local officials: Employers are most likely to participate in a school-to-work program when its purpose, benefits, and responsibilities are clearly articulated. They argue strongly for involving state and local trade associations in new school-to-work initiatives, both to represent local employers and to help educators persuade employers to participate.

Conclusion

In all sixteen school-to-work programs, employers and business-related intermediaries contributed substantially to program operations, improving the programs' design, curricula, and management and recruiting students and other employers. Employers' main reason for participating was their desire to help students and their community; they were also motivated by a need to recruit new workers and to upgrade workers' skills in their industry.

However, few employers provide more than three workplace learning positions for students. If school-to-work programs are to serve a substantial number of U.S. high school students, they must recruit additional employers and persuade currently participating employers to provide more positions. This will require energetic work by program staff and intermediary organizations, as well as major efforts to train employers in methods of supervising and training students.

Some programs have used wage subsidies to encourage employers to work with students, and tax credits have been proposed as another possible incentive for employers. The importance of employers' contributions to school-to-work programs means that it will be crucial to find ways to maintain and expand their participation in these programs.

Chapter Six

Overcoming
Implementation Challenges

In the preceding chapters, we have described the components of school-to-work programs: their curricula and instructional methods, the support structures they provide for students, and the learning experiences that students have in the workplace. In this chapter, we move beyond descriptions of program features to examine how schools and employers have solved the challenges they encountered as they set their new programs in motion.

Two types of implementation challenges that schools face are presented first: the programs' external relationships with the school system and the school of which they are a part, and the programs' internal efforts to improve content and instructional methods. (Additional issues of developing a vision and gaining broad support among employers and school staff are discussed in Chapter Two.) We then turn to the major implementation challenges faced by employers: deciding which students to accept for workplace experiences, working with those students, and responding to the concerns of adult employees.

Fitting In: Relationships with the Local
School System and the Host School

The bureaucratic politics required to mesh a school-to-work program with the daily operations of a large, complex school system are not exciting to most people, but they have a powerful effect on the ability of secondary schools to meet students' needs. Educational changes often depend on changing bureaucratic rules and procedures, and that is why course requirements, scheduling, finances, and articulation agreements are important to leaders of school-to-work programs. These rules and procedures affect the ability of high schools to change—to accept new kinds of teaching, learning, and support for students and new linkages with employers.

School-to-work advocates need to become experts on the standard operating procedures that must be changed to fit the programs successfully into a well-entrenched school system. Local school districts are big, complicated enterprises; in order to carry out their tasks, they have developed long-accepted ways of organizing their activities, fiscal priorities, and staff expectations that are based on habit and experience. Innovative programs frequently have difficulty fitting into the rules and relationships that govern the school district and its schools. The school-to-work programs we studied are no exception to this pattern. Their efforts to fit in demonstrate the problems that most new school-to-work programs encounter, and that program advocates must be prepared to deal with.

Curriculum and Graduation Requirements

Compared to many of the required courses in high school, school-to-work programs provide more occupation-related instruction, more math and science instruction, greater exposure to career opportunities, and more work-based learning experiences. This represents a major increase in instruction to be included in the regular school day and school year, and it pushes most school-to-work programs away from a traditional high school curriculum. At the same time, these programs must try to meet state and district graduation requirements and make sure that participating students can meet college entrance requirements. Achieving these goals is particularly difficult in youth apprenticeship programs, which include many hours at the workplace and sometimes remove students from the regular high school environment.

Teachers and administrators in the case study programs vary in their views of how far they should depart from the standard curriculum. Some programs simply add occupation-specific examples to traditional courses; others create hybrid, integrated courses that deviate from conventional topics and include substantial occupation-related instruction and applications-based lessons. Some programs confront tradeoffs between the traditional curriculum and their new emphasis on teaching critical-thinking and communication skills. In others, teachers are not yet certain how far they are willing to move away from the traditional curriculum.

Teachers and administrators often voice a desire for more guidance from state education officials and for more assurances from colleges and universities that their curriculum meets college entrance requirements. Many states are moving away from college entrance requirements tied to a specified number of hours of instruction (known as Carnegie units) in academic subjects, but in school-to-work programs being implemented before these state reforms are complete, staff members are concerned about jeopardizing students' future opportunities simply because the students happen to be in a pioneering program.

The experiences of the programs in Portland and Dauphin County illustrate how staff members have struggled with these issues. In the Portland occupational-academic cluster program, teachers' efforts to develop six new occupation-related course clusters are underway, and there are still many unresolved questions about how many courses students will take in their cluster and the extent to which academic courses will be included in the clusters. Teachers are discussing the balance between maintaining the standard curriculum and adopting occupation-related, cluster-based learning activities, and teachers and administrators are concerned about how innovative they can be and how far they can move from traditional course requirements and curricula. Some teachers are interested in combining several academic subjects into a single course (for example, combining English literature with government and American literature with U.S. history), so that more cluster-related courses can be added while the basic college requirements are still met. However, teachers are uncertain about how the state department of education will move from Carnegie units to outcome-based education as it implements the state's new school reform legislation. Currently in Oregon, there are a number of state school regulations that conflict with provisions of the school reform legislation, and the state recently asked schools to apply for waivers to implement new approaches. While there is strong support for this waiver strategy at the state level, Portland officials are cautious about charging ahead without clear guidance. For many programs in Oregon and elsewhere, meeting curriculum and graduation requirements is made more complicated by state systemic education reforms that are underway. These reforms typically increase the course requirements for students' graduation, adding to the difficulty of fitting occupation-related instruction and workplace learning into students' schedules. State policy makers who are responsible for building a school-to-work system will need to maintain close coordination with the ongoing systemic reform process.

In Dauphin County's cluster program, the academic courses follow a traditional high school curriculum with the addition of occupation-related assignments, rather than using applied academic courses. In English classes, when students studying the building trades read Macbeth, teachers use assignments on the construction and architecture of the Globe Theatre, and classes use construction trade magazines for reading instruction and vocabulary words. Thus the school, a pioneer in the clustering and curriculum-integration approaches, has kept its academic courses within the traditional curriculum. Two factors influenced this decision: the negative stereotyping of vocational education led the faculty to make their curriculum conform closely to traditional approaches, and the students already receive a substantial amount of technical instruction, so the academic classes do not need to provide it.

Graduation Requirements

While it is often difficult to fit new courses, work-based learning, and increased course requirements into the existing school day and year, most case study programs have not sought waivers of graduation requirements. There are several reasons for this. Program directors find that, in most districts and states, there is a great deal of flexibility within existing requirements, allowing for substantial innovation. Many of the new and revised courses address the same topics as the traditional curriculum, so waivers are typically not required, even when teaching methods are changed and subject matter is combined in nontraditional ways. And program managers believe that seeking waivers will be perceived as indicating that the school-to-work program is less rigorous than traditional high school instruction, which may undermine students' access to colleges and good jobs.

The only case study programs where waivers are currently being used are the youth apprenticeship programs; they encounter the most challenges meeting graduation requirements because the students spend up to half their time at a workplace for one or two years. For example, the Fox Cities youth apprenticeship program is a two-year program in which students are at the workplace three full days a week and attend classes at the local community college two days a week. During the program's first semester, students take only five hours of academic instruction each week. However, school administrators have decided to reduce the amount of technical training to allow for more instruction in English and social studies. Waivers have been obtained for some of the health, fine arts, and physical education course requirements, with varied implementation depending on what the student has already taken and which participating school district the student comes from.

The following changes are being discussed, although plans have not been finalized: entering students will be required to take classes that meet state graduation requirements during the ninth and tenth grades; during the eleventh and twelfth grades, students may be asked to take some courses outside the program on their own (such as foreign languages, unless they take these courses in grades 9 and 10); and some required courses will be offered through independent study. These changes will require students to plan ahead, starting in the ninth grade, if they want to enroll in the youth apprenticeship program in grade 11.

While the Fox Cities school administrators agreed to waive some requirements, such decisions are not taken lightly. The principal of one of the participating high schools received permission from his school board to waive any requirements that would prevent students from participating in the program, particularly during the first year of program operations. He was not comfortable with using waivers, particularly for basic subjects, but agreed to do so after seeing how much the students learn at the technical college and on the job. The Wisconsin Department of Public Instruction has supported district decisions to grant waivers for youth apprenticeship programs, but local program managers continue to seek more guidance on what requirements can be waived and which courses can be condensed or combined.

Some programs have adjusted their program design to avoid the need for waivers. The Tulsa youth apprenticeship program was originally designed to combine school-based and work-based experiences, similar to the Fox Cities program. However, plans were changed so that students spend the eleventh grade (when the program begins) in classroom academic and technical instruction and do not begin their work-based experiences until the summer after eleventh grade. This change was made because of the difficulty in meeting all graduation requirements when students spend many hours in the workplace and because employers want students to have some technical training before they begin their workplace experience. However, the program sought and received a waiver eliminating the requirement that students take a history and a physical education course. Because the program serves students from nine high schools, this waiver required approval from nine principals; this approval process will become even more cumbersome when the program grows to include districts outside Tulsa.

Some programs avoid the need for waivers by using independent study to meet course requirements that do not fit into students' schedules. For example, the West Bend youth apprenticeship program, rather than waiving the physical education requirement, has arranged for students to meet it on their own, under the rules governing credit for independent-study courses. Students must submit a plan for regular exercise and be periodically tested for physical fitness.

Maintaining Postsecondary Options

A major influence on decisions about curriculum changes is the need to maintain students' eligibility for two- and four-year postsecondary programs. It is too early in the history of school-to-work programs to assess whether participating students are at a disadvantage in enrolling in postsecondary institutions. Program staff said that many of their students do go to college, and their experiences in the programs are likely to make them more attractive—not less attractive—to colleges providing technical training.

While some postsecondary institutions are partners in school-to-work programs, most have not been consulted about the effect of work-based learning and applied academic curricula on college eligibility. However, these issues have been raised in some of the case study programs. The Tulsa youth apprenticeship program participated in a statewide debate about whether applied math courses would meet the entrance requirements of the four-year state university system, and the state regents board ruled that applied math courses were acceptable.

The Fox Cities youth apprenticeship program sought and received a letter from the Wisconsin Department of Higher Instruction assuring participants that they will be welcome to apply to the four-year state university system (including the University of Wisconsin at Madison, which has the state's most competitive admission standards), although discussions are continuing on whether occupation-related courses meet the requirements of the university system. In Oregon, the state education department and the department of higher education are discussing the skills and competencies that four-year university applicants are required to have, in an effort to move away from admissions standards based on specific required courses. More efforts of this type are needed to support the development and expansion of school-to-work programs.

As a national school-to-work system is being built, postsecondary institutions must adapt to the new kinds of courses and work-based knowledge that many high school students will have. A challenging process of adjusting postsecondary entrance requirements to take account of school-to-work initiatives will be required. This process has already begun with the creation of articulation agreements that mesh the content of school-to-work programs and the requirements of postsecondary institutions. The tech prep movement in particular has focused national attention on the goal of articulating, or connecting, the technical education that students receive in high schools with their subsequent technical courses in community college. Many tech prep programs are working to establish agreements with local community colleges under which tech prep students will receive community college credits toward a technical training degree for the applied academic and vocational courses they complete in high school.

Articulation agreements are intended to produce great benefits: faster progress for students pursuing a technical credential; increased motivation because students can get high-wage jobs sooner if they use articulation credits; savings for students and training providers; increased enrollment in community colleges; and increased communication between high school and community college educators, resulting in higher-quality instruction for students.

We found that when school-to-work programs try to establish

articulation agreements with local community colleges, the programs must provide assurances that their high school courses cover exactly the same material as the college courses for which students seek articulation credits. This typically requires a significant investment of time and work by program staff in the high schools; however, at least nine of the sixteen programs have articulation agreements with community colleges. Many of the school-to-work programs were among the first of any programs in their state to develop articulation agreements, so the negotiations involved a great deal of learning for all parties. School staff members in these programs find that the goal of increased communication with the colleges has been achieved and that this communication appears to have helped staff sharpen curricula and align them with the colleges' degree requirements.

Currently, few students (five to twenty per year) use articulation credits in most programs. The reasons are fourfold. First, students must meet numerous requirements to receive the articulation credits, beyond achieving an A or B in specified courses. Requirements may include taking a specified set of courses, passing exams given by the community college, obtaining a teacher's recommendation, achieving CPR and nurse's aide certification, or several of these. Articulation credits are usually available only after students have graduated from high school and enrolled in the community college. Taken together, these requirements require students to plan carefully and to pursue their articulation credits with extensive documentation—and energy. A considerable number of eligible students fail to complete the entire process.

Second, the informational and marketing effort—explaining to students their opportunity to obtain articulation credits and the process for doing so—is often weak and inconsistent. College admissions counselors who must process hundreds of students can easily lose track of the small number who may meet the specialized eligibility requirements for articulation credits, and some eligible students may not receive the information or reminders they need.

Third, students are rarely able to shorten the time required to complete a community college degree program, because the number of articulation credits that they can receive is usually very small. For example, many of the college programs offer only four to eight articulation credits—less than 10 percent of the ninety or more credits required for most technical credentials. An exception is the Fox Cities program, which provides up to one year of college credit toward an associate's degree. With so few articulation credits, students cannot reduce their enrollment time by even a single quarter or semester. However, articulation credits may modestly reduce the cost of obtaining a technical credential, since tuition is often tied to the number of course credits that a student takes.

Fourth, many four-year colleges do not accept articulation credits, limiting students' opportunities to transfer from a community college to a four-year college. Moreover, in many states, articulation credits are not portable; they can be used only at the particular college that has signed an articulation agreement with the school-to-work program. This reduces the incentive for students to seek articulation credits, and it can create significant problems for students who transfer to another college.

Local issues also affect student use of articulation credits. Socorro students who want to get technical training in a health specialty at the local community college currently face a long waiting list and uncertain chances for admission because the college's health programs are oversubscribed; program staff are working to improve their students' opportunities for admission. Wayne Township's agreement with Indiana Vocational Technical College has been affected by a state mandate that the technical college's course credits must be accepted by Indiana's four-year college system; this has increased the pressure on the technical college to ensure that credits are given only for college-level work. In addition, community colleges have no financial incentives to grant articulation credits. Similarly, high schools appear to lack financial incentives to help students obtain articulation credits.

These experiences suggest that policy makers should be cautious in projecting benefits from articulation agreements. It appears that the practical problems described here have greatly limited students' use of the articulation agreements that program staff have worked hard to establish, and the tech prep goal of linking high school and community college through the creation of articulation agreements appears to have been only partly realized. The process of creating articulation agreements helps teachers strengthen their courses but does not necessarily result in college credits for many students. More ambitious goals, such as shortening the time required for students to complete technical training and degree programs, are far from being fulfilled.

However, if policy makers want to design incentives for high schools and community colleges to help students take advantage of articulation agreements, there are innovative ideas available. They could offer high schools an incentive payment when a student's high school courses are accepted by colleges for credits. Similarly, community colleges might be paid a bonus by the state when a student graduates in a reduced amount of time. When the time required to attain a credential is shortened, the total cost of providing expensive training is lessened; the subsequent savings for the state would be greater than the costs of the incentive payments. These payments represent a way for states to encourage the use of articulation agreements by allowing high schools and colleges to share in the savings.

Time Demands on Students

The extra courses and work-based learning in school-to-work programs often mean that participating students have greater demands on their time than if they had not enrolled in the program. For example, students in the Oakland health academy take three or four science classes in their last three years of high school. Students in the Wayne Township tech prep program take chemistry, physics, and two years of math beyond algebra—far more science and math than they would take if they were not in the program. The applied academic courses in the Pickens County tech prep program are more demanding than the corresponding general education courses.

The occupation-related, work-readiness, and work-based learning experiences in school-to-work programs fit into students' schedules by using many or all of students' elective choices. For example, in the Socorro health academy, ninth graders take an introductory health occupations course and tenth graders take a two-period pre-employment lab course. The result is that participating ninth and tenth graders have only one elective selection available outside of the program. Some students complain about the restrictiveness of the programs, the limitations on their ability to take outside electives, and their limited access to the foreign language classes they need to apply to four-year colleges. For these reasons, most program developers work hard to ensure that language courses and other electives remain available for students.

Work-based learning experiences put additional pressure on students' schedules. In many school-to-work programs, participating students must be willing to extend their school day or participate over the summer in order to fit in the work-based experience. In programs with work-based experiences during the school year, the time at the work site can usually be accommodated by using all the students' elective choices, particularly in the senior year, when students have already met most graduation requirements. However, this may require students to take technical training courses before their senior year, further limiting their elective choices.

Some programs schedule work-based learning outside regular school hours, to maximize students' exposure to both school and work. For example, seniors in the Pickens County youth apprenticeship program take up to four academic classes in their home high school and also take at least part of the three-period electronics class at the vocational school—and then extend their day into the early evening at their workplace, putting in twenty hours of work a week. In the Little Rock youth apprenticeship program, students' time at hospitals and nursing homes is often during the evening or on weekends, when employers most need extra assistance. Many work-based learning experiences, including the academies' internships, take place during the summer. In the Tulsa youth apprenticeship program, students are in classes from 8:00 A.M. to 5:00 P.M., with an hour for lunch and breaks; this represents almost three hours more instruction per day than their secondary school peers receive. In addition, the program continues over the summer.

These demanding requirements appear to offer many benefits to participating students. However, they also have costs. Some students who could benefit from the program are reluctant to commit extra time for school and work because their friends do not have similar demands on their time. Students who want to earn spending money may be reluctant to participate in work experiences that pay less than jobs not connected to school. If students in a school-to-work program take more courses than they otherwise would, the school's instructional costs increase, and this may require increases in the resources provided to school systems—not easy to do in a time of tight budgets, even if there are clear benefits for students, employers, and society at large.

Scheduling Program Classes

Scheduling high school courses and teacher and student class assignments is already an extremely complex, time-consuming task. School-to-work programs add an extra burden to this process because they usually require block scheduling of several classes, common preparation periods for teachers, and time for students to participate in work-based learning (Dayton and Schneyer, 1992; Stern, 1991). Making such changes in a high school's schedule always creates a cascade of interconnected consequences because the school-to-work participants' other courses have to be fitted into a limited set of available time periods. This is particularly difficult for courses that are offered during only one time period, which includes many electives such as band, chorus, or Junior ROTC.

Some programs have had to reduce their block scheduling to

two class periods, with additional school-to-work classes scattered throughout the day. Others have had to close off some elective options, such as advanced placement classes, to participating students. And in at least one program, scheduling problems created highly unequal class sizes—fifteen students in one class, forty-five in another.

Program managers have devised creative solutions to these scheduling problems. Once the Wayne Township tech prep program enrolled enough students to fill two sections of its courses, it became easier to schedule students for electives (since an elective is unlikely to conflict with *both* scheduled times for a tech prep course). The academies in Baltimore and Socorro block schedule their ninth- and tenth-grade students for almost all their classes. Complete block scheduling may be easier to fit into a high school schedule than partial block scheduling because it creates a school-within-a-school. In addition, most ninth- and tenth-grade students take the same required courses and have few elective options other than the school-to-work program.

The Baltimore academy's block scheduling encountered resistance because some teachers and administrators believe that the relatively motivated academy students help other students in nonacademy classes, and both Baltimore and Socorro found that it was difficult to schedule teachers for the times when the academy needed their courses. Such scheduling problems are frequently cited as a source of tension between the school-to-work program and its host school. Strong support from the principal when decisions are made on competing schedule priorities is critical to the successful implementation of school-to-work programs.

The scheduling challenges are somewhat different in programs that involve schoolwide restructuring. Scheduling problems are still difficult, but since they affect the whole school they do not create tensions between competing interests. The most severe scheduling problems here stem from unequal numbers of students in the school's various career pathways. To balance enrollments in the career pathways, the Dauphin County program assigns students to occupational clusters on a first-come, first-served basis; Portland's cluster program is considering assigning some students to their second-choice career pathway. Also in Portland, the leaders of the career pathways and the department chairs (who assign courses to teachers) face challenging negotiations over teachers' schedules and course assignments. In the youth apprenticeship programs that provide academic instruction outside the high school, it has also been a challenge to allocate teachers' time efficiently. The Tulsa program hires part-time teachers and the Fox Cities program uses community college instructors.

These scheduling issues affect the very existence of school-to-work programs. If programs cannot schedule their classes at times that make it possible for interested students and teachers to participate, the programs will disappear. If the school's schedule conflicts with a program's needs, the resulting burdens on the program's teachers and students will take time and energy away from program activities; this has happened in several case study programs. The survival of school-to-work programs depends critically on the cooperation of the person responsible for the high school's schedule.

Other Effects on the Host School

In addition to scheduling conflicts, some programs have experienced other significant tensions with their host school or school district. Because they want to treat all teachers equally, principals are sometimes unwilling to provide extra meeting and planning time for program teachers. Department chairs and other administrators sometimes reject program staff members' requests for particular faculty members to teach program courses. In Oakland, as part of a plan to provide academies for a large proportion of the city's high school students, the district increased the size of academy classes to match the district's average class size, despite the fact that academy teachers perform considerable extra work in addition to their teaching. These examples show that school-level and district-level issues have sometimes caused school-to-work programs' requests to be rejected.

In the two Wisconsin youth apprenticeship programs, teacher union representatives expressed concern about students receiving instruction outside the school because of the potential reduction in the number of teachers needed at the school; plans now call for high school teachers to play a larger role in the program. And the teacher union in Portland expressed concern about the program's changes in teachers' planning and preparation periods, but withdrew its objections when the school's teachers said that they supported the changes.

However, our research found that most programs have also produced significant benefits for their host school. Teachers in school-to-work programs learn new instructional techniques, which they have found to be useful in their other courses. They cited applications-based instruction, occupation-related problem solving, project assignments, and students' work-based learning experiences as activities they have used to improve their teaching. When school-to-work programs succeed in motivating low-achieving students, engaging them in learning activities, and helping them earn credits toward graduation, the school's other staff members regard the program as beneficial to the school as a whole.

Researchers have found that some school-within-a-school programs engender hostility from teachers who are not part of the program (see Muncey and McQuillan, 1993); this apparently has not happened in programs that help the host school serve its difficult-to-teach students. In some schools, the principal and other administrators have recognized that the school-to-work program provides a model for the school's future development. Some tech prep programs and career academies have become the focus of their host schools' efforts to improve instruction in general. In addition, increased course taking by students in school-to-work programs has led to broadened support for the program. When students take more math, science, computer applications, and vocational courses, the whole school community benefits.

To increase their value to the host school and reduce tensions, some school-to-work programs have provided nonprogram teachers with several days of in-service education on the program's methods and informally briefed them about the program. These teacher-to-teacher explanations enable those who are not part of the program to have their questions and concerns addressed without feeling threatened. Moreover, many school-to-work programs have decentralized their decision making to engage teachers in the process of implementing the program and adapting it to meet students' needs. When teachers take on much of the responsibility for operating the program, their support for it becomes very strong.

Program-itis

Public education in the United States has often been described as suffering from program-itis, a disease in which a multitude of separately funded and separately administered programs targeted on various subgroups of a school's student body gradually dilute the school's mission and sap its strength. Program-itis is often a response to a compliance mentality among school and district staff, who feel obliged to show that they are carefully meeting the requirements of each federal and state program. When a new program, such as a school-to-work initiative, is launched, many educators wonder whether it will support or undermine the core activities of their school.

The programs we describe were started by local leaders and have deep local roots. Critically, they all serve a broad range of the school's students and have gained the support of most teachers and administrators. Because of this, it is not surprising that most school staff and community members involved with these programs believe that the programs are serving their schools' central missions. Many of the programs are squarely at the center of their schools' restructuring efforts, demonstrating that major school reform is consistent with the methods and structure of school-to-work programs. Instead of contributing to program-itis, they will probably either become a major part of the education of a large share of students in the school or, if they serve only a small number of students, they will disappear.

Perhaps the most important way for any school-to-work program to avoid contributing to program-itis is to integrate the worlds of academic and occupational instruction and to strengthen both. Historically, most vocational courses have been completely separate from the high school's academic curriculum. Students have taken vocational courses as electives that rarely have any systematic link to their academic courses. School-to-work programs that reject this traditional isolation of occupation-related instruction can revitalize their schools and avoid the stigmas created by separate, less-than-equal, and marginalized programs. Furthermore, policy makers and program staff need to pay as much attention to the goals and methods of the systemic school reform movement as to the school-to-work movement, and to face the challenge of using school-to-work programs as a lever for broader reforms. This will enable school-to-work programs to grow and reach large numbers of students as systemic school reforms spread.

Program Expansion

In our case studies, the possibility of expanding school-to-work programs is handled in one of three ways: by making the program a central part of the school's future plans, by allowing its staff to seek resources to support its expansion, or by leaving its future uncertain.

For programs placed at the center of their school's and district's future plans, expansion primarily requires good administration. For example, as the Portland cluster program moves toward including all the school's students, scheduling issues and teachers' course assignments are the focus of administrators' attention, and teachers are deeply involved in curriculum development.

The Wayne Township tech prep program director held a series of meetings with administrators, department chairs, and teachers on a discussion paper vividly entitled "Growing Pains," which explained the need for converting several classrooms into tech prep labs, purchasing additional equipment, and assigning additional teachers to new tech prep teams; it also showed the class periods when tech prep classes will meet. These meetings were aimed at gaining the cooperation of the many people who will be affected by the program's growth, through explaining the issues and demonstrating the administration's support for the expansion. Because of the administration's strong support, the meetings were businesslike and productive.

The Los Angeles medical magnet program will expand substantially when its new school building is completed; extensive discussions with the architects have enabled the program staff to make plans for its future use. Dauphin County school administrators, as we mentioned earlier, signaled their commitment to making the cluster program the center of the school's educational approach by abolishing the school's academic departments; teachers meet in cluster teams, not department groups. The restructured vocational education program in Cambridge has also received the strong support of the district's leaders, ensuring its growth.

Programs that must seek resources to sustain their growth are on shakier ground, but may succeed if they can build enough community support. Wisconsin's youth apprenticeships have strong support from the state government and the printing industry and seem poised to grow. The Little Rock youth apprenticeship program is working hard to build employer interest in providing training for students and has made useful contacts with health-sector and heating-contractor employers. Early plans called for the Tulsa youth apprenticeship program to double the size of its entering class, but the financial troubles of its cooperating employers required a decision to cut student stipends and to keep the number of new students constant. Expansion of these programs appears to depend on the response of employers, community members, and students to continuing marketing efforts.

Programs that are in a state of uncertainty about their future can be vulnerable to the actions of teachers and parents who are opposed to it. The Central Point cluster program has successfully created several schools-within-a-school, but many students (and their parents) and teachers remain outside them and there appears to be some tension between those who are "in" the schools-within-a-school and those who are "out." Similar tensions have affected the Oakland health academy. The expansion of these programs depends on changes in the climate of support from the host school and local district. In Oakland, the superintendent has strongly encouraged the expansion of the career academies; in Central Point, uncertainties remain.

Financing Issues in Multidistrict Programs

Many school districts belong to regional, multidistrict groups that share the costs of expensive vocational programs, jointly funding specialized training programs that recruit students from several school districts. This approach is used by three of the programs in this study (Dauphin County, Fox Cities, and Little Rock) and were scheduled to be adopted by a fourth (Tulsa). These programs provide some initial evidence on the issues that are likely to affect other programs that must fit into multidistrict funding systems.

When school districts pay a multidistrict unit for the cost of their students' education, they often make decisions based on financial incentives. We found that in the larger programs, participating districts were sometimes reluctant to make substantial payments to the school-to-work programs, presumably to save money. In the smaller programs, participating districts were reluctant to cede control of the program to a single host school or district, presumably to retain their traditional independence.

The Little Rock youth apprenticeship program and the

Dauphin County cluster program are operated by large vocational schools that are shared by a number of cooperating school districts (eighteen in Little Rock and six in Dauphin County). In both programs, students apply through the guidance counselors of their home high school, who pass the applications to the area vocational school. The "sending" districts make payments to the area vocational school based on the number of their students who enroll. Consequently, each vocational enrollment reduces the revenue available to the sending district. Some of the sending districts appear to respond by calculating the costs and benefits of having their students participate in the school-to-work program.

In times of increasing enrollments (which create pressures for hiring more teachers and building more classrooms), it is financially beneficial for districts to send more students to the area vocational school. It is also financially beneficial for these districts to send students who are relatively expensive to educate in a regular high school, including special-education students and students with behavior problems. In times of declining enrollments (which create pressures for laying off teachers and reducing school offerings), it is financially beneficial for sending districts to decrease the number of students sent to the area vocational school.

Staff members of the school-to-work programs in Little Rock and Dauphin County have learned that the number of applications they receive fluctuates with the financial incentives facing the sending schools. State education officials also believe sending districts adjust the flow of students to area vocational schools for financial reasons. It also appears that some sending districts encourage some students who are difficult to teach to attend the area vocational school. These practices are difficult to document and sending districts do not acknowledge that they exist (presumably because of the implication that student placement decisions are being made for economic rather than educational reasons), making it difficult to negotiate agreements to stabilize enrollments in the school-to-work programs. As described earlier, program leaders have responded to this situation by increasing their recruitment efforts and by targeting students in junior high schools, which do not have a direct financial stake in students' high school choices.

In school-to-work programs that serve a single school district, financial issues are addressed as part of the district's established budget allocation process. Typically, a district's internal budget negotiations reflect the priorities set by the district's leadership. In contrast, multidistrict financial decisions can easily turn into "I win, you lose" situations, as participating districts calculate their net revenue loss or gain and base their decisions on fiscal incentives rather than educational priorities.

In much of the United States, new school-to-work programs are likely to rely on multidistrict financing, so it is important for policy makers and staff to develop effective responses to the financial issues highlighted by the case study programs. Procedures such as the following can help avoid financial conflicts that undermine the programs:

- Establish basic funding levels to be paid by sending districts, regardless of the number of entering students from the sending district. This will create an incentive for sending districts to make sure that all of the slots for which they are paying are used by their students, rather than for them to reduce the number of applicants from their district.
- Have students apply directly to the program without having to obtain the approval of the sending school or district.
- Establish mediation procedures that can be used when sending districts and programs disagree on financial and policy issues.

The Fox Cities and Tulsa youth apprenticeship programs involve far fewer students than the school-to-work programs operated by large vocational schools; their participating districts send only one or two students to the apprenticeship program each year.

The Fox Cities program serves eleven school districts and the Tulsa program will open its doors to several surrounding school districts soon. For these programs, multidistrict financing creates problems of control. In the Fox Cities program, some of the smaller participating districts indicated that they did not want to locate the apprenticeship program in the high school of one of the larger districts; they wanted it on neutral territory, in the community college. (Space and equipment limitations may limit the college's ability to play this role in the future.) Some Tulsa school district officials have expressed dissatisfaction with locating the program at the area vocational school, which might reduce the district's control over the program. Control issues may increase when more school districts participate in the Tulsa program.

Midcourse Corrections: Making Content Better and Improving Instruction

In addition to managing all the challenges of fitting into an existing high school and school district, school-to-work programs must work at improving what they teach and how they teach it. Studies of new education programs have consistently found that, despite careful planning, innovations and reforms often fall apart when they encounter the realities of daily life in classrooms (Pauly, 1991). The reason is simple: it is impossible to anticipate how new instructional activities will work before teachers try them out with students. A careful planning process, while extremely valuable, does not diminish the need to adjust and refine a new school program to take account of classroom experiences.

The first years of any school-to-work program are a time of discovery. Teachers, employers, and program administrators are learning how the program works and discovering ways to improve it. They also become aware of problems and typically experiment with possible solutions to them. The pioneering programs in our study had no textbooks to tell them how to solve their problems; they had to invent their own solutions. Their experiences can serve as a textbook for others.

Staff of all sixteen programs made numerous adjustments and refinements in their curricula and instructional plans; in several programs, they made major changes, triggered by events in classrooms as teachers worked to put the new program into practice. In addition, decision-making processes changed: the programs became increasingly decentralized and teachers often used informal collaborative groups to devise solutions to the challenges they faced.

Adjustment Processes

Student responses to a new curriculum and new classroom learning activities are unpredictable, so it is not surprising that many teachers in school-to-work programs reported that they had to make changes in the program soon after implementing it. Many programs tried to do too much and fell behind schedule when the pace of classroom instruction turned out to be slower than anticipated. "We learned to be more realistic about how much material can be taught. Less is more if students really learn the material," one tech prep teacher said. When a newly developed, occupation-related lesson fails to work well with students, teachers are unwilling to use the lesson again until they can fix it, and the pressure to improve instruction when students respond poorly causes teachers to spend a great deal of time in a program's first few years altering and refining their lessons.

A more difficult issue was confronted when teachers in several programs discovered that starting the program in the eleventh grade left students with too little time to take the courses they needed to graduate, make up for courses they had failed, and learn the program's demanding occupational and academic material. Four of the sixteen programs changed their starting grade level for these reasons; the Baltimore and Socorro academies switched from starting in eleventh grade to starting in ninth grade, the Wayne Township tech prep program switched from starting in eleventh to tenth, and the Dauphin County cluster program added an extensive ninth-grade introductory program to its established program for grades 10 through 12.

These examples of changes in programs' instruction and structure underscore the importance of using feedback from classroom experiences to refine a new program. It is not always easy to incorporate the lessons of classroom experience into a new program, but the programs in this study all devised mechanisms to enable staff members to meet and discuss their classroom experiences, and these staff consultations led to the changes. Their adjustment mechanisms took three forms: informal, ad hoc staff meetings held when teachers are able to fit them into their schedules; formal staff meetings during time when teachers are released from regular classroom assignments; and teacher learning communities, in which peer groups of teachers analyze the practical problems in their classrooms and jointly devise solutions to them.

Formal, regular times for meetings and planning appear to improve substantially teachers' ability to make needed adjustments in their school-to-work program. When a program is just starting up, the burdens on teachers are particularly heavy, since many lessons are new and the work to be assigned is often as unfamiliar to the teacher as to the students. Implementing new lessons and assignments successfully requires quick responses to classroom events and a major investment of time by teachers. Trying simultaneously to meet these heavy work requirements and attend extra meetings to discuss the school-to-work program with other staff members is simply too difficult and too time-consuming for most teachers. Programs with resources that enabled them to reduce the teaching load of their staff, particularly in the early years of the program, were able to have more regular meetings, identify classroom implementation problems more quickly, and respond to them more readily than other programs.

The programs' capacity to make needed changes is also affected by whether the program coordinator has enough time to monitor events in classrooms and to respond to problems that arise there. When program coordinators were able to devote at least half their time to running the program, they served a crucial function as the communications link among the program's staff; when the coordinators had only one or two class periods free for program-related work, this need was less likely to be met. Particularly in the early years of a school-to-work program, providing substantial time for the coordinator to work closely with the staff appears to be worthwhile.

Staff development activities helped strengthen many programs. In schools, staff development typically consists of in-service education lectures and workshops in which teachers receive instruction related to their work. This approach, whose usefulness and effectiveness have received considerable criticism (see Lieberman and Miller, 1992), was used only occasionally in our sixteen programs. Instead, teachers often worked together to decide what they needed to learn and how they could best learn it.

Here are some examples of the staff development activities.

- Wayne Township tech prep teachers wanted to identify ideas for lessons that would allow them to teach the application of an academic concept to a work-related problem, so they arranged to visit local manufacturing plants and discuss production processes with experienced workers to find out about on-the-job problem solving in high-tech manufacturing. Like almost all teachers of academic subjects, they knew little about the work settings for which they wanted to prepare students, and the visits were an important source of ideas and stimulated development of new applications-based lessons.

- Little Rock's heating and ventilation youth apprenticeship teacher worked closely with the industry's apprenticeship coordinator and with employers to make changes in the occupation-related parts of his classes, increasing math instruction geared to jobs and adding customer relations instruction.

- The health academy teachers in Socorro contacted teachers in other health-occupations academies to learn about their curricula and their integration of academic and occupational instruction, and they used the information to strengthen their own curriculum.

- Finance academy teachers in Baltimore worked during the summer with computer firms to learn current industry standards and methods.

- Teams of teachers in Central Point, Portland, Fort Collins, and other programs worked to update their curricula substantially after the program's first year, identified many adjustments that needed to be made, and added much new material.

- The occupational-academic cluster programs used the regular meetings of cluster teachers to identify ways to increase the use of occupation-related material in their classes, often with the cluster's vocational teacher serving as leader and facilitator.

Instead of relying on experts to tell them what to do, these teachers devised ways to discover for themselves how to refine and improve their school-to-work program. Historically, many industries and most schools have relied on narrow and specific training for their staff; the new school-to-work programs appear to require new, broader kinds of teacher-led professional development, to help teachers connect their lessons with work-related skills and problem-solving methods, rather than more of the standard prescriptive training in highly specific pedagogical approaches.

In different ways in each of the sixteen programs, teachers worked together to identify and implement program improvements. Often, a few staff members became deeply engaged in converting the abstract plans for the new program into concrete lessons and classroom assignments. Using their daily experiences with students, and continuously updating each other on ideas that worked and others that did not, they gradually created and shared new teaching practices. Recent analyses done at the Center for Research on the Context of Secondary School Teaching have shown that these informal teacher learning communities appear to be a widespread grass-roots phenomenon in U.S. schools. The co-directors of the center point to impressive evidence of "the pivotal role that professional networks can play in teachers' interest [in] and capacity to learn new forms of teaching. . . . Teachers participating in these networks see them as critical contexts of their work and professional development" (McLaughlin and Talbert, 1993, p. 177).

In many of the school-to-work programs, teachers' willingness to change their instructional practices, their curriculum, and the kinds of student assignments they use appeared to be fostered by teacher learning communities. These informal collaborations kept teachers engaged in the process of adjusting their practice and provided them with ideas from their colleagues' classrooms. They also tended to prevent the conflicts that can easily arise when the program's director is the only person pressing teachers to change their practices. When teachers worked together to improve the school-to-work program, instructional changes were suggested and supported by the teachers themselves, rather than being imposed on teachers from above.

These processes of making midcourse corrections resulted in a remarkable degree of decentralized decision making. While district-level and school-level administrators usually played a significant role in planning and designing these programs, and always approved the basic program design, later decisions were increasingly made by program staff members responding to their experiences in classrooms, and curricula were extensively modified by teachers in many programs.

This decentralization of control over daily program operations suggests another important reason to allocate resources so that staff members can meet with each other even after the initial planning process has been completed. Once a program has been launched, information about its strengths and weaknesses comes principally from classrooms. That information is in the hands of teachers. So is the power to make changes in daily classroom practices. Providing teachers with time and support to identify problems and jointly solve them is the most straightforward way to use their information about classroom events and to encourage teachers' efforts to improve their classroom practices. Programs that skimp on planning time and meeting time for teachers are likely to lose important opportunities to obtain information about classroom problems and to motivate teachers' extra work on the school-to-work program.

Advice from the Front Line

When we asked school staff members what implementation advice they would offer to others, their responses contained several consistent themes.

• *Persist in efforts to make needed program adjustments pay off.* All sixteen school-to-work programs made numerous significant adjustments when classroom events signaled the need to alter the original program design. This underscores the fact that building a good program takes time and persistence to solve the problems that inevitably arise. Students, parents, teachers, and employers need to be assured that the program's leadership will persevere to implement the program successfully. It is always extremely challenging and time-consuming for teachers and students to change their deeply entrenched classroom behavior patterns; the support of program and school leaders is essential for these changes to be made.

• *Make sure the appropriate grade levels are included.* If entering students have difficulty completing all the courses they need to graduate, or if entry requirements screen out a significant number of students who could benefit from the program, it may make sense to start the program in an earlier grade or to establish a feeder program to help students prepare to enter the school-to-work program.

• *Identify instructional priorities and focus on achieving them.* Most of the school-to-work programs started with plans that were very ambitious and had to scale back in response to the realities of classroom experience. The adjustment process appeared to work best when teachers were involved in setting the program's instructional priorities or clearly understood what the priorities were; in these cases, the teachers could focus their energy on the most important issues.

• *Emphasize instructional changes that are occupation related.* Many teachers told the field researchers that the most valuable changes they made in their teaching were those built around work-related themes. They created new lessons in which occupation-related situations were used to help students learn how to apply the course's ideas to real-world problems. Developing these applications-based lessons required extra work, but it paid off in student learning.

• *Closely monitor relationships with employers.* Vocational educators learned long ago that a crucial part of their job is making sure that students who have little experience in the workplace receive the support they need to show up for planned meetings with employers, attend their work-based learning activity regularly, and meet the employer's expectations. They also know that some employers lack the experience and training needed to design and maintain a work placement that provides students with learning opportunities while meeting the employer's needs. When a school-to-work program is starting up, other demands may compete with the need to monitor the program's relationships with employers, but close contact with employers is essential if the program is to survive.

• *Use professional development to help teachers improve the program.* Traditional in-service education for teachers has often had limited effectiveness when it fails to engage teachers in the collaborative process of working with their colleagues to improve classroom instruction. Teacher learning opportunities that directly involve the teachers are particularly important in school-to-work programs. Support for teacher meetings, planning activities, visits to workplaces, and observation of other classrooms can stimulate program improvements that reflect teachers' direct knowledge of the program's problems and needs.

- *Do not try to do everything at once.* The school-to-work and school reform movements have produced an almost overwhelming number of innovative ideas. Program staff said that the most crucial elements of their program are the integration of academic and occupational learning in school, applications-based instructional methods, a strong and demanding instructional program, extra support for students through clusters or a school-within-a-school, and high-quality workplace learning experiences for students. Other program elements sometimes appear to distract staff from their core activities; for example, some of the programs in this study are beginning to work on such newly popular initiatives as replacing traditional tests with portfolios that contain students' best work, linking the school with community social service agencies to meet students' noneducational needs, and requiring students to donate their time to perform community services. When program staff try to undertake a large number of initiatives at one time, their classroom activities appear to suffer.

Midcourse corrections that reflect these lessons enable school-to-work programs to improve the quality of instruction for students while meeting both the work-related and school-related goals of the programs.

Employer Implementation Issues: Working Effectively with Students

The major implementation challenge for participating employers is to learn how to work effectively with students. It is crucial that school-to-work programs monitor the implementation process for each participating employer and respond quickly when problems arise. If programs are to maintain student access to high-quality workplace learning experiences, it is essential for workplace issues to be resolved before they threaten an employer's continued participation in the program.

Screening Students and Matching Them with Jobs

Many employers want to work with students who seem likely to perform well in their firm, and to screen out those who might lack needed skills or behaviors. But we found that employers are often uncertain about how to identify the students who are likely to perform well. Inappropriate selection criteria may close off workplace learning opportunities for some of the students who might benefit most from them. Also, most participating employers had little past experience to guide them. Few had worked with adolescents, or else they had experience only with students in positions different from the new workplace learning activities. Moreover, because of the heterogeneity of the jobs to be performed by students, different screening criteria are appropriate for each job. Even program staff themselves often have difficulty developing useful screening guidelines.

Most employers said that they value students' work-readiness skills more than their academic or technical skills. They want to work with students who are motivated, prompt, and respectful of supervisors and co-workers. However, a substantial minority of the employers also want assurances that students have good academic and technical skills.

In several of the programs in which employers provide extensive training to students, the employers participate in screening students for admission to the school-to-work program. These employers make a relatively large investment in their student workers and in the development of the program design, and to protect their investment, they seek to choose the students they will train. One employer's support for a youth apprenticeship program appeared to decline because it joined the program too late to select particular student apprentices. This suggests that for some employers the opportunity to screen students may be linked to support for the program. In programs that provide less extensive training, employers delegate work placement decisions to school staff. Many programs choose not to use screening criteria; instead they work hard to find well-matched placements for all students.

In the Fox Cities and Tulsa youth apprenticeship programs, a few students were admitted and subsequently dropped from the program because of poor academic performance and behavior problems at school or work. At the employers' request, more selective admissions criteria will be used in the future in both programs. Tougher screening will probably also result from an increased number of applications from higher-achieving students once information about the programs spreads and admission becomes more competitive.

The program staff who recruit employers typically have the most knowledge about the range of workplace learning positions available and the characteristics of students who might fill the positions. Consequently, these staff members usually match students with employers. Sometimes employers are asked to interview several students, giving students experience with the job interview process; usually, however, the program staff member simply introduces the employer to a student who the staff member thinks will perform well.

Students have preferences about workplace learning positions, too. Some students need to maximize their earnings, while others are willing to accept lower earnings (or no earnings) in order to receive valuable experience. In the Socorro health academy, staff try to give students a choice between a job in a field requiring post-secondary training (for example, a position in a medical laboratory or a surgical clinic) and a job without training requirements (such as a supply or pharmacy clerk), which can become permanent after the student's graduation.

Staff in all programs monitor the quality of workplace learning positions and employer compliance with written training plans. They negotiate with employers to provide students with learning opportunities and occasionally remove students from positions that lack such opportunities. The Fox Cities youth apprenticeship program removed a student from a printing firm that was following very little of the work-based curriculum. Similarly, the Dauphin County program's cooperative education teachers have stopped placing students with some employers whose jobs allowed for little learning, something that it is difficult to determine before a student starts work.

Supporting Workplace Supervisors

Just as teachers are critical to the success of the school-based activities of school-to-work programs, the students' job supervisors are critical to the workplace activities. Yet while teachers have training and experience in ways of providing instruction to high school students, many work-site supervisors have little, if any, experience working with adolescents. Consequently, training and other support activities for supervisors are vital.

In many programs, a student's workplace experience is overseen by one adult worker who performs the roles of supervisor, trainer, and mentor. This person provides on-the-job training, manages the student's work, and functions as a role model and source of career guidance. Performing these tasks for high school students is very different from working with new entry-level employees, since the students are being introduced to both the adult world and the work of the firm. This is a challenge for which supervisors' previous experience provides only limited guidance.

Just as students need to be oriented to the world of work, several supervisors reported a need to be oriented to the world of adolescence. Recognizing this, some programs provide training in methods of working with adolescents or forums for discussing supervisors' experiences with students. According to employer and program staff, these sessions result in useful suggestions for supervising, training, mentoring, coaching, and evaluating students. Tulsa's youth apprenticeship program organized fifteen sessions in which supervisors learned techniques for managing students' work and learning, discussed how to teach students the competencies included in the program's detailed workplace curriculum, and examined some of the behavior patterns typical of adolescents and effective ways to respond to them. In the West Bend and Fox Cities youth apprenticeship programs, training sessions were provided for the students' trainers and supervisors. Topics included how to communicate with students, building student motivation, providing constructive feedback to students, and techniques for teaching and assessing specific printing competencies. The supervisors' training materials were developed by the technical college faculty and by employer staff who had previously worked with high school students. These materials used discussions of simulated cases, which enabled the supervisors to try out their ideas and receive feedback on their effectiveness. For example, one case described a student's first day at work, and the employees were asked to critique the training that the student received and to suggest ways to improve it. These sessions were very popular with the production workers.

Supervisors find they face an inevitable conflict when their production responsibilities take them away from training or monitoring students. In both Wisconsin programs, supervisors designed special projects that students can perform independently when the supervisor has to carry out a high-priority printing job. These projects, prepared by the supervisor and the student in advance, enable the student to use unsupervised time constructively.

Supervisors' ability to work with students is also shaped by the school-based curriculum. Recommendations by supervisors to program school staff have resulted in curriculum changes that have improved students' workplace performance. When hospital supervisors in Socorro found that students were unfamiliar with the equipment used in the physical therapy department, they informed the co-op health teacher, who acquired an ultrasound system and maintenance manuals so that she could teach students how to operate, clean, and repair the equipment. This curriculum change reduces the training responsibilities of the supervisors and enables students to spend more of their workplace time working with patients. Similarly, the West Bend youth apprenticeship program's school staff responded to employers' requests to broaden the school curriculum to include price estimation for printing jobs, a topic that supervisors found themselves unable to cover sufficiently at the workplace. In the Central Point cluster program, teachers were asked by a participating hardware store owner to help a student learn about electricity, to improve the student's work in the store. The teachers arranged for the student to work on lessons from an electricity textbook at school. In these examples, program staff adjusted the program's curriculum to improve students' ability to benefit from the workplace experience while reducing the training burden on supervisors and making the students more valuable to employers.

When employers encounter student behavior problems, program staff are often able to intervene effectively as well. Cooperative education teachers typically have a great deal of experience dealing with students' workplace problems, and school-to-work programs that have co-op teachers use them to meet this need. In programs that do not include a co-op teacher, the program coordinator often meets with the employer and student to find a solution to the problem. Such case-by-case interventions were reported in several programs. Interestingly, students' problems were only occasionally rooted in their workplace experience; family, peer, and school problems were more frequently involved. In most situations, improving communication with the student and responding to the student's needs outside the workplace, rather than taking disciplinary action, appeared to resolve the problem.

Scheduling Workplace Activities

Students in school-to-work programs usually face scheduling constraints from both their school and employer; they must attend required school courses at the time they are offered and they must be present in the workplace when supervisors are available to work with them and when important work activities are occurring. Responding to both sets of scheduling constraints is a challenge, requiring creative responses from program coordinators. In some cases, students' hours at the workplace are reduced so that they can take required courses in school; in other cases, students' time in vocational courses is temporarily increased when employers' fluctuating staffing needs result in reduced time in the workplace.

When participating students must take many classes with nonparticipating students, there is little remaining time and little flexibility to schedule their workplace activity. Managers at one firm planned for their youth apprentices to spend ten to fifteen hours per week at the workplace, but when they learned that the students' course schedules required them to stay in school until 3:00 P.M., they reduced the workplace time to six hours a week. For many hospitals in the Socorro area, the day shift ends at 3:00 P.M., creating problems for students who attend school until that time. The school's program coordinator worked with hospital staff to find activities that students could perform during the late afternoon, evening, or weekend with supervision from experienced hospital staff.

Seasonal or business-cycle fluctuations in employers' workload also affect when they can work with students. The cooperating employers in Little Rock's youth apprenticeship in heating, ventilation, and air conditioning (HVAC) have little winter work when the season's weather is unusually warm. The HVAC teachers respond to this problem by substituting self-paced vocational training in school for work-based learning, while trying to provide as many students as possible with a workplace experience.

Overcoming Regulatory Barriers

Child labor regulations, licensing requirements, and workers' compensation rules affect employers' ability to provide high school students with a workplace learning experience. Regulations vary, depending on the state, the industry, the occupation, and the student's age. In addition, the application of these regulations may vary depending on a regulatory official's assessment of a workplace situation or interpretation of a state's rules, leading to considerable uncertainty about the tasks that employers can make available to students. Programs have addressed these issues by negotiating with employers, seeking exemptions or clarifications, and using intermediaries.

Health care is a highly regulated industry with many licensing requirements, and in some states these requirements make it difficult for high school students to perform many health care tasks. In other states, hospitals' internal policies (which aim to ensure consistently high quality care) determine whether students can participate in particular activities. For example, while few states regulate the type of experience and training required for hospital nurse's aides, the hospitals themselves set hiring requirements for them that sometimes exclude high school students. (In long-term care facilities, federal regulations require certification for nurse's aides based on classroom training, field experience, and passing a test.) The Socorro health academy's coordinator persuaded the local public hospital to revise its age and experience criteria, enabling Socorro students to work as nurse's aides after receiving training at school. Other school-to-work programs in the health care field, including the Little Rock and Oakland programs, are working with local hospitals to permit students to participate in workplace learning other than clerical and food service activities.

Employers in manufacturing and construction are also affected by child labor laws. Federal law prohibits people under eighteen from performing a number of tasks in these and some other industries, including tasks that use most types of metal-forming, woodworking, and paper-product machinery. Many states have additional regulations excluding teenagers from some activities not covered by the federal law. Exemptions from some federal and state prohibitions can be obtained for students in approved vocational education, cooperative education, and apprenticeship programs, and some school-to-work programs have received exemptions. However, Tulsa's metalworking youth apprenticeship program has not yet received the certification from the Bureau of Apprenticeship and Training that will enable its students to work with restricted equipment. Some employers cooperating with the Dauphin County cluster program work only with high school students who are eighteen or older because the firms use lifting equipment that is restricted to adult workers.

Uncertainty about the implementation of child labor regulations affects some programs' willingness to place students in some workplaces, thereby limiting the programs' growth. The co-op supervisor in one program does not refer students under age eighteen to firms that use hoisting equipment, because of uncertainty regarding the employer's liability if a student were involved in an accident with such equipment. Based on previous experience with the state regulators, the co-op supervisor believes that a regulatory decision on this situation would depend on which child labor enforcement official acts on the case. In Oregon, widespread uncertainty about the application of child labor regulations to workplace learning led the Bureau of Labor and Industry to publish a booklet clarifying its rules for school-to-work programs.

Some employers are reluctant to participate in school-to-work programs because increased workers' compensation premiums might result if a student is injured on the job. In several firms, the research team was told that employers feared that workers' compensation costs might double if a student were injured. One solution to this problem, used in both Tulsa and Little Rock, is to create an intermediary agency to hire the students and pay workers' compensation costs; so far, this has substantially reduced these costs, since there have been few accidents. The employers pay the agency for the students' work, much as they would pay an agency providing temporary workers.

Addressing the Concerns of Co-Workers and Unions

When employers decide to participate in a school-to-work program, the adult employees and unions may have concerns about how the program will affect job security, wages, and access to technical training. Addressing these concerns and negotiating solutions are essential if the program is to gain the support of the workers who will provide students with supervision, training, and mentoring. Even in small and nonunion firms, students' opportunities to learn on the job depend on the cooperation and support of production-level workers.

Unions have objected to employers participating in school-to-work programs that appear to provide better training to students than to employees, to pay students lower wages than adult workers doing the same tasks, to displace current employees, or to pay students who are subsequently hired for regular jobs more than other new workers. In the Tulsa metalworking youth apprenticeship program, for example, American Airlines' unions did not want the students hired for lower wages than adult workers received for the same work. This problem was resolved by having students paid by Craftsmanship 2000, the organization that operates the program, rather than by American Airlines; this response was acceptable to the unions. To address the unions' desire for a fair distribution of training opportunities, American Airlines also created an adult apprenticeship program for its workers.

A firm that participates in Dauphin County's occupational-academic cluster program encountered concerns from laid-off workers that they would be displaced by the high school students. The firm committed itself not to hire the students as full-time, permanent workers as long as any workers remained laid off. Under this agreement, students can work for the firm half time while they are in school.

Several programs have worked hard to develop good working relationships with unions. The Oakland health academy's advisory board has several members from local hospital workers' unions, and they are working with the academy's staff to develop a union-led mentoring and job shadowing program for tenth-grade academy students. In an effort to build worker support for youth apprenticeship in four of its plants, one corporation has moved to strengthen its programs for upgrading the skills of current workers. Although this does not eliminate workers' concerns about possible displacement, it reduces them by demonstrating the firm's commitment to investing in its current workers. Other employers' participation in school-to-work programs has also triggered decisions to upgrade the skills of adult workers.

In one firm that participates in the Fox Cities printing youth apprenticeship program (and whose top management and union leadership strongly supported the program), opposition from workers blocked the assignment of students to the firm for a year; the students received somewhat different training from one of the firm's subsidiaries. This incident underscores the need for programs to involve affected workers during the development of the workplace learning activity and not to rely exclusively on the support of employer administrators and union leaders.

Sometimes individual workers become involved in conflicts with students. We were told of such conflicts in two programs. Program staff worked to transform these conflicts into learning opportunities in which the student is challenged to respond to a difficult working relationship, thereby learning conflict-resolution skills that can be applied in any job. When a student's co-worker appeared to feel threatened by the student's work, the co-op teacher explained how and why co-workers might feel this way and suggested ways that a student could make the co-worker "look good" to supervisors, thereby gaining the co-worker's confidence. By responding quickly and skillfully to resolve workplace conflicts, program staff can maintain a firm's willingness to provide students with workplace learning experiences; without these interventions, the participation of many employers would be jeopardized.

The Need for Careful Monitoring

These employer implementation problems will probably be faced by many new school-to-work programs, which may benefit from the experiences of the programs described here. In addition, there is a broader lesson from these implementation experiences: school-to-work programs must be prepared to work individually with each participating employer, its unions, and its workers to develop acceptable program designs and to respond to their concerns about how the program will affect them. There are no blanket solutions to employer implementation problems; case-by-case monitoring and problem solving are needed to build each workplace learning opportunity.

When program staff respond quickly and skillfully to the issues posed at each participating firm, they increase the likelihood that the firm's managers will accept more students. Identifying the concerns of current employees, and acting to allay those concerns, are necessary to gain the support of the people who actually provide students with on-the-job instruction. Effective responses to implementation issues in the workplace may also produce higher-quality learning opportunities for students: for example, carefully matching students to jobs can increase student motivation; providing customized training to students can make them more desirable workers; and training students' supervisors can enhance the students' work-based learning. For all these reasons, the staff of school-to-work programs need to reserve sufficient time for making workplace visits and for working closely with the staff of each participating employer.

Conclusion

To achieve effective implementation, constant vigilance is needed. Since it is extremely difficult, perhaps even impossible, to design a program that anticipates all the implementation challenges that will ever arise, program staff need to monitor their program and its surrounding context for all signals indicating that a problem is on the horizon.

This chapter shows program staff where to look for potential problems. They should look at the fit between the program and its host school, scheduling conflicts, teachers' experiences implementing the program in their classrooms, students' work-based learning activities, and the concerns of students' workplace supervisors and co-workers. In responding to the challenges that will inevitably arise, program staff will benefit from consulting with all affected parties and maintaining a flexible stance as they make adjustments in the program.

Chapter Seven

Conclusion: Recommendations for Policy and Practice

The School-to-Work Opportunities Act became law in May 1994. Its goal is to stimulate states and local communities to build a nationwide system of school-to-work programs. This ambitious legislation will doubtless lead to many efforts to launch innovative and effective programs. We would need a crystal ball to tell whether these efforts will succeed. But as educators and employers focus on the future, we urge them to learn from those who have gone before. The fragile framework contained in the legislation—with its requirements for school-based activities, work-based activities, and activities connecting the two—is no substitute for the pragmatic experience of the pioneers whose programs made this book possible.

Overall, our sixteen case study programs clearly demonstrate that it is feasible to create and operate innovative programs that combine learning in high school and in the workplace. It remains to be seen whether these and similar programs will be able to expand into state and local school-to-work systems that can serve large numbers of high school students nationwide.

While implementation challenges must be surmounted for programs to succeed, the pioneering programs described here should provide encouragement for educators, employers, and community leaders who see school-to-work programs as an important method of improving young people's preparation for postsecondary education, training, and rewarding careers. This chapter discusses three policy issues of overriding importance for policy makers and practitioners, plus a set of implementation issues for schools, teachers, and employers.

Policy Issue: The Content and Design
of School-to-Work Programs

Policy makers should be wary of prescriptive formulas and formats. U.S. schools and employers are devising their own customized, hybrid school-to-work programs, which draw their core components from several models and add components over time. Major program characteristics that cut across most generic school-to-work models include the integration of academic and vocational learning, the provision of workplace experiences, and efforts to offer extra support to students.

As efforts to create a national school-to-work system continue, there may be even fewer distinctions between program types and even greater need for a shared set of activities drawn from several different approaches. In general, program staff will need to design, adapt, and refine their programs to meet the needs of students; consequently, efforts to enforce the use of prescribed program designs are likely to provoke considerable local opposition. Prescriptive policies also run the risk of becoming obsolete when schools and employers discover ways to combine existing ideas and adapt new ones.

We suggest that policy makers should consider requiring the use of broadly specified program components, such as work-based instruction, but allow these components to be used in a wide range of differing, locally customized programs, rather than limiting funding to a small and tightly regulated group of program models. This would stimulate local schools and employers to adapt and shape the new programs to meet local needs while implementing the priority components specified by policy makers.

The evidence in this book shows that school-to-work programs can provide educational and work-based experiences that are *qualitatively different* from the experiences of most high school students. Programs can replace traditional instructional methods with substantially different, innovative teaching methods; use new kinds of learning activities instead of traditional assignments; and drastically change the context of students' learning from a school setting to a workplace setting. Both large and small programs can provide several years of classroom instruction and one or more years of training in a high-tech workplace. They can induce their students to take more science, math, and technical courses than are required for graduation and more of these courses than their peers who are not enrolled in the school-to-work program.

A technical assistance effort by states and the federal government could disseminate ideas from existing programs and reduce the cost of starting new programs, resulting in improved program quality. We believe that policy makers should support technical assistance to enable local school-to-work programs to learn about the innovations developed by pioneering programs.

Policy makers must never lose sight of the fact that there is no single, simple transition from school to work. Participating students combine secondary schooling, postsecondary education and training, and employment in a variety of ways, and students' choices do not necessarily correspond to the programs' plans for students. When programs provide highly developed career counseling and career exposure to help students decide how to prepare for a good career, this information about a wide range of options enables students to make informed program choices and can reduce their dropping out of expensive technical training programs such as those provided by youth apprenticeships and community colleges. Career information can also boost students' motivation to work hard in their work-related academic and occupational courses, while increasing their satisfaction with their career choice. Again, this information should be provided in the early high school years, so that students will use program resources more efficiently.

Programs that do not prepare students to meet college entrance requirements can easily become stigmatized. States should help maintain access to college, thereby attracting a broad range of students to school-to-work programs, by making sure that state-funded postsecondary programs do not exclude students who participate in school-to-work programs. This will require informing the higher education community about what students learn in such programs.

Policy Issue: Student Targeting

We found that a wide variety of students, including disadvantaged and low-achieving students, can and do participate in school-to-work programs. Most of the case study programs use open eligibility and admissions policies; students are subsequently screened by employers before they enter work-based learning activities.

Recruiting messages can appeal to all kinds of students with messages explicitly refuting the traditional stigma of vocational programs. Programs can also attract students by building support among the school's guidance counselors and teachers who are not part of the program; these school staff are very effective recruiters.

Policy makers should be wary of requiring entering students to have received a certificate of initial mastery or to meet other entry criteria. These requirements can have the unintended consequence of excluding low-achieving students who might do well in the program. Technical assistance on successful recruiting and instructional practices would help many programs. Also, rather than mandating entry criteria, programs can use exit standards to assure that students have mastered important skills.

An important message that emerges from all sixteen programs we studied is that school-to-work programs appear to be able to maintain program quality while serving a broad cross section of students. Program staff and employers report little difficulty in working with many students who are relatively low-achieving and disadvantaged; teachers say that many low-achieving students appear to learn more successfully in school-to-work programs than they had previously in other classes; and these students often performed well in the work-based learning activities. Therefore, state and federal policy makers should encourage efforts to include disadvantaged and low-achieving students in school-to-work programs.

It seems clear that some students need to enter a school-to-work program well before the eleventh grade. Many program staff members think that it is essential for programs to start in the first or second year of high school in order to motivate students, engage them in schoolwork, improve their achievement, prevent their failing and dropping out, and prepare them for success in the workplace. Policy makers, schools, and employers should consider beginning programs in the ninth or tenth grade. The first two years would include career exploration, academic and work-related learning, and broad support for students, to prepare them for training and work-based learning in grades 11 and 12.

Finally, we suggest that screening for workplace learning slots focus on work readiness, not academic performance. Employers typically screen students in school-to-work programs before offering them a work-experience position. However, the use of grades and test scores as criteria for these screenings has uncertain accuracy and validity. Employers have worked with low-achieving students despite having reservations about their suitability, and there is no consistent pattern of success or failure based on students' school achievement. This suggests that many low-achieving students may learn and perform better in workplaces than in school. Any mechanism for student screening should be examined carefully for its true usefulness.

Policy Issue: Resource Requirements

The startup and continued operation of school-to-work programs require three principal types of resources: program funding for staff, equipment, materials, and other expenses; staff time; and student compensation.

Startup costs are affected by the intensity and length of planning activities (which can require from a few months to two years), the amount of curriculum development and employer preparation needed, and the number of students in the program. The sixteen case study programs met their startup costs by reallocating existing resources; using donated staff time from schools, employers, and intermediary organizations; and using special funding.

Reallocation of existing local school funds and additional special funding seem always to be crucial. The special funding can come from school districts (often from Carl Perkins Act vocational education dollars), special state funding for demonstration efforts, federal demonstration funding, contributions from business partners, and grants from foundations. Schools, intermediary organizations, and employers can donate large amounts of time for planning and early program coordination activities, but it is important to note that the value of this time depends on whether the donors have the skills needed to build the program and to engage employers and school staff in it. Thus, funding to pay for a coordinator is often important. Without these funds, the school and employer staffs can be overloaded; for staff members to launch a program while continuing to perform their usual duties can produce severe, perhaps insuperable difficulties.

Local, state, and federal funding sources can expedite the process of starting school-to-work programs by providing needed startup funding. The creation of large numbers of school-to-work programs will probably depend on the stimulus and support of both state and federal governments, which can use their funding as leverage to shape the programs by identifying key program activities to be developed with the special funding. By using both technical assistance and special funding, states can encourage local programs to build on the experience and accomplishments of existing programs.

School-to-work programs' operating costs are affected primarily by their use of staff, both on the school side and the employer side. Major expenditures by schools often include hiring a program coordinator, reducing the number of students per teacher, and paying school staff for their planning time. Employers' costs include both donated staff time and students' wages.

While some schools use regular allocations of school staff and donated staff time, other programs spend up to $1,500 per student per year for additional school staff and smaller class sizes. The cost of ongoing program operations is primarily supported by school districts and employers, with some use of state and foundation grants, particularly for smaller classes and program coordinators. Existing vocational education funds are used in many programs to pay ongoing costs.

Employers typically donate the staff time used for supervising and training students. This time varies considerably among programs. Although only limited cost information is available from employers, the value of their contributions may amount to $1,000 to $2,000 per student when programs are new, and could fall once programs have expanded and reach a steady state. Students' wages, usually paid by employers, are an additional expense. However, some programs use Job Training Partnership Act and summer youth employment funding for students' wages.

Existing local resources, including vocational education funds, can support much of the cost of operating school-to-work programs. However, important activities such as recruiting employers and helping them design and supervise students' work-based activities, and creating new school activities that integrate academic and vocational learning, will affect programs' operating costs. Again, state and federal funding can be used to supplement ongoing local program operations and to leverage improvements in local programs by requiring program operators to add the broad program elements that policy makers want to encourage.

Not surprisingly, launching new school-to-work programs is very time-consuming. Programs may spend a year or more on planning, and program revisions typically continued for the first three to five years of operation.

Finally, program operators must never lose sight of the fact that ongoing program operations require substantial staff time, whether donated or paid—to arrange and monitor students' work-based activities, adapt new lessons and materials for the program, and carry out the basic program activities in school and in the work-place. Both school staff and employers must expect to spend sub-stantial additional time working with students—a cost factor that policy makers, too, need to be aware of.

Implementation Issues for Schools

We identified significant implementation tasks facing local school-to-work programs.

• *Support for teachers' professional development and new respon-sibilities*. School-to-work programs often use innovative instructional methods such as project-based assignments, hands-on tasks, team-work, instruction in problem-solving and communication skills, multiple methods of presenting course material, new kinds of assess-ments, and instruction aimed at achieving competence in skills rather than memorizing information. A theme of much school-to-work instruction is "experiential learning," with teachers using care-fully selected occupation-related tasks and assignments as the basis for each lesson. Students and teachers often find experiential lessons the best parts of their work.

School-to-work programs should provide teachers with paid time to develop and adapt experiential lessons for their courses and to learn new instructional techniques. To prepare the new lessons, they need to visit workplaces, interview skilled high-tech workers and supervisors, and learn about their program's occupational field. A high priority for programs should be providing sufficient paid time for teachers to learn the ideas and methods necessary to teach expe-riential lessons.

• *Organizational changes to increase support for students*. Many programs have changed the organizational structure of school and the roles of teachers to create new ways of providing support to stu-dents. Such support structures as schools-within-a-school and teacher-student clusters appear to be far more important parts of school-to-work programs than previously believed. These intimate, familylike structures provide support that contrasts sharply with the environment provided by most large comprehensive high schools. Other support structures include giving teachers responsibility and time to work on students' problems, having teachers call students' homes when they are absent, keeping the same students and teachers together for two or three years, and providing tutoring for students.

These efforts appear to foster greater engagement by students in their schoolwork, improved attendance and retention in school, and increased student interaction across ethnic, racial, and socio-economic lines. All these can be particularly important for students who are at risk of dropping out or having low achievement in school.

Policy makers and local school officials should assist in the development of new student support structures by providing technical assistance on this topic. Localities seeking special funding for school-to-work programs can be encouraged by funders to consider making organizational changes to increase the support that students receive.

• *Consensus-building among all constituencies.* Important elements in the creation of new school-to-work programs include committed leadership; the participation of employers, school staff, and district staff early in the development process; and effective marketing to parents and students. Policy makers should be alert to opportunities to encourage the active involvement of all concerned constituencies, who must learn how to work together effectively if the program is to succeed.

• *Support from intermediary organizations.* Local organizations such as chambers of commerce, business and professional groups, and trade associations have made crucial contributions to many programs, bringing schools, community colleges, and employers together, and serving as brokers between groups that have little experience dealing with each other. They can also dedicate staff to the program, recruit employers, and design curricula. Program developers should make every effort to involve local intermediary organizations in planning and implementing the school-to-work program.

- *Support from parents.* While many students are attracted by the programs' supportive atmosphere and sense of community, parents often express reservations. They like the programs' work-related activities and the chance for students to learn about a wide range of occupations, but want reassurance that students' opportunities to attend college will not be limited. Program marketers should keep this finding in mind as they approach students and parents. Although parents are initially skeptical because of the poor reputation of much vocational education, they are often converted into supporters when programs emphasize preparation for both college and work.

- *Input from teachers and guidance counselors.* These two groups of educational staff play essential and central roles in developing and implementing school-to-work programs. Teachers were among the key program developers and usually are responsible for creating or adapting a program's curriculum. They are the people responsible for providing classroom instruction to students, and their central involvement in designing and refining the school-based components of the program is essential. Support for teachers' planning activities, visits to workplaces, meetings with other participating teachers to develop solutions to instructional and curricular problems, and observation of other teachers' classrooms can strengthen program development and stimulate subsequent improvements.

Guidance counselors are gatekeepers for school-to-work programs. Consequently, involving counselors in the program and informing them about its benefits for students are important tasks for programs. Seeking their input when the program is being developed is likely to give them a sense of ownership and investment in it. They should also be kept closely informed about the kinds of students who have benefited from the program.

• *Articulation credits.* Although students can receive credit toward a college degree or training certificate based on their school-to-work courses, few appear to be using such credits. Many current programs do not materially shorten the time required for students to complete postsecondary technical training and degree programs. Existing efforts to communicate to students the requirements for receiving articulation credits are often ineffective, and students must often meet burdensome deadlines and requirements.

If policy makers want to increase students' use of articulation credits, they should consider creating financial incentives for high schools and community colleges to help students use them. For example, states could offer high schools an incentive payment when students' high school courses are accepted by colleges for credits. Community colleges might be paid a bonus by the state when students graduate in a reduced amount of time by using articulation credits. Both approaches would probably save money for the state, because of the students' reduced postsecondary training time.

• *Fitting in.* School-to-work programs often have difficulty fitting into the patterns of rules and standard operating procedures that govern school districts and schools. Particular sources of tension include curriculum and graduation requirements, the need to maintain students' postsecondary options, complex scheduling requirements, program expansion issues, and financing issues in multidistrict programs. Program leaders must be prepared to spend a significant amount of time and consensus building to craft solutions that support the school-to-work program.

Local school officials need to work closely with school-to-work program staff to resolve scheduling problems without undermining programs' operation. State education officials should identify ways to support local programs by providing waivers from regulations that limit students' access to college.

• *The need for persistence*. We found that all sixteem programs made major adjustments in response to the implementation problems they confronted in classrooms, demonstrating that building a good program takes time and persistence. Local schools and employers should anticipate that substantial amounts of staff time will be required to deal with these inevitable problems.

Implementation Issues for Employers

The evidence in this book clearly shows that it is feasible for school-to-work programs to go beyond simple work experience, giving students a wide range of contextual learning experiences in workplaces and connecting these experiences to their schooling. Students can learn how to apply skills to work tasks, receive training in specific job skills, observe and learn about various occupations through job shadowing and serving rotations in several parts of a workplace, and receive instruction in academic topics at the workplace. However, substantial time is required to recruit employers and to persuade them to offer high-quality work-based activities for students. When program staff have limited time to recruit and work with employers, the quality of students' experiences is likely to suffer.

Students are likely to benefit most from work-based learning that has several key features. It should draw on students' academic and vocational courses in school; provide relationships with adult workers; teach work-oriented motivation, attitudes, and behaviors; and use the contextual learning opportunities of the workplace to teach real-world applied problem solving. It appears that many employers will cooperate in making these contextual learning opportunities available, even though self-interest might incline them to push for greater amounts of productive work and narrow, job-specific training.

Valuable workplace learning opportunities are not restricted to any particular programmatic model; programs can develop workplace contextual learning opportunities in many different ways. Local programs should allocate substantial time to recruiting and assisting employers to develop and maintain high-quality workplace activities for students. Technical assistance is particularly valuable for employers that have little experience working with teenage employees.

Our study of the sixteen case study programs illuminated several implementation issues relating to employers.

- *Nature and scale of work-based learning positions for students.* There is a tradeoff between providing intensive work-based learning for relatively few students and expanding programs rapidly to serve large numbers of students with less intensive activities such as internships. Policy makers must be aware that employers have to invest substantial amounts of time and money to create intensive work-based learning activities for students. Because of these high costs, programs that included intensive workplace activities are able to serve fewer students than less intensive programs.

There is reason for concern about the scale of employers' participation in programs. We found that few employers provide more than three work-based learning slots for students. If this continues, many more employers must be recruited—or many students will miss a chance for work-based learning.

- *Recruiting employers.* Programs use numerous creative methods to recruit employers and facilitate their participation in school-to-work programs. Potential tools for involving employers include marketing and support from business intermediary organizations, subsidies for training and supervision (which can be time limited), and tax credits. Many strategies are aimed at decreasing the costs of participation for employers and increasing their awareness of the personal and societal benefits of participation.

Intermediary organizations are effective in facilitating employers' participation because their broad membership and financial base enable them to provide assistance to participating employers while spreading the costs of their recruiting work among many local employers. Intermediaries are also able to reassure individual employers that they are not bearing a disproportionate share of the community's task of preparing young people for employment. In some programs, JTPA funds are used to pay students' wages until the students receive enough training to merit the employer's paying them.

- *Workplace regulations.* Some employers are affected by child labor laws, safety rules, workers' compensation costs, and licensing requirements that limit their ability to provide students with work experiences. The employers in each state can provide policy makers with information on the regulations and enforcement practices that limit their participation. Regulatory relief could expand the opportunities for students to have valuable workplace experiences.

- *Support for supervisors.* School-to-work programs can develop innovative strategies to train and support students' supervisors at work. Program staff can provide special training sessions for supervisors to discuss shared problems and to offer useful suggestions on mentoring, coaching, communicating, and evaluating students at work. A particular need for employers is information and training on maintaining effective working relationships with adolescents, a subject on which school staff have special expertise.

It will take enthusiasm and dedication as well as appropriate policies to build the school-to-work programs that the U.S. needs. It is important to do so, because school-to-work programs have broad appeal to students, and they can improve the quality of education students receive while motivating and preparing them to seek valuable and rewarding careers. Indeed, the economic well-being of the next generation of American families may well hinge on the success of school-to-work programs in guiding students through the passage from high school to adulthood. Traditional high school instruction is a poor guide for students concerned about their future, and employers cannot do the job alone. A new partnership is required, and the pioneering programs described in this book show how to make that partnership work.

The future of school-to-work programs will be determined by the answers to three questions:

Will classrooms become dynamic learning environments for a broad range of students?

Will employers come forward in large numbers to share in the training of young people?

Will students commit themselves to becoming more engaged in school and achieving academic and occupational mastery?

The answer to these three questions will depend on us. The sixteen school-to-work programs that provide this book's lessons clearly show that it *is* possible to answer these questions affirmatively. But it remains to be seen whether schools and employers will be able to expand their school-to-work programs to serve large numbers of students with high-quality programs nationwide.

Appendix

Profiles of Programs

This book is based on case studies of sixteen pioneering school-to-work programs; this appendix describes them. The information presented pertains to the 1992–1993 school year, and may have changed since then.

Career Academies

Academy of Finance: Lake Clifton–Eastern High School Baltimore, Maryland

Community Setting. Baltimore is a large, ethnically mixed city. Its leading employment sectors are services, manufacturing, retailing, and business and finance. The Academy of Finance is part of Lake Clifton–Eastern High School, a comprehensive neighborhood high school with 2,100 students in grades 9 through 12. The academy is one of several citywide magnet programs in Baltimore high schools; all Baltimore eighth graders may apply to enter the academy in the ninth grade. Most of the academy's students are African-American.

Origins. District staff, the principal of Lake Clifton–Eastern High School, and business and community leaders created Baltimore's Academy of Finance to bolster the reputation of the comprehensive high school and achievement levels of its students, and to improve access to careers in financial services for minority students.

261

The National Academy Foundation, a nonprofit organization that promotes and supports the academy model in several professional fields, provided extensive planning support on the program model, curriculum, and staff development activities.

School Elements. The Baltimore Academy of Finance is a school-within-a-school that encompasses grades 9 through 12. Approximately seventy academy students in each grade take their classes together; throughout the four-year program, they maintain close contact with the academy director and two academy teachers. The academy has a distinct identity within the comprehensive high school, and its small school-within-a-school structure helps promote positive relationships between students and teachers.

Academy students take all of their courses together in grades 9 and 10, including academic and finance-related classes; in grades 11 and 12, they take three or four finance-related courses together each year. Finance courses include exploring financial careers, introduction to personal computers, computer science, economics, world of finance, banking and credit, college accounting, security operations, and international finance. The courses are closely linked with each other, use cooperative learning methods, and cover both specific skills and broad concepts.

Academy students also take brief personal development seminars on interviewing and resume writing, presentation skills, time management, career planning, and other topics. The academy provides support services, including academic advising and after-school tutoring. The program promotes college attendance, and more than 95 percent of the graduates go on to college. Workshops on how to apply to college and obtain financial aid and PSAT and SAT preparation help students achieve this goal; students who complete the program in good standing receive a certificate of financial studies.

Workplace Elements. After completing grade 11, academy students participate in a nine-week, paid summer internship. Participating employers represent a cross section of the financial services sector. Students select a field of interest for the internship and are interviewed by several employers in that field. All students who are certified by academy staff as being prepared for an internship receive one; the internships develop generic work-readiness skills and finance-related skills. Students write an internship report and attend summer seminars linking their internship with school-based instruction. A small number of internships are also available for students completing grades 10 and 12.

During the school year, students are assigned a business mentor and participate in job shadowing, spending a day at the workplace with their mentor every other month and in other settings several times a semester over two years. At the mentor's workplace, students learn about the firm, its specific job tasks, and required skills. Field trips to local businesses and the Federal Reserve Bank expose students to diverse finance careers and work environments.

Postsecondary Elements. In grade 12, most academy students take a three-credit introductory finance course at Morgan State University.

Recruitment. The academy recruits students completing the eighth grade who are slightly above Baltimore's average in achievement and attendance and who want to succeed in high school and attend college. (Historically, the city's most academically successful students have attended established college preparatory high schools; the Academy of Finance attracts mid-range students.) The academy's marketing efforts stress individual attention, hands-on instruction, insight into the world of money and finance, paid summer internships, mentors, field trips, and preparation for college.

The academy's students are recruited from twenty-six middle schools and are selected through a citywide ranking process. Students learn about the program through presentations at the middle schools, open houses at the high school, posters, pamphlet mailings, a brochure distributed to all eighth graders listing all high school programs in the district, and referrals by guidance counselors and academy students.

Cost Factors. City businesses and the school district provided startup funding. The district funds a secretarial position for the academy; other district expenditures for the academy are comparable to expenditures for other high school programs. The academy receives $100,000 each year from business partners and the Fund for Educational Excellence for the director's salary, the summer salary of the program coordinator, books and materials, field trips, PSAT and SAT preparation, after-school tutors, a wilderness team-building field experience, computers, and part of the fees for the college finance class taken by seniors.

Scale. The Academy of Finance enrolls 200 students and is expected to remain at that size.

King-Drew Medical Magnet High School
Los Angeles, California

Community Setting. Los Angeles Unified School District is the second largest school district in the United States; it enrolls more than 600,000 students in the highly urbanized Los Angeles metropolitan area. The region's diverse economy has been deeply affected by a lengthy and deep recession. King-Drew Medical Magnet High School, located in South Central Los Angeles, is a citywide magnet program; students from throughout the city are eligible to attend, and approximately one-quarter of the school's students live in its neighborhood. King-Drew's students are for the most part minorities, with 65 percent African-American, 22 percent Latino, and 6 percent Asian-American. Almost all of the school's graduates attend college or postsecondary training.

Origins. Faculty members of the Medical College of Charles Drew University of Medicine and Science (which specializes in training physicians to work in urban settings and serves the South Central Los Angeles community), wishing to increase the interest of minority youth in becoming health care professionals, conducted a summer program for high school students in 1981 and subsequently worked with community members to seek support for a medical high school. This group submitted a proposal to the Los Angeles Unified School District, which was then working to create magnet programs to foster integration. With support from the district superintendent, the community, and leaders of local medical institutions, the magnet school opened in 1982.

School Elements. King-Drew Medical Magnet High School includes grades 10 through 12, and shares the campus of the Charles Drew University of Medicine and Science; the M. L. King Jr. Medical Center is across the street. The school's curriculum, focused on the academic courses needed to enter college, emphasizes science, math, and other courses related to the study of medicine. Three years of English, science, and math are required.

Medical examples, vocabulary, and related assignments are used in many courses. Students use their work-based experiences in school assignments, including class presentations, report writing, and junior and senior research projects. Students also take workplace-linked courses in career exploration, health, hospital careers, and health occupations. After-school tutoring is provided daily, and a voluntary math review class is offered after school at the end of each semester.

King-Drew's small size—it has only ten teachers—enables students and staff to develop strong relationships; students typically have the same teacher for two or more courses during their three years in the school. The sixty to eighty students in each grade level interact extensively, and the school has a strong group identity. The school's guidance counselor and program coordinator meet with students more frequently than would be possible with a larger student caseload. King-Drew has an active advisory group that includes medical professionals from Charles Drew University and M. L. King Jr. Medical Center.

Workplace Elements. Work-based learning and work-readiness skills are a central part of the school's program. All students participate in a workplace rotation session each week, enabling each student to observe and assist professionals in ten health care settings during the three-year program (see table A.1).

Table A.1. King-Drew Medical Magnet Rotation Schedule.

Grade	Length and frequency of rotation	Rotations per year
10	3-hour weekly rotation	4
11	5-hour weekly rotation	4
12	5-hour weekly rotation	2

M. L. King Jr. Medical Center, UCLA Medical Center, local clinics, medical offices, and veterinary hospitals provide unpaid workplace learning positions in a wide range of fields, including sensitive areas such as emergency rooms and radiology labs. Students identify areas of interest that school staff try to match, if possible. A training plan is developed for each rotation, including a list of experiences that students are expected to carry during the rotation and competencies they are expected to master. Students' rotations are monitored by a workplace supervisor; school staff maintain contact with supervisors and regularly visit students at the workplace. Each semester students take a course linked to their workplace rotation; to receive credit, students complete a journal documenting the activities that occurred during each workplace session, along with related assignments. During the summer, many students work in university medical centers or health maintenance organizations.

Postsecondary Elements. King-Drew has a strong relationship with Charles Drew University, which gives students and faculty access to its library and learning laboratories. King-Drew and the university currently are developing a curriculum that would enable students to begin an allied health program while still in high school.

Recruitment. King-Drew is one of more than forty magnet high school programs in the Los Angeles Unified School District. Marketing efforts rely heavily on a booklet distributed to all students in the school district that describes all of the district's magnet programs, including King-Drew. In addition, the program's faculty and students visit some junior high schools to recruit students. All students entering the tenth grade are eligible to apply to King-Drew; there are no academic or other admission requirements. More students apply to King-Drew than it can accommodate, and district rules are used to select students based on the goals of reducing enrollments in overcrowded schools and promoting integration.

Cost Factors. The program received a foundation grant to support its initial planning and curriculum development. Like many magnet programs in Los Angeles, the school's ongoing costs are somewhat higher than those in larger high schools. A program coordinator, funded by the school district, develops workplace rotations, summer jobs, training agreements, and other activities. Bus transportation is provided for students who do not live in the school's area, and shuttle buses take students to the more distant workplace rotations. Cooperating medical professionals donate their time to work with the students.

Scale. King-Drew has 220 students. In 1997, the school plans to move into a new building and increase its enrollment to 1,700 students. Plans call for the creation of several schools-within-a-school, to retain King-Drew's distinctive small-school character. Negotiations with health care providers are underway to create a large number of additional work-based learning opportunities.

Health and Bioscience Academy:
Oakland Technical High School
Oakland, California

Community Setting. The city of Oakland, California, is ethnically and economically diverse, and includes a large African-American community as well as growing Latino and Southeast Asian populations. The economy is based on industrial and service employers. Oakland is a regional center for hospitals, related health industries, and the emerging biotechnology industry, all of which are growing. While some entry-level jobs are available, there is also substantial unemployment. Oakland Technical High School, one of the city's large comprehensive high schools, serves inner-city, disadvantaged students from grades 9 to 12; approximately 67 percent are African-American and 23 percent are Asian-American, including many students whose families are recent immigrants.

Origins. In 1985, California's state education department held a competition for grants to replicate the career academies that recently had been established south of San Francisco. Oakland Tech's principal was interested and received support from the Oakland Alliance (a community-based organization whose staff had worked with career academies) and from local hospitals whose recruitment efforts had been limited by the weak preparation of many high school students.

The design of the Health and Bioscience Academy was based on the Peninsula academies in a school district south of San Francisco, the Philadelphia Health Academy, and the High School for the Health Professions in Houston. People active in the Peninsula academies were consulted during the design and implementation process, and a program planner was hired to spearhead the development effort.

The academy's goal is to reduce dropouts among at-risk and disadvantaged students and to prepare them for postsecondary education and for skilled health careers.

School Elements. The Health and Bioscience Academy is a school-within-a-school for students in grades 10 through 12 (with some students in grade 9). Academy classmates take three or four courses each year, including biology, biomedical lab, advanced biology, double-period physiology, chemistry, math (three years), English (three years), social studies (three years), computer applications, health occupations, community service, and advanced electives. Courses focus on science- and health-related themes, and the science courses emphasize medical vocabulary and applications. Each twelfth-grade student prepares a major health-related project and receives comments from an adult mentor working in the health field.

Academy teachers have developed numerous health-related curriculum units over the years, adding interest to the program and tailoring it to the needs of Oakland Tech's students. Multiple instructional approaches are used, including graphs, diagrams, and computers, and an array of new and challenging materials has been obtained through aggressive grant seeking. Team projects and portfolio assessments are used in English, social studies, science, and science laboratory courses. Academy teachers are developing a multidisciplinary, project-based curriculum and have introduced competency assessments, reflective learning activities, and other innovations into their program.

Field trips, speakers, and job-shadowing opportunities are used to inform students about a wide range of health and bioscience careers; these experiences are then used in classroom writing and research assignments to emphasize the connection between school and work. Community service opportunities, employer- and union-provided mentors, special job-related workshops, and tutoring (before school, after school, during students' free period, and in class) are also provided. Academy students have a strong feeling of program identity based on shared classes, activities, and parent involvement.

The recognition received by the Health and Bioscience Academy has led the school district to support the development of eleven additional career academies in other occupational fields and to use the career academy approach as a central part of the district's high school restructuring efforts.

Workplace Elements.   In tenth grade, academy students are matched with career mentors and do 100 hours of community service in local hospitals; students and mentors meet monthly for one semester. During eleventh grade, students are given the opportunity to rotate through a series of after-school career-exploration and job-shadowing experiences. More than 90 percent of academy students are placed in a health-related work internship during the summer after eleventh grade. The quality of internships varies, and efforts are being made to upgrade the positions to focus on hands-on medical training rather than clerical activities.

Training plans are made for each placement, and students are paid by the employer, the Oakland Redevelopment Authority, or the Summer Youth Employment Program. Academy staff visit interns and their supervisors daily to assess the implementation of the training plan, check student attendance and work behavior, and respond to any problems that arise. Students attend workshops related to their internships during the summer.

Approximately one-third of academy twelfth graders participate in internships after school; they earn wages or school credits, sometimes both. Many students continue their internships during the summer after graduation. Efforts are also underway to develop intensive youth apprenticeship training positions for grade 12 students.

The Health and Bioscience Academy has an active advisory group that includes employer representatives.

Postsecondary Elements.   Academy staff counsel students to take the courses required for college admission, including college-prep math. In addition, the academy has arranged for local community colleges to offer several English, science, and allied health courses (medical terminology and multimedia first aid) at Oakland Tech.

The courses enable students to earn college credits and to learn the work and study habits they will need in college, and they are open to all Oakland Tech students; more than fifty academy students take the courses.

The academy has two tech prep articulation agreements with local community colleges, one in allied health and one in biotechnology. In addition, the academy has a partnership with a local private nursing and physical therapy college.

Recruitment. The academy targets students who are middle and low achievers at Oakland Tech, a recruitment process that results in a relatively low-achieving, disadvantaged group of students. The school district recently included the academy in the citywide magnet program, which may increase the representation of students from other schools.

Students apply to the Health and Bioscience Academy during the spring of their ninth-grade year and enter the academy in tenth grade. Academy teachers and students visit ninth-grade Oakland Tech classes with concentrations of low achievers to encourage students to apply, and write notes to those who they think would benefit from attending the Health and Bioscience Academy. Academy staff also recruit at the district magnet fair, junior high schools, and in local African-American churches.

An application form and parent interviews are used for most students—not for screening purposes but to increase the engagement of students and their parents. A few ninth-grade students (most of whom are repeating grade 9) and eleventh-grade students enter the academy by special request.

Cost Factors. State funds were used during the program's development phase to pay for the program coordinator, curriculum development, materials and equipment, student support services, and reduced class sizes. Currently, the size of academy classes is roughly equal to the school's average class size. Costs for the academy are higher than the district average due to special staffing, teacher released time, equipment, and student stipends. Funding from the state, city, Oakland Redevelopment Authority, school district, foundations, and the federal government pays for reduced teaching loads for the program coordinator and some academy teachers in addition to coordination, curriculum development, developing internships, support staff (an industry liaison, parent liaison, and tutors), student stipends, field trips, other special student activities, and information dissemination.

Scale. During the 1992–93 school year, the program had approximately 175 students: 10 in grade 9, 60 in grade 10, 55 in grade 11, and 50 in grade 12. The academy planned to serve 215 students in the 1993–94 school year.

Socorro High School for the Health Professions: Socorro High School El Paso, Texas

Community Setting. Socorro, Texas, is a predominantly urbanized area on the U.S.–Mexico border about ten miles east of El Paso. El Paso and the surrounding U.S. communities have a population of over 600,000, and Ciudad Juarez, Mexico (which borders El Paso), has a population of over 1 million; these cities constitute one of the world's largest population centers on an international border. The economy on the U.S. side of the border is based on assembly plants, education, retailing, the military, and the processing of chiles, pecans, onions, and premium cotton grown on area farms.

The Socorro Independent School District serves approximately 17,000 students and is one of the fastest growing school systems in Texas. The district's students are predominantly Mexican-American and often first-generation U.S. citizens; many families in the district are economically disadvantaged. Socorro High School, one of two high schools in the district, serves over 2,000 students in grades 9 through 12.

Origins. The Socorro High School for the Health Professions (SHSHP), a health academy program, was created in 1991 in response to the area's high demand for health care workers. It grew out of a successful two-year health occupations program. Health occupations teachers saw that many eleventh- and twelfth-grade students were interested in health occupations classes and cooperative education jobs they could not take because their schedules were filled by makeup English and math courses—classes they had failed during their early high school years. In response to this situation, the teachers designed a program that enabled them to work with students from the beginning of high school, to help students pass required courses, succeed in school, and prepare for good jobs in the health field.

The teachers were supported by the district's vocational director, who obtained the necessary district approval, supplies, and a small stipend for extra work done by academic and vocational teachers implementing the program. The Socorro health academy's development was also aided by the vocational teachers' close relationship with other area high school and community college health occupations teachers, their membership in local professional organizations, and their participation in a pilot project sponsored by East Texas State University to develop curricula integrating academic and vocational instruction related to health occupations.

Socorro's health academy was designed to address the underrepresentation of minorities in the health care field owing to students' lack of information about health careers, appropriate role models, and study skills. To meet these needs, the program has an integrated curriculum, work internships, and student leadership activities. While many high school health occupations programs focus on helping students obtain the nursing assistant credential, Socorro's program emphasizes the wide array of jobs available in the health care industry.

School Elements. Socorro's health academy is a school-within-a-school in which students are block scheduled for almost all of their classes in grades 9 through 12, including English, math, social studies, science, and health occupations. In the ninth grade, academy students take a double period of math (prealgebra and algebra I), English, world history, biology, and an introductory health occupations course. In the tenth grade, students are block scheduled for most of their classes: math, English, world geography, science, and a two-period preemployment health occupations lab. Eleventh-graders take math, English, social studies, and science, and a health occupations field experience course in which they rotate through job-shadowing and observation positions to explore a range of health occupations. Grade 12 students take English, social studies, and (optionally) math and science, reserving two to three periods for health occupations co-op placements.

A team of eight teachers, including two health occupations teachers, works almost exclusively with SHSHP students; the team meets weekly to discuss the integration of students' academic and occupational instruction, address individual student needs, and plan academy events. Occupation-related assignments for students include writing biographical sketches of medical pioneers in English courses, developing a health care reform agenda in social studies, and math word problems using medical applications such as temperature conversions in the human body, drug dosage conversions, and intravenous-solution dilution calculations. Efforts are underway to strengthen the program's school-within-a-school identity and increase the integration of health themes in academic and occupational courses.

Most SHSHP students participate actively in the school chapter of the Health Occupations Students of America (HOSA) and in its local, state, and national competitions, including public speaking, CPR skills, and responding to mock trauma cases. HOSA activities build unity among health occupations students and reinforce their classroom experiences by bringing them into contact with other students who have similar aspirations and by expanding their knowledge of health professions. In addition, the teachers receive information and support through their involvement in this national network of health occupations educators.

Workplace Elements. Grade 12 students participate in year-long co-op placements in hospitals, public health clinics, and nursing homes; they work a minimum of fifteen hours a week and attend a one-period health occupations class each day. Throughout their work experience, students are mentored by department supervisors and other medical professionals, who make sure that they learn the essential elements of the job, which are specified in individual training plans signed by the supervisor, student, parent, and high school co-op coordinator.

In an innovative use of JTPA funding, initially students are paid by the school district using funds from the local private industry council (PIC); employers subsequently pay part-time salaries to half of the students. The employers' co-op supervisors are certified PIC trainers. This arrangement relieves employers of the responsibility of paying students receiving initial training, while putting experienced students first in line for paid positions.

Postsecondary Elements. Health occupations courses completed at Socorro High School can be accepted for degree credit by El Paso Community College under articulation agreements approved by the state. Students can earn up to eight credits, which otherwise would cost $100 each. While the utilization of articulation credits has been limited, staff are working to make students more aware of articulation opportunities while reducing the paperwork required for articulation credits. Community college staff have developed a certificate that students can show to community college counselors to obtain articulation credits. In addition, they are exploring ways to weight SHSHP students' articulation credits to bypass long waiting lists and the time-consuming special admissions process instituted to deal with the high demand for health occupations courses.

Recruitment. SHSHP's selection criteria are being refined as the program evolves and staff assess which students are best served by the academy approach. The main criterion for selection is the student's interest in health careers, since the teachers have seen that students' interest motivates them to do well in school. In the program's first year of operation as an academy, recruiting efforts yielded just enough applicants to fill the program. In the program's second year, its participation in MDRC's National Career Academies Demonstration and Evaluation required a broader marketing and recruitment effort, which reached all eighth graders planning to attend Socorro High School. Over 100 students applied, and a lottery was used to determine which students were accepted.

Cost Factors. Startup costs for the program were paid by redirecting a modest amount of the district's Carl Perkins Act funds. Ongoing operational costs are approximately $50 to $100 more per student than the cost of the regular high school program to pay for equipment, supplies, and program development efforts, although much of the development work is done by teachers during conference periods or on their own time. SHSHP classes are the same size as other classes in the high school. Some JTPA funding administered through the school district is used to pay students for some or all of their co-op internships.

Scale. SHSHP admits 50 to 55 ninth graders each year, and has a total of 200 students in grades 9 through 12.

Occupational-Academic Cluster Programs

Crater High School
Central Point, Oregon

Community Setting. The Central Point school district serves a largely rural, blue-collar, low socioeconomic status community just outside Medford, Oregon. Local industries include timber, agriculture, medical services, retail trade, and tourism. The decline of the timber industry has created the need to train new workers and retrain displaced workers. Unemployment has been high, but the economy appears to be growing, particularly in service industries. Crater High School serves a mostly white population of approximately 1,300 students in grades 9 through 12; about 38 percent of its graduates attend a two- or four-year college.

Origins. The initial development of Crater's occupational-academic cluster program preceded the passage of Oregon's school reform legislation (H.B. 3565), and the school is one of six high schools receiving state demonstration funding to develop the reforms; earlier state grants supported teachers' work on program design and curriculum development.

Crater's cluster program consists of four schools-within-a-school: the schools of business, social services, humanities, and Rogue ecology (so named because Central Point is located in the Rogue Valley). The School of Humanities was not included in the research for this book because it does not have an occupational focus. The high school also has a community-based education program for at-risk students in which students spend half the day in school and half at the workplace. The principal and faculty decided to focus on reducing the dropout rate and strengthening the connection between school and work, and the principal challenged the faculty to devise ways to improve students' learning and commitment to education. Each school was created by a group of teachers who responded to this challenge and were given responsibility by the district and high school for creating a school-within-a-school. The first of these, the schools of business and social services, opened in the 1991–92 school year.

School Elements. The schools-within-a-school have differing designs, reflecting the talents and interests of their teachers. The schools of social services and Rogue ecology serve students in grades

10 to 12; the school of business includes grades 11 and 12. These schools-within-a-school share the following elements: students have a daily four-period block of time with the school's team of teachers, and are mixed across grade levels; team teaching and individualized instruction are used extensively; basic skills, higher-level thinking skills, and applied learning are emphasized; and technology is a key tool for learning. When participating students are not attending their school-within-a-school, they take traditional classes with other students.

Curricula and courses have been extensively revised. The four-period blocks cover academic and occupation-related subjects, with integrated instruction across subjects. Each day's schedule varies; teachers use the amount of class time they need to cover each topic and project, and do not have to stay within fifty-minute periods. Students are regrouped depending on the activity.

The school of social services' integrated curriculum emphasizes the life cycle and explores human development from the prenatal stage through death, and includes skills and concepts from the language arts, social studies, and health. The school of Rogue ecology offers an integrated curriculum in mathematics, science, and social studies; its goal is to promote active participation in understanding people's place in the Rogue Basin ecosystem. Students study stream enhancement, fish and wildlife habitats, forest ecology, pollution, and fish raising. Students' projects include operating a fish hatchery and helping government agencies gather data and disseminate information. The school of business's curriculum integrates business courses (including marketing, personal finance, advanced keyboard skills, Lotus 1–2–3, and WordPerfect), English, social studies, and economics.

Teams composed of two or three teachers in each school plan courses together. The schedules of each team are arranged so that team members have common planning and lunch periods, enabling them to coordinate instruction. Teachers use whole-group instruction, team projects, and small-group or individualized instruction.

Project-based assignments, in which teams of students work in the community, are common. Students work with teachers to decide on the focus of project activities.

Workplace Elements. Students in the schools of business and social services participate in work-based experiences one day a week for a four-period block of time; these experiences are intended to give students an opportunity to explore a career and develop work-readiness skills. There are no formal training plans; a student and his or her supervisor decide what the student will do.

Business students also participate in job shadowing to observe operations, interning in businesses related to their career interests (in two nine-week internships) and operating one of the school's businesses. Internships are with local employers: banks, a graphic arts firm, the school district's business office, retail stores, and a radio station. The school's businesses include a branch of First Interstate Bank serving the school community, an electronic publishing firm (Multimedia Designs), and the school store; students also staff an adult business night school for community members.

Social services students have internships in local social service agencies and schools, experiences that are used as material for school assignments and discussions. Internships include elementary and junior high schools, Head Start programs, shelters, and hospitals; students help teachers and service providers and provide peer counseling. Rather than having individual internships, Rogue ecology students work on group projects for various government agencies concerned with the environment.

Postsecondary Elements. Crater High School has numerous articulation agreements with nearby community colleges, mostly with Rogue Community College (RCC). Students who participate in the school of business for two years earn up to sixteen credits toward an RCC associate's degree in business.

Recruitment. The schools-within-a-school are open to all students in the eligible grades; no effort is made to target specific kinds of students. The school of Rogue ecology has had more applicants than it could accommodate, an oversubscription that was resolved through a lottery. Other schools have accepted all applicants. Recruitment efforts include presentations by the school-within-a-school faculty and students as well as brochures aimed at parents and students describing each school. Students must obtain their parents' consent to their choice of a school-within-a-school.

Cost Factors. Crater High School received several small grants from the Oregon state department of education to support curriculum development during the summer, teacher planning time, travel to conferences, and other tasks. The school receives funding as one of six demonstration high schools for Oregon's school reform legislation; this funding supports a clerical staff person who develops job-shadowing and internship opportunities. Some additional costs in staff salaries are incurred because school-within-a-school classes are slightly smaller than traditional classes. Teachers have time for coordination and planning efforts when students are at the workplace.

Scale. In 1992–93, the school of Rogue ecology had ninety students in its first year of operation; the schools of social services and business had sixty-five and forty-two students, respectively, in their second year.

Dauphin County Technical School
Harrisburg, Pennsylvania

Community Setting. The Dauphin County Technical School, known as Dauphin Tech, is supported by six school districts in the suburban area surrounding the city of Harrisburg, a predominantly

white, middle-class community. Major industries include government, small manufacturing and construction companies, and agri-
culture-based enterprises. The school has a higher percentage of
low-income students and minorities than the community at large.
Approximately 40 percent of the school's graduates enter postsecondary education or training (20 percent upon graduation, 20 percent later); another 10 to 15 percent join the military. The other
graduates obtain full-time jobs immediately after graduation, 60 to
65 percent in their training field or a related field.

Origins.   Dauphin Tech was created in 1970 as a full-time comprehensive vocational high school, with a traditional structure of
academic and vocational departments. By 1981, Dauphin Tech's
board of directors and faculty recognized that substantial numbers
of the school's students were failing, and there were few trades for
those without postsecondary education or training. A respected
guidance counselor in the school was appointed director; while
doing graduate work at Temple University he chose an assistant
director, and they jointly designed Dauphin Tech's cluster program.

Drawing on the work of Donald Maley of the University of
Maryland, who developed an early approach to clustering in vocational education, they sought to create clusters of related vocational
shops, integrating academic and vocational instruction within these
clusters. The goal was to help students uninterested in traditional
academic instruction see the relevance of academic skills to the
vocational field they wish to pursue, and to facilitate cross training
so that these students are better prepared to respond to changing
technologies in all occupational areas.

School Elements.   Dauphin Tech has reorganized its academic
courses and its twenty-one vocational shops into four occupational
clusters that operate as schools-within-a-school: technical, communication and transportation, construction, and service occupations. Academic departments were disbanded, and teachers from

traditional academic disciplines were reassigned to each cluster, in which vocational courses are linked with courses in language arts, math, science, social studies, health, and physical education.

Students enter the school in tenth grade or through the ninth-grade exploratory program. Before starting the tenth grade, students select a particular vocational shop that determines their cluster. The school uses a "week-about" system, in which students devote all of their time to academic classes for one week and to vocational classes the following week. Each cluster has approximately fifty students. Thus, during a given week, twenty-five tenth-graders in the construction cluster take academic classes while the other twenty-five tenth-graders in the construction cluster are in various construction shops all day, in classes containing students from grades 10 to 12. The following week, the two groups switch places. Each cluster of fifty students and the academic and vocational teachers assigned to it stay together for grades 10 through 12.

The teachers within a cluster integrate vocational material into the academic curriculum to make the instruction relevant to and supportive of the technical instruction students receive in their shops. For example, reading and vocabulary assignments are drawn from the cluster's vocations; when Shakespeare is read in the construction cluster's English class, students study the construction and architecture of the Globe Theatre. In grade 11 English classes, students write a technical report explaining a procedure they learned in shop; these reports are reviewed by shop teachers for technical accuracy. Academic and vocational instruction are outcome-based.

The school's ninth-grade exploratory program consists of academic courses, career exploration, self-esteem building, and experience in each of the school's shops. It operates as a school-within-a-school with a team of four academic teachers and one program coordinator. Teachers control the flexible schedule, and some occupation-related applications are used in the math and science courses. Teachers provide ongoing support to students and make regular contact with their parents.

Workplace Elements. Students work in co-op education place-ments during the twelfth grade, replacing their vocational course work. Students work full time every other week, taking academic courses in school during alternate weeks. Almost half of the seniors participate in co-op education work. Some students do not meet the co-op eligibility requirements (a 2.0 average and no more than ten unexcused absences in the junior year), and it is difficult to find co-op placements in some occupational areas (local hospitals do not like the week-about arrangement, and students in the criminal jus-tice field do not meet the minimum-age requirements for most jobs).

Co-op placements are monitored by two co-op coordinators who recruit employers and work with them to develop training plans. Most students are placed in existing entry-level positions, many of which become permanent upon graduation. Students are paid for their co-op work and receive vocational education credits. Co-op students meet weekly with their shop teachers to discuss what they are doing on the job and write regular reports. Some shop teachers assign additional reading and writing exercises to co-op students.

Postsecondary Elements. Dauphin Tech has articulation agree-ments with the Harrisburg Area Community College in math, Eng-lish, and all of the school's technical areas. Students can earn up to eighteen college credits while in high school; however, few students use these credits (see the discussion of this issue in Chapter Six).

Recruitment. Dauphin Tech introduces its program to all eighth graders in the junior high schools of the six school districts it serves; most eighth graders tour the school and hear presentations by cur-rent students. Videos and brochures are also used. Marketing efforts directly address the stereotypes of vocational education, emphasiz-ing the benefits of preparing for both college and work. Students apply for admission in grade 9 or 10 through guidance counselors in their area schools. Applying students mostly come from the lower-achieving 30 percent of their area schools; the school has numerous special-needs students to whom it offers ongoing supportive services.

Cost Factors. During the planning of the cluster program, Dauphin Tech received funding to support curriculum development efforts. Existing staff development funds were also used for planning activities. The school does not receive additional operating funds on an ongoing basis.

Scale. The school serves 800 students in grades 9 through 12.

Roosevelt Renaissance 2000: Roosevelt High School Portland, Oregon

Community Setting. Roosevelt High School serves North Portland, a low-income, working-class neighborhood geographically separated from the rest of Portland, with a high percentage of minorities and the state's largest housing projects. Approximately 20 percent of the graduating seniors plan to attend a four-year college and 30 percent plan to attend a two-year college. Portland's economic base is shifting away from natural resources, with growth in financial services, high-tech industries, light manufacturing, and government services.

Origins. At the time the Roosevelt Renaissance 2000 initiative (RR2000) was developed, the high school had the district's highest rates of absenteeism and early leavers; 49 percent of the school's ninth-graders dropped out before graduation. Roosevelt staff developed a five-year plan for the high school; the planning process revealed that the faculty felt they were not meeting the needs of the majority of students, and they formulated a plan that foreshadowed the RR2000 initiative.

At the same time, the deputy commissioner of the Oregon Bureau of Labor and Industry was developing a plan that would expose high school students to apprenticeship occupations and encourage them to enter apprenticeships. He approached district and school administrators, who joined the planning effort, along with a new program coordinator and an active business advisory committee.

Teachers' participation at this stage of planning increased slowly; after a year of discussions, a series of retreats for teachers, employers, and some parents produced a shared vision of a restructured high school that became the Roosevelt Renaissance 2000 initiative. While planning for the initiative preceded passage of Oregon's school reform legislation, the RR2000 initiative closely resembles these legislative reforms. Roosevelt High School is one of six demonstration schools receiving state funds to pioneer school reforms.

School Elements. The RR2000 initiative has created six occupational pathways (essentially clusters of courses, teachers, and students) for students in grades 10 through 12. Each pathway will provide occupation-specific courses, and academic courses will include some integration of occupation-related and career exploration themes. After a ninth-grade exploratory course, students select a pathway in one of the following areas: information systems and processing; health and human services; manufacturing technology and engineering; natural sciences and resource management; professional, public, and commercial services; and trade and tourism. Instruction uses applied and integrated academics, hands-on learning through work experience opportunities and project-based classroom work, and evaluations of student performance based on demonstration of skills.

In 1992–93, all of the school's ninth graders took the introductory Freshman Focus class, which includes career exploration, life skills instruction, self-esteem building, problem solving, decision making, group work skills, and an introduction to the six occupational pathways. It uses hands-on, team-based learning. Students rotate among four teachers to explore each of the pathways. Ninth graders also participated in monthly men's and women's Freshman Forums, created by local businesses under the leadership of the Business Youth Exchange, an intermediary group associated with the local chamber of commerce that promotes business-education initiatives. In these sessions, small groups of students discuss employment-readiness skills with a business person.

Courses and integrated lessons in the occupational pathways are being created by teams of teachers with input from business advisory committees. In grade 10, students take one course introducing the occupational area. In grades 11 and 12, students will take an occupational course and an occupation-related academic course in their pathway. There will be some block scheduling of students in each pathway.

Workplace Elements. Ninth graders who have a passing grade in the Freshmen Focus class and exhibit workplace-appropriate behavior participate in at least one three-hour job-shadowing experience. The students write responses to a questionnaire and a reflection form about what they learned. Plans call for additional job shadowing in grade 10 and for structured work experience opportunities in grades 11 and 12. Work-experience placements will range from three weeks to one semester in length and will be guided by training plans. Students also will be able to participate in the state's youth apprenticeship pilot program.

Postsecondary Elements. Roosevelt High School has several articulation agreements with Portland Community College. In addition, each career pathway's community college advisers work with pathway teams to expand the articulation agreements and to smooth students' transition to the community college.

Recruitment. The RR2000 program serves all the students in the school, therefore no recruitment effort is needed. Assignment to the school is based on residence.

Cost Factors. Roosevelt High School received state demonstration funds to implement the state's reforms. Additional funding came from a state grant, the district's federal Chapter 2 funds, and a small foundation grant. The resources were used for hiring additional staff, paying staff for extra work, paying for conferences and visits to other schools to gather ideas, hiring consultants, conducting off-site planning meetings, and paying teachers who participated in externships.

Scale. During the 1992–93 school year, Roosevelt High School's ninth-grade class of approximately 275 students participated in RR2000. In each successive year, the program will include an additional class of students until all students in the high school participate. The school's enrollment is approximately 1,200 students.

Restructured Vocational Education Programs

Rindge School of Technical Arts
Cambridge, Massachusetts

Community Setting. The Rindge School of Technical Arts (RSTA) is the second oldest vocational school in the country. It is now part of the Cambridge Rindge and Latin School, the only high school serving the city of Cambridge. Cambridge is an economically and ethnically diverse city adjacent to Boston; its major industries include biotechnology, health, and higher education. RSTA is one of the high school's six "houses"—that is, schools-within-a-school. Of the houses, RSTA has the highest proportion of economically and academically disadvantaged students, most of whom come from the two poorest sections of the city. Nearly half (46 percent) are defined as having special needs, and many are at risk of dropping out. Approximately half of RSTA graduates receive post-secondary education.

Origins. In the past, RSTA has lost many of its students because they had failed in academic classes and did not have enough time to take vocational courses. The district superintendent, acknowledging the need to restructure RSTA, asked a successful and innovative former carpentry teacher at the school to become the director of vocational education and to restructure RSTA's program.

The director previously had been active as a leading advocate for change in the 1990 Carl Perkins Vocational Education Act, and RSTA's innovations are aimed at fully implementing the provisions and intentions of the Perkins Act. RSTA teachers are closely involved in the restructuring process, which seeks to link vocational and academic learning, train students in all aspects of their chosen industry, and link vocational education with community economic development efforts.

School Elements. Before the restructuring effort, students took their academic classes in the larger comprehensive school and RSTA provided their vocational courses. Currently, RSTA provides special academic courses that both integrate vocational and academic instruction and strengthen academic skills. RSTA's vocational training gives students experience in several of the school's shops, uses project-based instruction extensively, and emphasizes all aspects of operating a business.

Changes are in place for grades 9 and 10, and planning is underway for changes in grades 11 and 12. Entering ninth graders take a group of courses with a range of innovative techniques—CityWorks, CityLife, and CitySystems—that are the cornerstone of the school's instruction.

CityWorks is a hands-on, project-based course in which students use the city of Cambridge as their classroom and explore varied occupations taught at RSTA. Students work on community development projects that involve multiple trades; for example, one class planned and designed four businesses by finding locations, completing paperwork for regulations and construction approval, creating models of the buildings, developing marketing plans, and other tasks. CitySystems combines math and science with vocational themes; similarly, CityLife links English and social studies with vocational themes. Both use projects and hands-on instruction.

Instructors for these three courses meet regularly to plan, coordinate, and share information. Previously, ninth graders were only at RSTA for one class a day; they now spend five periods a day with the same classmates, an increase that enables RSTA staff to offer strong support to entering students.

For the tenth grade, staff are developing integrated academic classes and projects that involve multiple shops and focus on community development needs identified during the CityWorks course. In one project, students investigate the technology and market for electric cars and for converting cars to electric power as a new industry for the community. For grade 11 and 12 students, plans call for creating school-based enterprises to enable students to learn about all aspects of an industry.

Workplace Elements.   RSTA offers two youth apprenticeship programs; juniors and seniors in all the high school's houses may apply. Students may choose to participate in the internship for one or two years.

In the youth apprenticeship linked with Polaroid, students work with building trades workers who support the operation of the corporation's plants and office buildings. Participating students are assigned to one of eight shops at Polaroid: carpentry, electronics, multicraft, control center (record keeping and accounting), computer technology, plumbing, and heating/air conditioning. Students are mentored by shop supervisors and work with a number of skilled craft workers to learn about different aspects of the shop's work. Apprentices spend half the day at school and the remainder working at Polaroid and participating in a seminar that combines English and social studies with work-site experiences, which are used as a source for seminar writing and presentation topics; history lessons emphasize the development of industries. Polaroid staff visit the seminar to discuss various aspects of the corporation's operations. Students are paid for their work at Polaroid.

A youth apprenticeship in elementary education is offered by RSTA, Lesley College, and the Cambridge school district. Participating students work in a classroom in the primary grades two mornings a week for three hours. Students assist teachers, work with a small group of children on an activity, or help individual children with an assignment. After they acquire some experience, youth apprentices participate in planning activities and lessons for the students. The program coordinator and a Lesley College professor visit the classrooms each week to assess students' work and respond to any problems.

During the other three mornings each week, students go to Lesley College for a seminar taught by an RSTA English teacher and a Lesley College education professor. The course emphasizes written and oral communication skills and integrates workplace experiences with instruction in teaching techniques, English, and social studies. In the afternoon, students take academic classes in the high school.

Postsecondary Elements. Students participating in the education apprenticeship program earn three Lesley College credits for the seminar. Lesley College offers scholarships to study teaching for minority students graduating from the Cambridge and Boston public school systems; at least one youth apprentice has received this scholarship.

Recruitment. Students select a house within the high school at the end of the eighth grade. RSTA and district staff make presentations to all eighth graders at the feeder schools; RSTA accepts all students who select the program. In addition, some students from other houses enter RSTA if they are not performing well. The youth apprenticeship programs are open to all students in the high school; recruitment efforts include informational sessions for interested students and referrals by teachers and guidance counselors.

Entry into the youth apprenticeship programs is competitive; approximately thirty-five students typically apply for eight positions in the Polaroid building trades program and forty students apply for sixteen positions in the Cambridge-Lesley teaching program. Selection criteria are flexible and emphasize students' level of interest and performance during a group interview. Polaroid staff interview applying students and seek students of average achievement with no attendance problems; Lesley College staff are willing to accept at-risk students who may benefit from a nontraditional program.

Cost Factors. The district's Carl Perkins funds have been used to develop the restructuring efforts. RSTA's director has redirected existing school resources to curriculum development and applied academics (including hiring academic teachers). RSTA has sought and received several foundation grants that support the CityWorks program, the use of its approach in higher grade levels, and technical assistance to other vocational education programs. Most ongoing costs are supported by the school's regular budget.

Scale. Of the 2,100 students in its host high school, RSTA has approximately 250 students; an additional 100 students from other houses take electives in RSTA. Approximately 70 ninth graders took the CityWorks course in the 1992–93 school year. The youth apprenticeship program at Polaroid serves 8 students each year and the Cambridge-Lesley program serves 16 students.

Professional and Career Experience (PaCE):
Poudre R-1 School District
Fort Collins, Colorado

Community Setting. Fort Collins is a mostly white, middle-class community, with many small employers and several large ones, including Colorado State University, Hewlett-Packard, and Kodak. The Poudre R-1 school district has three comprehensive high schools with a combined enrollment of 3,600 students and a small alternative high school with 200 students. Approximately 65 percent of the graduates attend a two- or four-year college. The local economy is very healthy, with unemployment below national and state averages.

Origins. The Professional and Career Experience (PaCE) program was developed by two vocational teachers who received support from the school district to design a vocational program that would reach a broader range of students, provide high-quality career exploration instruction, and increase the number and diversity of cooperative education and placements. Prior to PaCE, access to vocational instruction was restricted to students who enrolled in two-year specialized vocational programs requiring several hours each day; many students with the potential to benefit from career-related instruction were not able to participate in the program.

School Elements. PaCE is available at all district high schools. Its cornerstone is the career development (CD) course, which students usually take in grade 10. The one-semester CD course was developed by district staff collaborating with the local chamber of commerce, Job Training Partnership Act (JTPA) agency, and business community. The curriculum provides exposure to a wide range of careers and teaches work-readiness skills, interpersonal and time management skills, budgeting, and personal finance. Students also develop a preliminary career plan and a job search portfolio. Activities in the CD class include community service, research projects on careers, and job shadowing.

Students participating in a co-op work experience must simultaneously take a related academic or vocational course and attend a weekly seminar led by a PaCE director to discuss work-related issues. All students attending the alternative high school take the CD course, and most participate in a work experience as well.

Workplace Elements. Students who complete the CD course with a grade of C or better are eligible to participate in paid work experience, unpaid internships, service learning, and unpaid job shadowing. With the help of counselors, students identify placements of interest and employers interview them; if both student and employer agree, the student begins the work experience. Students who receive satisfactory ratings from their work-site supervisors, complete the required related courses, and attend the weekly seminars can obtain up to twenty-five high school course credits for their placements.

Students work in co-op placements in a range of fields including high-tech electronics, health care, and the public sector. To maintain the quality of placements, PaCE program directors and employers prepare training plans describing the skills students are expected to acquire.

Recruitment. The career development course is open to all students in grades 10 through 12. Marketing efforts include presentations to all ninth-grade civics classes; a video, brochures, and a handbook describing the PaCE program; personal letters to students and parents who may be interested in the program; and articles about the program in the school and local newspapers.

Cost Factors. The program's initial planning and curriculum development were supported by in-kind donations by staff members, schools, the local chamber of commerce, JTPA agency, and employers' staff. The district also received a small grant from Carl Perkins Act funds.

Scale. PaCE currently serves 550 students in four high schools.

Tech Prep Programs

Pickens County School District
Easley, South Carolina

Community Setting. Pickens County is a largely rural area in northwestern South Carolina. The decline in the area's textile industry has been mostly offset by the development of manufacturing, education, and tourism jobs. Approximately 12 percent of the district's 2,500 high school students receive free or reduced-price school lunches. Half of the county's high school graduates enroll in two- or four-year colleges.

Origins. The Partnership for Academic and Career Education (PACE) Consortia was formed by Tri-County Technical College in 1987 to promote tech prep in northwestern South Carolina. Area businesses are increasingly replacing cheap labor with skilled workers capable of maintaining advanced production processes, and educators recognize their need to change to meet the changing needs of industry. Educators in Pickens County envisioned a public education system that would prepare students for productive careers at all levels of industry.

PACE staff worked closely with school district administrators, principals, and teachers to inform them about tech prep, provide applied technology curriculum materials, update career guidance material, and provide training in new teaching techniques. The first tech prep applied academic courses were offered at Liberty High School in Pickens County in 1990 and have since been imple-

mented in all four district high schools. In 1992 a youth apprenticeship program was added for vocational students, providing
intensive work-based learning opportunities and guidance by workplace mentors.

School Elements. Under its districtwide tech prep initiative, the
Pickens County School District has begun replacing high school
courses in the "general education track" (that is, courses that are
less demanding than the highly academic college preparatory and
advanced placement courses) with tech prep applied academic
classes, expanding career awareness activities for all students and
strengthening links to postsecondary programs. All four district high
schools have implemented applied math (math for the technologies I and II), applied English (communication for the workplace
I), and physics for the technologies; three high schools offer applied
biology and chemistry.

Tech prep classes are offered primarily in grades 10 through 12.
There is no fixed sequence or minimum number of tech prep
courses that students must take. Tech prep courses differ substantially from traditional, lecture-style classes; they include cooperative learning methods and multiple instructional approaches (video,
brief lectures, exercises requiring student participation), and use
examples that simulate workplace activities and engage students in
learning. The math, measurement skills, and science knowledge
taught in tech prep courses have improved students' preparation for
vocational courses.

Extensive career counseling activities are used in kindergarten
through grade 12. Focusing on the career implications of a student's
choice of courses, secondary school guidance counselors help students plan for careers, use articulated college credits, and seek indus-
try-sponsored tuition reimbursement.

Workplace Elements. Local employers participate in tech prep
advisory committees, speak to tech prep classes and career work-

shops through a speakers' bureau established by PACE, offer summer internships for tech prep teachers, and provide work-based learning for youth apprentices.

Students in the youth apprenticeship in electronics receive twenty hours of work-based learning per week, replacing most of the time they would have spent in vocational courses. Participating seniors take up to four classes at their high schools, part of the three-period self-paced vocational class at the vocational center, and extend their day into the early evening at their work-based learning assignment.

Work-based learning develops competencies that have been specified by the electronics teacher and the chairman of the industrial and engineering division of the technical college, with input from employers. These competencies include technical math, reading, communications, problem solving, and teamwork. Workplace activities start in grade 12 and continue for two more years, through the completion of an associate's degree. Employers pay students for their time at the workplace.

Postsecondary Elements. Articulation agreements enable students to receive credit for approximately forty specified high school courses in fourteen fields at Tri-County Technical College. Students earn college credits for high school classes through the Technical Advanced Placement (TAP) process. TAP requirements are developed separately for each college course and are reviewed annually by high school and technical college faculty.

TAP credits usually require one or more of the following: passing a TAP exam (given free of charge by the college); receiving a recommendation from the secondary school course teacher; having a high school teacher complete a competency checklist certifying that the student has the skills to receive TAP credit; presenting portfolios of high school work; successfully placing into higher-level college courses; and, in some cases, completing a brief independent study course to develop skills not covered in high school courses.

TAP credits are not accepted by four-year universities (although efforts are underway to change this), so students who plan to transfer to a university are discouraged from seeking TAP credits.

Recruitment. Tech prep classes are designed for average students, including those at risk of dropping out. Most students enroll in several tech prep classes (such as applied English, math, and science), and teachers estimate that about three-quarters of students who take tech prep courses also take vocational courses at the district's career center. Tech prep courses are open to all students.

The youth apprenticeship program is designed for the most advanced vocational students with good grades and attendance at the district's career center. Apprenticeships are available in computer electronics, business management, auto mechanics, and industrial electricity.

Cost Factors. Pickens County and PACE have received state funds to support the implementation of tech prep classes. The district uses local funds for staff training, curriculum development, and instructional materials. The district also funds a youth apprenticeship coordinator position.

Scale. Tech prep classes are offered at all four Pickens County high schools. During the 1992–93 school year, over 2,500 students took tech prep classes and four students participated in a youth apprenticeship in computer electronics.

Ben Davis High School
Wayne Township (Indianapolis), Indiana

Community Setting. The Wayne Township school district in Indianapolis is an ethnically mixed, urbanized area; previously mostly white-collar, its employment base is now both blue- and white-collar. It has a substantial industrial tax base, but its economic and population growth has slowed. Ben Davis High School serves over 2,500 students in grades 10 through 12; approximately 50 percent of its graduates attend a two- or four-year college. Job openings in the local labor market are mostly with small employers.

Origins. District and school officials and teachers recognized that at least half of their students were graduating or leaving school without adequate preparation for good jobs or college. In the program director's words, they wanted to create a "viable alternative to the college prep program." The state of Indiana's 1987 announcement of a competition for funding to develop tech prep programs (using the state's Carl Perkins Act funds) provided a useful way to further the district's goals, and the district sought and received state funding to start its program.

Members of the school's vocational department supported the plan in order to gain access to more and higher-achieving students. The state funding enabled academic and vocational teachers to meet with and visit employers, receive suggestions from postsecondary faculty, and work together to design the program. The first classes began in September 1989.

School Elements. The tech prep program is designed to replace the school's "general track" with courses focusing on the applications of technology. Tech prep students in grades 10 to 12 take a required, structured set of courses: two years of communications (English), two years of math beyond algebra, and one year each of chemistry, physics, introduction to technology, and computer applications. All these courses use curricula specifically designed for the tech prep program, with many lessons based on applications of industrial technology. Numerous vocational courses and an internship or cooperative education experience are available as electives.

The tech prep program has a distinct identity within the high school, and only tech prep students may take tech prep courses.

Tech prep students and teachers are grouped into teams; a team of teachers (for example, teachers in math, communications, industrial technology, and computer applications) works with several classes of students and meets together during weekly common preparation periods to discuss student and curricular issues. Students in the team "travel together" through the school day, taking their tech prep classes with the same classmates. This scheduling approach creates, in effect, a school-within-a-school for most tech prep students.

Tech prep courses at Ben Davis use applications-based lessons as their primary instructional tool. The lessons require students to solve brief, hands-on, work-related problems, working singly or in cooperative learning teams. Classes use a businesslike, get-the-work-done-in-class approach, with little homework but with strict standards for completing assignments (resembling the requirements of many workplaces). Material is retaught until mastered, and many courses use competency checklists to assess students' progress.

Science teachers report that 25 percent of instruction is by lecture and 75 percent by lab work or teamwork. Teachers of math, technology, and science coordinate the scheduling of topics and occasionally integrate instruction to build on material taught in other classes. Skills taught in the computer applications course are used by most tech prep courses, including spreadsheets, data bases, science data collection, Lotus 1-2-3 formulas, drafting, and word processing. Communications courses use work-related applications such as writing the instructions for a work task and interpreting graphs in *USA Today*.

Technology-based themes, examples, and assignments are used throughout the tech prep courses. The tech prep program requires students to take more math and science courses than the general education track requires.

Workplace Elements. Work internships are offered to twelfth-grade tech prep students; these resemble co-op placements, with formal training agreements and regular workplace visits by a co-op teacher. The internships vary, depending on the interests of participating employers, which are mostly small businesses that previously have had co-op students.

Student interns are covered by the district's liability insurance policy, which excludes workers' compensation coverage. For internships in occupational fields for which the high school lacks a state-approved co-op program, the district uses its "work-release" authority to approve the activity.

Postsecondary Elements. This is the only tech prep program in Indiana with an articulation and credit agreement with the Indiana Vocational Technical College (Ivy Tech). Tech prep courses in communications (English), math, and computer applications can be accepted for credit (if the student earns a B or higher) toward Ivy Tech degrees in numerous programs, including electronics technology. Tech prep science and technology courses are accepted toward credit for only a few programs.

Most Ivy Tech programs require thirty-six to eighty credits; students can receive up to nine credits for their tech prep courses. The articulation credit agreement is based on a careful review of the course curriculum by Ivy Tech faculty, who determine whether tech prep courses cover the topics in Ivy Tech's courses.

One benefit of the articulation agreement is its stimulus for joint discussions between high school and postsecondary faculty, for better orientations during high school for students entering Ivy Tech, and for upgrading math levels to prepare students for postsecondary instruction.

Recruitment. Recruiting efforts emphasize the value of tech prep for students who want a high-wage job but may not want to attend a traditional four-year college. The district's policy is to target "the middle 50 percent" of students for the tech prep program, but lower-achieving students are accepted if they pass algebra or prealgebra and keyboarding. Junior high and high school guidance counselors, who work with all students as they select their courses, identify many who have no specific school plans and encourage them to consider tech prep.

Tech prep recruiting includes presentations to classes with concentrations of low-achieving students. The tech prep program currently enrolls a diverse group of students, with a higher proportion of minorities and males than the schoolwide average.

Cost Factors. State funds were used during the project's development phase to pay for teachers' released time and summer curriculum development and for a part-time program coordinator. The district now pays for a part-time coordinator and for modest summer planning work by new tech prep teachers. Equipment and other capital expenses are also funded by the district, which has chosen the tech prep program as the central part of its high school restructuring effort. A state dissemination grant pays for the program's involvement with other central Indiana high schools initiating tech prep programs.

Scale. The program had 22 students in its first year (1989) and 89 in 1992–93; approximately 250 students were expected to enter the program in fall 1993. Plans call for the initiative to be fully implemented by 1996, at which point it will serve approximately 900 students (about 35 percent of the student body).

Youth Apprenticeship Programs

Fox Cities Printing Youth Apprenticeship
Appleton, Wisconsin

Community Setting. The Fox Cities area, located 100 miles north of Milwaukee, includes the cities of Appleton, Neenah, Menasha, and Kaukauna; the villages of Little Chute, Kimberly, and Combined Locks; and the adjoining towns of Menasha, Grand Chute, Greenville, Buchanan, and Vandenbroek. The area's population exceeds 170,000 and includes a small minority population.

The youth apprenticeship program is overseen by the Education for Employment Council, a consortium of eleven of the area's school districts, the Fox Valley Technical College, local employers, and the Fox Cities Chamber of Commerce. The three largest school districts in the consortium are Appleton, Neenah, and Menasha. The percentage of graduates from these districts who continue on to two- or four-year colleges ranges from 30 percent to 50 percent. Employment in the area is predominantly in manufacturing industries.

Origins. The Fox Cities program is one of the pilot sites for Wisconsin's youth apprenticeship initiative. Development of the program at the local level was spearheaded by a vice president of a large printing firm and a district school superintendent who had participated in state-level youth apprenticeship planning efforts; they approached the Education for Employment Council about sponsoring a youth apprenticeship program, and the council and its participating districts agreed. Fox Valley Technical College was recruited as another major partner. Officials from the state departments of public instruction and industry, labor, and human relations provided technical assistance and political support.

School Elements. Students in grades 11 and 12 participate in the program, attending academic and technical classes at Fox Valley Technical College two days a week and participating in workplace learning three days a week. They do not attend their original high schools except for sports and other extracurricular activities.

The college charges each district a tuition fee of approximately $4,000 per student per school year for the two days of instruction— roughly comparable to the participating districts' per-student expenditure. Students are instructed by technical college teachers in classes reserved only for youth apprentices. The development of this component of the program was complicated by the fact that the participating districts have different graduation requirements and do not offer the same courses.

At the participating employers' request, first-year instruction emphasizes math and chemistry—necessary background for the students' workplace experiences. Students' classes at the technical college are not scheduled in traditional class periods; students spend half the day in math class and the other half in printing class. Classes are individualized and competency-based. Math and science classes focus on technical applications, and English and social studies courses organized around the theme of industry and technology are being developed.

The program uses a competency-based printing curriculum developed to guide technical instruction in the classroom and at the work site. This curriculum, commissioned by the Wisconsin department of industry, labor and human relations, is being developed by instructors from the Moraine Park and Fox Valley Technical Colleges. It builds on skills identified by industry experts, drawing heavily from a curriculum developed by Printing Industries of America. The first semester is an introduction to the printing industry; the second semester focuses on electronic publishing. Youth apprentices are expected to specialize in lithographic or flexographic techniques by the end of their second year.

Workplace Elements. Students' workplace experiences are designed to focus on training and giving the students wide exposure to the printing industry: without being placed in preexisting jobs, students observe and receive instruction, rotating through different sections of a printing company. After a year of instruction, they are expected to become more involved in production and will work in positions that closely resemble those of regular employees.

Each participating employer has a head mentor who provides overall guidance to the students, coordinates the program for the employer, and determines how instruction will be delivered at the workplace, deciding which competencies will be addressed in particular work areas and who will train the apprentices. Students carry a list of technical competencies specified in the curriculum for the current semester that may be checked off by the classroom instructor and head mentors when a competency has been met; some competencies can best be taught in the classroom or at the workplace, while others can be taught in either setting. The head mentors and printing instructors meet regularly to coordinate the program and discuss issues of implementation.

Students are paid for their time at the workplace. Most of the apprentices are hired by participating employers during the summer between grades 11 and 12. Students receive a single grade for printing on the basis of their performance both at the workplace and in the technical class. Grades are based on competencies, attendance, teamwork, and communication, and are jointly determined by the printing instructor and head mentor at the student's workplace. Apprentices earn a certificate of occupational proficiency from the department of industry, labor and human relations after they successfully complete the program.

Postsecondary Elements. The state of Wisconsin allows secondary students to receive technical college credits for high school courses through dual credit arrangements. In addition to their dual-credit courses, some of the apprentices' courses are drawn from the technical college's curriculum (the first-semester technical math course is a standard requirement for an associate's degree) and will result in college credit.

The technical college is considering adding a third (postsecondary) year to the program; this would enable youth apprentices to obtain an associate's degree in printing and publishing. Students will also be able to transfer technical college credits to the University of Wisconsin at Stout (and possibly at Platteville), where they can pursue a four-year degree in printing management.

Recruitment. The program aims to recruit students from the middle fifty percent of tenth graders, but has accepted more educationally disadvantaged students. Each school district conducts recruitment activities in its high schools. Recruitment efforts typically involve identifying students with an interest in graphics. The program is marketed as an opportunity to learn printing skills, get firsthand exposure to the printing industry, and earn college credits toward an associate's degree in printing. Guidance counselors and vocational instructors meet individually with students to discuss their interest in the program; some schools include parents in these discussions.

Students must meet state eligibility criteria that include enrollment in school with eleventh-grade standing in the year they start the program; mastery of basic skills used in the youth apprenticeship curriculum (this requirement will eventually be replaced with satisfactory completion of the state's tenth-grade gateway assessment); and prior participation in career exploration and planning activities. Students complete an application that requires a statement by parents on why their child would be a good candidate for the program.

All applications that meet these eligibility criteria are sent to the Education for Employment Council. The council's staff director distributes the applications to participating employers, who select students to interview and then select students for the program. If more than one employer wants a student, an agreement is negotiated between employers; the student does not choose among employers.

Cost Factors. The development and initial operation of the printing youth apprenticeship program was primarily supported by donations of staff time from employers, schools, the technical college, and the chamber of commerce. The state of Wisconsin financed the development of the technical curriculum for use by all of its printing youth apprenticeships. Participating school districts redirected existing funds to pay the technical college's tuition. The program received a corporate foundation grant to support expansion and some staff for coordination activities.

Scale.   In the program's first year (1992–93), nine eleventh-grade students started the program; two were dropped because of behavior and performance problems. A second cohort of eleven students planned to begin the program during the 1993–94 school year. Also in 1993–94, a youth apprenticeship in banking and finance is planned for the Fox Cities, and a health occupations youth apprenticeship currently is being planned for the future.

Little Rock Youth Apprenticeship
Metropolitan Vocational Center
Little Rock, Arkansas

Community Setting.   The Metropolitan Vocational Center is a regional district vocational high school serving Little Rock and eight surrounding school districts. The local economy is concentrated in the service, trade, and government sectors and has grown in the past five years, particularly in services. Metropolitan's students take academic courses in their area high schools and come to Metropolitan for vocational courses.

Metropolitan serves over 700 students, mostly in grades 11 and 12. Approximately half of its graduates attend a two- or four-year college, and another 30 percent secure some other postsecondary training. Nearly two-thirds of Metropolitan's students are classified as disadvantaged either because their grade average is below 2.0, they are more than two years below grade level in math or reading, they are a parent, or they are pregnant.

Origins.   In 1991, the Arkansas legislature created the Youth Apprenticeship/Work-Based Learning Program; the state sought proposals for grants to develop and support local programs, and

Metropolitan received one of these grants. For its youth apprenticeships, Metropolitan sought to strengthen its cooperative education program, create articulation agreements with postsecondary institutions, and develop instruction providing students with credentials for high-skill, high-wage careers.

Youth apprenticeships have been developed in two of the school's eighteen vocational areas: health occupations and heating, ventilation, and air conditioning (HVAC). The health occupations field was selected because the state had targeted that industry for youth apprenticeships and because Metropolitan already had co-op jobs in health fields; the HVAC program was selected on the basis of strong support from local employers and two trade associations.

School Elements.   The youth apprentices are selected from students in Metropolitan's health occupations and HVAC programs. In addition, one of Metropolitan's students in the commercial food industry is a youth apprentice. First-year apprentices attend the same vocational courses as other students and take a weekly work-readiness class, which focuses on problem solving, teamwork, and coping skills. Second-year apprentices participate in workplace learning and study advanced technical skills at Metropolitan, conducted as part of the vocational courses taken by other Metropolitan students.

The health youth apprenticeship program includes ten health occupations. First-year students take the core curriculum, including human anatomy, nutrition, and microscope lab work. A course module enables students to obtain a nurse's aide certificate. Second-year students work independently on special reports relating to specific health occupations. Outside speakers make presentations describing their jobs, the challenges they confront at work, and the education required in their work.

The HVAC youth apprenticeship uses curriculum materials developed by the Association of Building Contractors (ABC) for its four-year adult apprenticeship program; that curriculum includes technical skills (soldering, fabricating ducts, and some electrical work), safety, applied math, and human relations. The human relations module provides students with practice in dealing with difficult work situations involving supervisors and customers. The local ABC affiliate has persuaded employers to donate valuable equipment to Metropolitan's HVAC shop, with which students learn workplace skills.

Metropolitan has also created an Apprenticeship Academy that sponsors meetings in which parents, students, teachers, and employers discuss the goals and structure of the youth apprenticeship program and current efforts to strengthen it. As part of the academy's activities, Metropolitan staff are developing youth apprenticeships in computer-aided design, welding, and computer programming, with plans for team teaching and expanded work-based learning.

Workplace Elements. Most youth apprentices participate in work-based learning jobs during their second year at Metropolitan (usually the twelfth grade); a few work during their first year or the summer preceding their second year. Students' hours of work vary. Their jobs resemble co-op positions, with training plans and regular visits by the program coordinator.

The health jobs include certified nursing assistant (CNA) and general assistant positions in long-term care facilities, serving and delivering food in hospitals, and clerical positions in a hospital. The CNA jobs provide contact with health professionals and patients as well as opportunities to apply and develop technical skills; for example, students take vital signs, operate whirlpool baths, and help patients extend their range of motion. Teachers are working to place students in a wider array of health occupations and enhance the intensity of their training in health jobs.

The HVAC work-based activities are somewhat more developed than the health youth apprenticeships and offer more learning opportunities. Youth apprentices work in small HVAC firms, where they fabricate ducts and install grills, insulation, and ducts in customers' homes. They receive substantial on-the-job training from co-workers and supervisors, complementing their courses at Metropolitan. Employers plan to train experienced students to solder copper piping and install thermostats. The students' work counts toward the four-year requirement for journeymen established by the Bureau of Apprenticeship and Training.

A student in the commercial food industry created a youth apprenticeship with a local country club, where he is learning to become a pastry chef. He receives on-the-job training from the head chef and sous chefs, building on his course work at Metropolitan.

Postsecondary Elements. Metropolitan staff are working to link the health youth apprenticeship program with a one-year surgical technology program offered by a local college. Students will receive one of the thirty-two credit hours required by the surgical technology program. Metropolitan is also developing articulation agreements in other fields, including computer-aided drafting and computer programming.

Recruitment. The youth apprenticeship program targets all high school students with the exception of those who have failed many academic courses. Students can apply and be admitted at any time. Most recruitment activity has focused on students who have already applied to or are currently attending Metropolitan's health and HVAC programs.

Metropolitan's guidance counselors recently began advertising the youth apprenticeships to middle and high school students. Counselors make presentations to all Little Rock eighth graders and to many area high school students in schoolwide assemblies, English, and science classes. In addition, employers in local HVAC associations have met with high school teachers, students, and counselors to inform them about the HVAC youth apprenticeship program and employment opportunities in the industry.

To remain in Metropolitan's youth apprenticeship program,

students are asked to maintain an average grade of 2.5 in their most recent Metropolitan courses; alternatively, their program's lead teacher needs to be persuaded that they will be successful in the program. Youth apprentices may have no more than six unexcused absences per semester. Health youth apprentices are slightly less likely to be academically disadvantaged than other Metropolitan students, and HVAC youth apprentices are somewhat more likely to be academically disadvantaged. Metropolitan requires HVAC apprentices to have access to cars so they can get to their jobs; many health apprentices can get to their jobs by walking or using buses.

Cost Factors. A state grant of $130,000 paid the salary of the program coordinator (who also teaches the work-readiness classes), part of the salary of a guidance counselor, the cost of new equipment and materials, special events and workshops, and staff time for curriculum development. Other program costs are supported through Metropolitan's existing budget.

Scale. In 1992–93, there were ten first-year apprentices (five in health and five in HVAC) and thirteen second-year apprentices (seven in health, five in HVAC, and one in commercial foods).

Pickens County Youth Apprenticeships
Pickens County School District
Easley, South Carolina

This program is described jointly with Pickens County School District's tech prep program (see above).

Craftsmanship 2000
Tulsa, Oklahoma

Community Setting. Craftsmanship 2000 (C2) is a metalworking youth apprenticeship program serving students in the Tulsa School District and thirteen surrounding school districts. Employment in the Tulsa metropolitan area is concentrated in services, wholesale/retail, and manufacturing. Two of the largest manufacturing subsectors involve metalworking: fabricated metal products and nonelectrical machinery. During the last five years, wholesale/retail employment has grown, while manufacturing employment has been stable. Approximately 18 percent of ninth graders in Tulsa County do not graduate from high school, and 38 percent of those who complete high school attend a two- or four-year college.

Origins. The idea of a metalworking youth apprenticeship program was developed by executives of the Hilti Corporation, a Liechtenstein-based manufacturer of construction fasteners with a large facility in Tulsa. Hilti staff invited local public and private leaders to observe the apprenticeship system in Liechtenstein; Hilti's human resources vice president recruited additional employer sponsors and became C2's chairman. The Tulsa Chamber of Commerce became a key C2 partner, helping design the program and building its political support base.

Employers and school staff operated a pilot program for fifteen students in the summer of 1991; it highlighted supervisors' need for training in working with adolescents. In the fall of 1993, C2's first class of eleventh graders started at the Tulsa Technology Center (Tulsa Tech), a regional vocational high school.

School Elements. C2 is a four-year program beginning in the eleventh grade and leading to an associate's degree from Tulsa Junior College; every year except the first includes some in-plant training for students. C2 students take vocational and academic courses at Tulsa Tech, thereby reducing transportation time from their area high school to the vocational school. At the request of employers, the school day was extended by two hours until 5:00, which increases instructional time by approximately three hours a day.

In their first year, students take English, history, physics, applied math, and an intensive introductory machining course. The academic courses (except history) incorporate applied components relevant to manufacturing. Much of the academic and vocational course work is done by four-student teams. Second-year courses are English, geometry, advanced machining, drafting, metal finishing, electronics, hydraulics, and machine repair. Third-year courses include welding, to meet employers' need for this skill. While the program meets state graduation requirements, local requirements for U.S. history and physical education were relaxed for C2.

The machining curriculum was developed by a Tulsa Tech curriculum specialist, with extensive input from Tulsa Tech machining instructors and employers (who made suggestions for verifying learner outcomes and emphasizing the use of hand tools).

Workplace Elements. All students receive in-plant training during the summer and, beginning in twelfth grade, during the school year. Work-based activities increase from 360 hours in the summer after the students' first year to 920 hours in their fourth year.

C2 provided fifteen training sessions for mentors (the employer staff who supervise students) on methods for training and supervising high school students, developing detailed training plans, and defining and assessing students' competencies in six skills (safety, blueprint reading, measurement, basic metalworking, turning, and milling).

Employers pay the first group of students substantial stipends for their school and work time—approximately $50,000 over four years, with bonuses for grades and attendance. To attract additional employers, stipends for subsequent cohorts of students were cut by 40 percent, and welding instruction was added. Students are employees of C2 rather than of sponsoring firms, which avoids displacing adult workers and reduces the cost of workers' compensation premiums.

Postsecondary Elements. During their third and fourth years, students take courses at Tulsa Junior College and Tulsa Tech on computer numerically controlled machining, statistical process control, inventory control, metallurgy, general management, basic computer software and hardware systems, social studies, speech, and writing. Tulsa Junior College will extend credit toward an associate's degree for students' in-plant training and Tulsa Tech course work.

Recruitment. C2 is targeted to all Tulsa County high school students interested in a career in metalworking manufacturing. C2 staff make presentations in high schools, highlighting opportunities for high-wage jobs and a junior college degree. Students apply during the tenth grade and are selected on the basis of grades, scores on standardized achievement and technical skills tests, written statement of interest, and interviews.

Cost Factors. Tulsa Tech paid for the curriculum development specialist, who worked for almost a year on C2's course plans; the local chamber of commerce paid for the early cost of the program coordinator. C2 received $250,000 from the U.S. Department of Labor to pay for the program coordinator, curriculum development, tools, and textbooks. A Tulsa public utility donated $20,000 and a staff person to train the students' supervisors. During the program's first year, the Tulsa school district paid for the academic teachers, and Tulsa Tech paid for the vocational teacher and guidance counselor. The employer sponsors pay students' stipends and contribute staff time for developing and refining the curriculum and supervising and training students.

Scale. Sixteen eleventh-grade youth apprentices entered the program in 1992. Twelve first-year apprentices were accepted for the program in 1993.

West Bend Printing Youth Apprenticeship
West Bend, Wisconsin

Community Setting. West Bend, Wisconsin, is located thirty miles north of Milwaukee and has a population of 26,000. The growing local economy is based on manufacturing and has low unemployment. Many residents work in Milwaukee. The community is economically varied, with a small minority population. West Bend has two high schools, East and West, which are collocated and serve 2,393 students. In a typical year, approximately 55 percent of its graduates enter a four-year college; 35 percent of graduates later complete a four-year degree.

Origins. West Bend's youth apprenticeship program in printing resulted from the state's development of a youth apprenticeship initiative, the leadership of a local employer, and the school district's interest in strengthening the transition from school to work. The program was spearheaded by the chief executive officer of Serigraph, Inc., a large screen-printing company in West Bend, who served on the Governor's Commission for a Quality Workforce and attended high school in West Bend. In February 1992, he approached the school district about developing a printing youth apprenticeship program linked to the state's initiative and pledged to provide work-based learning for all of the first-year youth apprentices.

The superintendent, principal, and school board quickly accepted the proposal and began planning; students entered the program in August 1992. The local technical college, Moraine Park, became the program's third partner. The state's department of public instruction and department of industry, labor and human relations provided technical assistance, political support, and some funding for development efforts.

School Elements. West Bend's two-year youth apprenticeship program serves students in grades 11 and 12. The youth apprentices divide their day between morning classes with other students at the high school and a printing course and workplace learning activities in the afternoon. Since the youth apprenticeship program takes up all of their time for electives, students' morning classes are those required for graduation.

The high school is creating applied academic courses as part of an occupational cluster approach that includes a tech prep pathway, with youth apprenticeship options, and a college prep pathway. In the program's first year, youth apprentices took a newly developed applied technical math course; in grade 12, they will take an applied English class integrated with business computer applications and an applied chemistry class.

The program uses a competency-based curriculum to guide technical instruction in classrooms and in the workplace. This curriculum, commissioned by the Wisconsin department of industry, labor and human relations, is being developed by instructors from the Moraine Park and Fox Valley Technical Colleges. It builds on skills identified by industry experts and draws heavily from curricula developed by Printing Industries of America.

The first-semester printing course is an introduction to printing; the second semester focuses on screen printing, the technology primarily used by local employers. Instruction in the second year emphasizes prepress and offset techniques. The printing course is jointly taught by a technical college instructor and the high school graphics instructor. The course was initially taught at Serigraph in a mobile classroom but has since been moved to the high school because of the need for equipment.

Workplace Elements. The work-based component emphasizes students' learning opportunities and broad exposure to the printing industry: without being placed in preexisting jobs, students rotate through several parts of the host company. After a year, they become more involved in production and may work in positions that closely resemble those of regular employees.

Youth apprentices work in pairs and are assigned to line-level trainers, who teach them the competencies identified in the curriculum. Trainers are selected by the head mentor, who coordinates the youth apprenticeship program for Serigraph, and by division supervisors. Since the same list of competencies guides both classroom and workplace instruction, a great deal of reinforcement exists between classroom instruction and workplace learning. The trainers work on specific competencies in their area and check off those that students have met. The youth apprentices participate in some of Serigraph's formal training for its staff, and are also paired with mentors who provide overall guidance. Students are paid for their time at the workplace.

Students develop portfolios from their work-based activities that include a list of their competencies, test results from their training, and work samples. Grades for workplace experience and the printing course are determined jointly by classroom instructors, head mentor, and program coordinator. Apprentices earn a certificate of occupational proficiency from the department of industry, labor and human relations after they successfully complete the program.

Postsecondary Elements. The state of Wisconsin allows secondary students to earn high school and technical college credits simultaneously through dual credit arrangements; the West Bend high schools offer these technical college credit courses. Youth apprentices receive technical college credits for their applied communications, psychology, and computer applications courses. Printing and occupational experience courses will be eligible for technical college credit in the future.

Recruitment. The program aims to recruit the middle 50 percent of tenth-grade students. Program admission was competitive from the beginning; twenty-four students applied for twelve slots the first year. The state has specified student selection criteria (described for the Fox Cities program, above), and the district has additional criteria: good attendance, a 2.0 grade average, three references, and students must be on schedule to graduate within two years. An introductory graphics course has been added as a prerequisite.

Recruitment efforts include program presentations to all tenth-grade English and introductory graphics classes, brochures distributed to all tenth-grade students and their parents, media coverage of the program, and an open house at Serigraph. Program advertising emphasizes the opportunity to earn a youth apprenticeship certificate, course credits for working and credits accepted by the technical college, and the opportunity to learn skills for work.

Cost Factors. The district received Carl Perkins Act funds from the state department of public instruction to support staff visits to other schools, participation in conferences, and hiring consultants to inform program development (for both the youth apprenticeship program and the school's occupational clusters). The district used its strategic planning budget and Carl Perkins Act funds to support a part-time project coordinator, teachers' released time for creating applied courses, and payment for the technical college instructors who instruct the youth apprentices. The state financed the development of the technical curriculum as part of its youth apprenticeship initiative.

Scale. During the 1992—93 school year, twelve students participated in the printing youth apprenticeship program; this was scheduled to grow to a total of twenty students the following year. In addition, a youth apprenticeship program in banking and finance with ten students is planned.

References

Berryman, S. E., and Bailey, T. R. *The Double Helix of Education and the Economy.* New York: Institute on Education and the Economy, Teachers College, Columbia University, 1992.

Burtless, G. "Are Targeted Wage Subsidies Harmful? Evidence from a Wage Voucher Experiment." *Industrial and Labor Relations Review,* 1985, 39(1), 105–114.

Carnegie Council on Adolescent Development. *Turning Points: Preparing American Youth for the 21st Century. The Report of the Task Force on Education of Young Adolescents.* New York: Carnegie Corporation of New York, 1989.

Council of Chief State School Officers. *European Lessons from School and the Workplace.* Washington, D.C.: Council of Chief State School Officers, 1991.

Commission on the Skills of the American Workforce. *America's Choice: High Skills or Low Wages!* Rochester, N.Y.: National Center for Education and the Economy, 1990.

Dayton, C., and Schneyer, R. *California Partnership Academies 1990–91 Evaluation Report.* Berkeley, Calif.: Policy Analysis for California Education, 1992.

Grant Foundation Commission on Work, Family and Citizenship. *The Forgotten Half: Pathways to Success for America's Youth and Young Families.* Washington, D.C.: William T. Grant Foundation Commission, 1988.

Hamilton, S. F. *Apprenticeship for Adulthood: Preparing Youth for the Future.* New York: Free Press, 1990.

Hill, P. T., Foster, G. E., and Gendler, T. *High Schools with Character.* Santa Monica, Calif.: Rand Corporation, 1990.

Jobs for the Future. *Learning Through Work: Designing and Implementing Quality Worksite Learning for High School Students.* New York: Manpower Demonstration Research Corporation, 1994.

Kemple, J. J., Doolittle, F., and Wallace, J. W. *The National JTPA Study: Site Characteristics and Participation Patterns.* New York: Manpower Demonstration Research Corporation, 1993.

Levy, F., and Murnane, R. J. "U.S. Earnings Levels and Earnings Inequality: A Review of Recent Trends." *Journal of Economic Literature*, 1992, 30(3), 1333–1381.

Lieberman, A., and Miller, L. "Professional Development of Teachers." In M. C. Alkin (ed.), *Encyclopedia of Educational Research* (6th ed.), vol. 3. New York: Macmillan, 1992.

McLaughlin, M. W., and Talbert, J. E. "Understanding Teaching in Context." In D. K. Cohen, M. W. McLaughlin, and J. E. Talbert (eds.), *Teaching for Understanding: Challenges for Policy and Practice*. San Francisco: Jossey-Bass, 1993.

Marshall, R., and Tucker, M. *Thinking for a Living: Education and the Wealth of Nations*. New York: Basic Books, 1992.

Muncey, D. E., and McQuillan, P. J. "Preliminary Findings from a Five-Year Study of the Coalition of Essential Schools." *Phi Delta Kappan*, 1993, 74(6), 486–490.

Murnane, R. J., and Levy, F. "Education and Training." In H. J. Aaron and C. L. Schultze (eds.), *Setting Domestic Priorities: What Can Government Do?* Washington, D.C.: Brookings Institution, 1992.

National Assessment of Vocational Education. *Summary of Findings and Recommendations*. Washington, D.C.: U.S. Department of Education, 1989.

National Assessment of Vocational Education. *Final Report to Congress*. Washington, D.C.: U.S. Department of Education, 1994.

National Center for Educational Statistics. *Dropout Rates in the United States: 1991*. Washington, D.C.: U.S. Department of Education, Office of Educational Research and Improvement, 1991.

National Center for Research in Vocational Education. "Entering a New Era in Vocational Education: Highlights of the June, 1992, NCRVE Tech Prep Leadership Summit." Berkeley, Calif.: National Center for Research in Vocational Education, 1993.

National Commission on Excellence in Education. *A Nation at Risk: The Imperative for Educational Reform*. Washington, D.C.: U.S. Department of Education, 1983.

Nothdurft, W. E. *Schoolworks: Reinventing Public Schools to Create the Workforce of the Future*. Washington, D.C.: Brookings Institution, 1990.

Odden, Allan R. (ed.). *Education Policy Implementation*. Albany: State University of New York Press, 1991.

Osterman, P. *Is There a Problem with the Youth Labor Market and If So How Should We Fix It?* Cambridge, Mass.: Sloan School of Management, Massachusetts Institute of Technology, 1991.

Osterman, P., and Batt, R. "Employer-Centered Training for International Competitiveness: Lessons from State Programs." *Journal of Policy Analysis and Management*, 1993, 12(3), 456–477.

Pauly, E. *The Classroom Crucible: What Really Works, What Doesn't, and Why.* New York: Basic Books, 1991.

Resnick, L. "Learning In School and Out." *Educational Researcher,* 1987, *16*(9), 13–20.

Sarason, S. B. *The Culture of the School and the Problem of Change.* Needham Heights, Mass.: Allyn & Bacon, 1982. (Originally published 1971.)

Sarason, S. B. *The Creation of Settings and the Future Societies.* Cambridge, Mass.: Brookline Books, 1988. (Originally published 1972.)

Secretary's Commission on Achieving Necessary Skills (SCANS). *What Work Requires of Schools: A SCANS Report for America 2000.* Washington, D.C.: U.S. Department of Labor, 1991.

Smith, M. S., and O'Day, J. A. "Systemic School Reform." In S. Fuhrman and B. Malen (eds.), *The Politics of Curriculum and Testing.* Bristol, Pa.: Falmer Press, 1991.

Stasz, C., and others. *Classrooms That Work: Teaching Generic Skills in Academic and Vocational Settings.* Santa Monica, Calif.: Rand Corporation, 1993.

Stern, D. *Combining School and Work: Options in High Schools and Two-Year Colleges.* Washington, D.C.: Office of Vocational and Adult Education, U.S. Department of Education, 1991.

Stern, D., Dayton, C., Paik, I., and Weisberg, A. "Benefits and Costs of Dropout Prevention in a High School Program Combining Academic and Vocational Education: Third-Year Results from Replications of the California Peninsula Academies." *Educational Evaluation and Policy Analysis,* 1989, *11*(4), 405–416.

Stern, D., and Nakata, Y. "Characteristics of High School Students' Paid Jobs, and Employment Experience After Graduation." In D. Stern and D. Eichorn (eds.), *Adolescence and Work: Influences of Social Structure, Labor Markets, and Culture.* Hillsdale, N.J.: Lawrence Erlbaum Associates, 1989.

Stern, D., Raby, M., and Dayton, C. *Career Academies: Partnerships for Reconstructing American High Schools.* San Francisco: Jossey-Bass, 1992.

Stern, D., Stone, J. R. III, Hopkins, C., and McMillion. M. "Quality of Students' Work Experience and Orientation Toward Work." *Youth and Society,* 1990, *22*(2), 263–282.

Stern, D., and others. *School to Work Transition and the Relevance of Vocational Education to Subsequent Employment.* Berkeley, Calif.: National Center for Research in Vocational Education, 1993.

University-Oakland Metropolitan Forum. *Support of Academies in the Oakland Public Schools by the Oakland Redevelopment Agency: Final Report for the Evaluation of the First Year, Executive Summary.* Oakland, Calif.: University-Oakland Metropolitan Forum, 1991.

University-Oakland Metropolitan Forum. *Support of Academies in the Oakland*

Public Schools by the Oakland Redevelopment Agency: Interim Report from Project Evaluators. Oakland, Calif.: University-Oakland Metropolitan Forum, 1992.

U.S. General Accounting Office. *The Job Training Partnership Act: Youth Participant Characteristics, Services, and Outcomes.* GAO/HRD-90–46BR. Gaithersburg, Md.: U.S. General Accounting Office, 1990.

U.S. General Accounting Office. *Transition from School to Work: Linking Education and Worksite Training.* GAO/HRD-91–105. Gaithersburg, Md.: U.S. General Accounting Office, 1991.

Wentling, T. L., Leach, J. A., and Galloway, J. R. *Evaluation Report: Technology Preparation Pilot Test, School Year 1989–1990.* Urbana, Ill.: Evaluation Consultants, 1990.

Wentling, T. L., Leach, J. A., and Galloway, J. R. *Evaluation Report: Technology Preparation Pilot Test, Year 2, School Year 1990–91.* Urbana, Ill.: Evaluation Consultants, 1991.

Witte, J. F. *Choice and Control in American Education: An Analytic Overview.* Madison: University of Wisconsin, 1989.

Selected MDRC Publications

Programs for Youth

The School-to-Work Transition Project

A study of innovative programs that help students make the transition from school to work.

The School-to-Work Transition and Youth Apprenticeship: Lessons from the U.S. Experience. 1993. Thomas Bailey, Donna Merritt.

Learning Through Work: Designing and Implementing Quality Worksite Learning for High School Students. 1994. Susan Goldberger, Richard Kazis, Mary Kathleen O'Flanagan (all of Jobs for the Future).

The JOBSTART Demonstration

A test of a program combining education, training, support services, and job placement for very disadvantaged young high school dropouts.

The Pilot Phase: A Case Study of Five Youth Training Programs. 1985. Michael Redmond.

Launching JOBSTART: A Demonstration for Dropouts in the JTPA System. 1987. Patricia Auspos.

Implementing JOBSTART: A Demonstration for School Dropouts in the JTPA System. 1989. Patricia Auspos, George Cave, Fred Doolittle, Gregory Hoerz.

Assessing JOBSTART: Interim Impacts of a Program for School Dropouts. 1991. George Cave, Fred Doolittle.

JOBSTART: Final Report on a Program for School Dropouts. 1993. George Cave, Hans Bos, Fred Doolittle, Cyril Toussaint.

The Career Beginnings Evaluation

An evaluation of a program that seeks to increase college attendance and improve job quality among disadvantaged high school students.

Career Beginnings Impact Evaluation: Findings from a Program for Disadvantaged High School Students. 1990. George Cave, Janet Quint.

The Youth Incentive Entitlement Pilot Projects (YIEPP) Demonstration

A test of a school-conditioned job guarantee for low-income youth.

Lessons from a Job Guarantee: The Youth Incentive Entitlement Pilot Projects. Monograph. 1984. Judith Gueron.

Programs for Teenage Parents on Welfare

The New Chance Demonstration

A test of a comprehensive program of services that seeks to improve the economic status and general well-being of a group of highly disadvantaged young women and their children.

New Chance: Lessons from the Pilot Phase. 1989. Janet Quint, Cynthia Guy.

New Chance: Implementing a Comprehensive Program for Disadvantaged Young Mothers and Their Children. 1991. Janet Quint, Barbara Fink, Sharon Rowser.

New Chance: An Innovative Program for Young Mothers and Their Children. Brochure. 1993.

Lives of Promise, Lives of Pain: Young Mothers After New Chance. 1994. Janet Quint, Judith Musick, with Joyce Ladner.

New Chance: Interim Findings on a Comprehensive Program for Disadvantaged Young Mothers and Their Children. 1994. Janet Quint, Denise Polit, Hans Bos, George Cave.

The LEAP Evaluation

An evaluation of Ohio's Learning, Earning, and Parenting (LEAP) Program, which uses financial incentives to encourage teenage parents on welfare to stay in or return to school.

LEAP: Implementing a Welfare Initiative to Improve School Attendance Among Teenage Parents. 1991. Dan Bloom, Hilary Kopp, David Long, Denise Polit.

LEAP: Interim Findings on a Welfare Initiative to Improve School Attendance Among Teenage Parents. 1993. Dan Bloom, Veronica Fellerath, David Long, Robert Wood.

LEAP: The Educational Effects of LEAP and Enhanced Services in Cleveland. 1994. David Long, Robert G. Wood, Hilary Kopp.

Project Redirection

A test of a comprehensive program of services for pregnant and parenting teenagers.

The Challenge of Serving Teenage Mothers: Lessons from Project Redirection. Monograph. 1988. Denise Polit, Janet Quint, James Riccio.

The Community Service Projects

A test of a New York State teenage pregnancy prevention and services initiative.

The Community Service Projects: A New York State Adolescent Pregnancy Initiative. 1986. Cynthia Guy.

The Community Service Projects: Final Report on a New York State Adolescent Pregnancy Prevention and Services Program. 1988. Cynthia Guy, Lawrence Bailis, David Palasits, Kay Sherwood.

The National JTPA Study

A study of sixteen local programs under the Job Training Partnership Act (JTPA), the nation's job training system for low-income individuals.

Implementing the National JTPA Study. 1990. Fred Doolittle, Linda Traeger.

The National JTPA Study: Site Characteristics and Participation Patterns. 1993. James Kemple, Fred Doolittle, John Wallace.

A Summary of the Design and Implementation of the National JTPA Study. 1993. Fred Doolittle.

Welfare-to-Work Programs

From Welfare to Work (Russell Sage Foundation). Book. 1991. Judith M. Gueron, Edward Pauly. A synthesis of research findings on the effectiveness of welfare-to-work programs. Chapter 1, which is the summary of the book, is also published separately by MDRC.

Reforming Welfare with Work (Ford Foundation). Monograph. 1987. Judith M. Gueron. A review of welfare-to-work initiatives in five states.

Papers for Practitioners

Assessing JOBS Participants: Issues and Trade-offs. 1992. Patricia Auspos, Kay Sherwood.

Linking Welfare and Education: A Study of New Programs in Five States. 1992. Edward Pauly, David Long, Karin Martinson.

Improving the Productivity of JOBS Programs. 1993. Eugene Bardach.

Working Papers

Child Support Enforcement: A Case Study. 1993. Dan Bloom.

Learning from the Voices of Mothers: Single Mothers' Perceptions of the Trade-offs Between Welfare and Work. 1993. LaDonna Pavetti.

Unpaid Work Experience for Welfare Recipients: Findings and Lessons from MDRC Research. 1993. Thomas Brock, David Butler, David Long.

The Impacts of California's GAIN Program on Different Ethnic Groups: Two-Year Findings on Earnings and AFDC Payments. 1994. Daniel Friedlander.

The GAIN Evaluation

An evaluation of California's Greater Avenues for Independence (GAIN) Program, which is currently operating as the state's JOBS program and features upfront basic education as well as job search and other activities.

GAIN: Planning and Early Implementation. 1987. John Wallace, David Long.

GAIN: Child Care in a Welfare Employment Initiative. 1989. Karin Martinson, James Riccio.

GAIN: Early Implementation Experiences and Lessons. 1989. James Riccio, Barbara Goldman, Gayle Hamilton, Karin Martinson, Alan Orenstein.

GAIN: Participation Patterns in Four Counties. 1991. Stephen Freedman, James Riccio.

GAIN: Program Strategies, Participation Patterns, and First-Year Impacts in Six Counties. 1992. James Riccio, Daniel Friedlander.

GAIN: Two-Year Impacts in Six Counties. 1993. Daniel Friedlander, James Riccio, Stephen Freedman.

GAIN: Basic Education in a Welfare-to-Work Program. 1994. Karin Martinson, Daniel Friedlander.

GAIN: Benefits, Costs, and Three-Year Impacts of a Welfare-to-Work Program. 1994. James Riccio, Daniel Friedlander, Stephen Freedman.

The JOBS Evaluation

An evaluation of welfare-to-work programs operating under the Job Opportunities and Basic Skills Training (JOBS) provisions of the Family Support Act of 1988.

From Welfare to Work (Russell Sage Foundation). Book. 1991. Judith M. Gueron, Edward Pauly. A synthesis of research findings on the effectiveness of welfare-to-work programs. Chapter 1, which is the summary of the book, is also published separately by MDRC.

The Evaluation of Florida's Project Independence

An evaluation of Florida's JOBS program.

Florida's Project Independence: Program Implementation, Participation Patterns, and First-Year Impacts. 1994. James Kemple, Joshua Haimson.

The Saturation Work Initiative Model (SWIM)

A test of the feasibility and effectiveness of an ongoing participation requirement in a welfare-to-work program.

Interim Report on the Saturation Work Initiative Model in San Diego. 1988. Gayle Hamilton.

Final Report on the Saturation Work Initiative Model in San Diego. 1989. Gayle Hamilton, Daniel Friedlander.

The Saturation Work Initiative Model in San Diego: A Five-Year Follow-up Study. 1993. Daniel Friedlander, Gayle Hamilton.

The Self-Employment Investment Demonstration (SEID)

A test of the feasibility of operating a program to encourage self-employment among recipients of AFDC.

Self-Employment for Welfare Recipients: Implementation of the SEID Program. 1991. Cynthia Guy, Fred Doolittle, Barbara Fink.

The Parents' Fair Share Demonstration

A demonstration aimed at reducing child poverty by increasing the job-holding, earnings, and child support payments of unemployed, noncustodial parents (usually fathers) of children receiving public assistance.

Caring and Paying: What Fathers and Mothers Say About Child Support. 1992. Frank Furstenberg, Jr., Kay Sherwood, Mercer Sullivan.

Child Support Enforcement: A Case Study. Working Paper. 1993. Dan Bloom.

Matching Opportunities to Obligations: Lessons for Child Support Reform from the Parents' Fair Share Pilot Phase. 1994. Dan Bloom, Kay Sherwood.

Index